The Great Elector

John Sisismund
&
George William
&
Frederick William

PROFILES IN **POWER**

General Editor: Keith Robbins

The Great Elector

Derek McKay

Longman

An imprint of **Pearson Education**

Harlow, England · London · New York · Reading, Massachusetts · San Francisco
Toronto · Don Mills, Ontario · Sydney · Tokyo · Singapore · Hong Kong · Seoul
Taipei · Cape Town · Madrid · Mexico City · Amsterdam · Munich · Paris · Milan

Pearson Education Limited
Edinburgh Gate
Harlow
Essex CM20 2JE
United Kingdom

and Associated Companies throughout the world

Visit us on the World Wide Web at
www.pearsoneduc.com

First published in 2001

© Pearson Education Limited 2001

ISBN 0582 49482 6 PPR

British Library Cataloguing in Publication Data
A CIP catalogue record for this book can be obtained from the British
Library.

10 9 8 7 6 5 4 3 2 1
05   04   03   02   01   00

Typeset by 35 in 10/12 pt Janson Text
Produced by Pearson Education Asia Pte Ltd.
Printed in Malaysia, LSP

For Frances

CONTENTS

CONTENTS

ACKNOWLEDGEMENTS

Much of the material in chapter 8 appeared in an article in the collection *Royal and Republican Sovereignty in Early Modern Europe*, edited by Robert Oresko, G.C. Gibbs and H.M. Scott (Cambridge, 1997). I am grateful to Cambridge University Press for letting me use this. Over the past 30 years Hamish Scott has always been generous with his time and help, never more so than in the writing of this book. Christopher Storrs has helped in many ways. Professor Peter Cole of the Royal Brompton has kept me in one piece; my wife, Frances, our daughters and grandson have made sure that I enjoy living beside the seaside.

Brighton,
2000

CHRONOLOGY

1608 Accession of John Sigismund as elector of Brandenburg
1609 Death of John William of Cleves-Jülich
1613 Elector John Sigismund becomes a Calvinist
1614 Treaty of Xanten provisionally settles the Cleves-Jülich succession
1616 Marriage of Crown Prince George William and Elizabeth Charlotte of the Palatinate
1618 Death of Duke Albert Frederick of Prussia and succession of John Sigismund; Bohemian rebellion and outbreak of Thirty Years War (May)
1619 Ferdinand II elected Holy Roman Emperor
1620 Accession of George William as elector of Brandenburg and duke of Prussia (Jan.); birth of Frederick William, the Great Elector (Feb.); defeat of Frederick V, Elector Palatine, outside Prague (Nov.)
1621 Outbreak of Dutch-Spanish War
1625 Beginning of Swedo-Polish War (till 1629); Christian IV of Denmark enters Thirty Years War (till 1626)
1626 Imperialists under Wallenstein occupy Brandenburg
1629 Further treaty between Brandenburg and Pfalz-Neuburg over Cleves-Jülich
1630 Gustavus Adolphus of Sweden enters Thirty Years War
1631 Alliance between Brandenburg and Sweden (Jun.)
1632 Election of Władisław IV as king of Poland; death of Gustavus Adolphus (Nov.)
1635 France enters the Thirty Years War; Saxony and Emperor make Peace of Prague, which Brandenburg joins (Sept.)

1637   Death of Bogislav XIV of Pomerania; succession of Ferdinand III as Holy Roman Emperor; Brandenburg joins the Emperor and Saxony against Sweden

1638   George William flees to Prussia

1640   Death of George William and accession of Frederick William (Dec.)

1641   Death of Schwarzenberg (Mar.); Brandenburg-Swedish armistice (Jul.)

1643   Frederick William returns to Brandenburg (Mar.)

1644   Danish-Swedish War begins (May) (to 1645)

1646   First Berg War begins (Nov.) (till April 1647); marriage of Frederick William and Louise Henrietta (Dec.)

1648   Peace of Westphalia ends the Thirty Years War in Germany (Oct.); election of John Casimir as Polish king (Nov.)

1651   Second Berg War ('Cow War') (Jun.) (till Oct.)

1653   Agreement (*Landtagsrezess*) with Brandenburg Estates (July)

1654   Imperial decree (*Reichsabschied*) (May); accession of Charles X of Sweden

1655   War of the North begins (Jul.) (till 1660)

1656   Brandenburg-Swedish alliances of Königsberg (Jan.) and Malbork/Marienburg (Jun.); battle of Warsaw (July); Brandenburg-Swedish alliance of Polessk/Labiau (Nov.)

1657   Emperor Ferdinand III dies (April); Charles X leaves Poland (Jul.); Brandenburg-Polish peace treaties (Sept., Oct.)

1658   Brandenburg-Polish-Imperial alliance (Feb.); election of Leopold I as Holy Roman Emperor (Jul.); Frederick William enters Denmark (Sept.)

1659   Frederick William leaves Denmark (Sept.); Franco-Spanish Peace of Pyrenees (Nov.)

1660   Death of Charles X (Feb.); Peace of Oliwa (May); *Rezess* made with Cleves-Mark Estates (Dec.)

1661   Death of Cardinal Mazarin, beginning of Louis XIV's personal rule

1662   Frederick-William Canal begun; Frederick William subdues Königsberg (Oct.)

1663   Prussian Diet accepts Frederick William's sovereignty (May)

1664   Franco-Brandenburg alliance (Mar.)

1665   Bishop of Münster attacks Dutch Republic (Oct.)

1666 Frederick William mediates Münster-Dutch Peace (April); final Brandenburg-Pfalz-Neuburg settlement (Sept.)

1667 France begins War of Devolution (May) (till 1668); death of Electress Louise Henrietta (Jul.); Franco-Brandenburg alliance (Dec.); introduction of first excise tax in Brandenburg

1668 Marriage of Frederick William and Dorothea (Jun.)

1669 Election of Michael as king of Poland (June)

1670 Franco-Brandenburg alliance (Jan.)

1671 Dissolution of last Prussian Diet (Sept.); Jewish families invited to Brandenburg

1672 Execution of Kalckstein (Jan.); Brandenburg-Dutch Alliance (May); France begins Dutch War (June) (till 1678/9)

1673 Franco-Brandenburg Peace of Vossem (Jun.)

1674 Military occupation of Königsberg (May); election of John Sobieski as Polish king (May); Brandenburg rejoins anti-French alliance (Jul.)

1675 Swedes invade Brandenburg (Jan.); battle of Fehrbellin (Jun.)

1678 Frederick William takes Szczecin (Jan.); Franco-Dutch Peace of Nijmegen (Aug.); Frederick William's campaign in Prussia (Dec.–Feb. 1679)

1679 Franco-Imperial peace (Feb.); Franco-Brandenburg Peace of St Germain (Jun.), followed by alliance (Oct.); Grumbkow appointed head of the *Generalkriegskommissariat*

1680 Brandenburg privateering war with Spain; Franco-Brandenburg alliance (Nov.)

1681 Establishment of first Brandenburg trading post in West Africa (May)

1682 Franco-Brandenburg alliance (Jan.); foundation of Brandenburg Africa Company (March)

1683 Knyphausen given control of finances; defeat of Turks outside Vienna (Sept.)

1684 Final Franco-Brandenburg alliance (Jan.); truce of Regensburg/Ratisbon (Aug.)

1685 Accession of James II in Britain (Feb.); Brandenburg-Dutch alliance (Aug); revocation of Edict of Nantes (Oct.); edict of Potsdam (Nov.)

1686 Brandenburg-Imperial alliance (April)

1688 Death of Frederick William (May); William III invades England (Nov.)

Chapter 1

THE INHERITANCE OF
THE GREAT ELECTOR

Few rulers can have had such an inauspicious start in life as Frederick William, the Great Elector of Brandenburg-Prussia. He was born at the beginning of the Thirty Years War, which was to ruin much of Germany, including his own scattered and impoverished inheritance. When he came to the throne in 1640 in the middle of the most destructive stage of the war, there were doubts whether his dynasty and territories would survive. Yet the achievements of Frederick William's long reign have led even such a cautious and sober historian as Francis Carsten to write: 'No other ruler has exercised such a far-reaching influence on the history of modern Germany'.[1]

. . .

GERMANY IN THE EARLY
SEVENTEENTH CENTURY

An 'irregular body . . . like some mis-shapen Monster'[2] was how the seventeenth-century philosopher and historian Samuel von Pufendorf described his native Germany. Known grandiosely as the Holy Roman Empire of the German Nation, the country was a grotesque mosaic of hundreds of states, ruled by lay and clerical princes.[3] It straddled the European continent from the Baltic to the Alps and from the Rhineland to the Polish and Hungarian plains. The various states ranged in size from tiny principalities to such crowded Imperial cities as Hamburg and such large compact duchies as Bavaria and Saxony which had some significance outside the Empire. Unity of a sort was provided by the Imperial Diet, the *Reichstag*, which elected

1

Germany's overlord, the Holy Roman Emperor. Even here, however, only a few of the more important princes took part in the election. These were the seven electors: the three archbishops of Cologne, Mainz and Trier and the four rulers of Brandenburg, the Palatinate, Saxony and Bohemia. Their choice since the mid-fifteenth century of a member of Europe's leading family, the Habsburgs, had been consistent, and increasingly predictable. By the 1600s this remarkable dynasty still ruled most of Christian Europe. From Madrid the Spanish branch reigned over the Iberian peninsula, the Southern Netherlands and lands in Italy; from Vienna (or briefly Prague under Emperor Rudolf II) the German branch, as well as being elective emperors, provided the hereditary rulers of Austria and elective kings of Bohemia and the rump of the old kingdom of Hungary.

Germany's political fragmentation was compounded by the religious division and conflicts it shared with most European countries. The Peace of Augsburg of 1555 had reconciled the Catholic Emperor with the Protestant Lutheran princes and established a *modus vivendi* between Catholic and Lutheran rulers who could now impose their faith on their own subjects. Although the peace had not recognised the rights of Protestant Calvinist rulers or princes, it ushered in a long period of apparent quiet in Germany at a time when western Europe was plagued by the French Wars of Religion and the Revolt of the Netherlands against Spain. The conservative German Lutheran rulers, including those of the larger states of Saxony and Brandenburg, had been determined to keep out of these wars and in any case had little sympathy with the politics or religion of the Calvinist rebels in France and the Netherlands. In the first two decades of the seventeenth century the Lutherans also hoped they could continue to stand aside when the struggle between the Calvinists and the Catholic Counter-Reformation spread to Germany, just as it came to a temporary halt in the Netherlands (1609) and a more permanent, if still uncertain, one in France (1598).[4]

The great conflict of the Thirty Years War (1618–48), which engulfed Germany after 1618, stemmed from a mix of German and wider European problems. The most important European issue in the first years of the war, and of great weight throughout, was the continuation of the struggle between Spain and her rebellious former subjects in what had become the Dutch Republic. Tension between Catholic Spain and the Calvinist Dutch, and their jockeying for allies and advantage, dominated international relations in western

2

and central Europe from the truce of 1609 till the two countries renewed their own war in 1621. Spain's dynastic and religious connection with her Habsburg cousins in Austria and their increasing political cooperation in the late 1610s, together with the Dutch search for Protestant friends in Germany and Scandinavia, meant that any quarrel within the Holy Roman Empire acquired a much wider dimension. This developed further when first Denmark (1625) and then Sweden (1630) entered the Thirty Years War to pursue their ambitions on the southern Baltic. The old feud between Bourbon France and Habsburg Spain (both Catholic monarchies after the conversion of the French Henry IV in 1593) was to be far less important until the 1630s, when France also entered the conflict.

Tension within Germany itself in the 1600s and 1610s came from two sources. The first was the growing military character of confrontations between Calvinist and Catholic princes and communities in the Empire, and the second was the attempt by the Austrian branch of the Habsburg family to rejuvenate itself under a Counter-Reformation banner. Calvinist militancy was centred on the electorate of the Palatinate in the Rhineland.[5] Here the Wittelsbach electors, Frederick IV (1583–1610) and Frederick V (1610–23), made Heidelberg the centre of a network of political and military relationships with other German Calvinist princes and cities and with some European states, especially the nearby Dutch Republic. They aimed to have Calvinism accepted in Germany on the same legal basis as Lutheranism and Catholicism in the Peace of Augsburg and at the same time to resist and to drive back the tide of the Catholic Counter-Reformation. While their main European enemy was Spain, seconded by her Austrian cousins, their German one was the ambitious Catholic Duke Maximilian of Bavaria (1598–1651), who also happened to be a Wittelsbach and dynastic rival of the Palatinate electors. By 1608–9 the Palatine–Bavarian antagonism had produced two military leagues within Germany, the Protestant (although almost exclusively Calvinist) Union and the Catholic League. These were directed from the Palatinate and Bavaria and patronised over the next years from outside, chiefly by the Dutch and Spaniards. Open conflict was avoided for almost a decade for three reasons: the foreign patrons were not yet ready for war, the two weak emperors, Rudolf II (1575–1612) and Matthias (1612–19), were reluctant to become involved, and the large German states of Brandenburg and Saxony were eager to keep the peace. Unfortunately, the emergence of the tough and enthusiastic Catholic Ferdinand of Styria, supported by the Spanish Habsburgs, as heir to the childless Emperor Matthias tipped the scales heavily towards war.

Before Matthias died in 1619 Ferdinand had already been elected king of both Bohemia and Hungary (1617). He then inherited the Austrian lands and was also elected Emperor Ferdinand II (1619–37). However, in 1618 the predominantly Protestant Estates in Bohemia deposed him only a year after his election as their king because of clear signs that he intended to pursue a Catholic and absolutist policy there. The Estates' offer of the Bohemian throne to the Calvinist Frederick V of the Palatinate, and his acceptance, was provocative and led to the outbreak of the Thirty Years War. Maximilian of Bavaria's Catholic League, backed by the Spaniards, came to Ferdinand II's aid, defeated the forces of the Protestant Union, expelled Frederick from Bohemia and also occupied his Palatinate lands. The Emperor subsequently deposed Frederick, transferring his electoral title and some of his lands to his Wittelsbach relative, Maximilian. There the whole affair should have been settled, but the renewal of the Spanish–Dutch war in 1621 meant that the Dutch Republic had an interest in encouraging further conflict in Germany to destabilise control of the military corridor of the Rhineland by the Habsburgs and their Catholic League allies. For the moment, disaster had struck the Calvinist cause in the Empire and it looked as if it would soon be obliterated there. No one was happier to see this than the German Lutherans, especially their acknowledged leader, the Elector of Saxony, John George I (1611–56). He had even joined in the attack on Frederick of the Palatinate. Although the Emperor Ferdinand's offer of territory in Lusatia/Lausitz was one motive, more important was John George's hatred of Calvinism and his concern over rebellion against the Emperor and disruption of the constitutional *status quo* in the Empire.[6] While the attitude of Saxony and of most German Lutherans was to remain consistent until the late 1620s, this was not true of the other large Protestant state, Brandenburg.

. . .

BRANDENBURG BEFORE THE ACCESSION
OF FREDERICK WILLIAM IN 1640

The north-German electorate of Brandenburg (*Kurbrandenburg*) was in the most backward part of the Empire. It was originally a frontier

4

region, created over centuries from lands conquered by German Christian princes from pagan Slavs. By the seventeenth century it was made up of five provinces or *Marks*. The Altmark, on the left bank of the River Elbe, was the most westerly province, with Stendal as its main town; then the Mittelmark in the centre between the Elbe and Oder was the most important province and included the main towns of Brandenburg, Berlin-Cölln[7] and Frankfurt an der Oder; on the north-west border of the Mittelmark on the right bank of the Elbe around Perleberg was the Prignitz; east of the Prignitz stretching to the Oder was the Uckermark, with its chief town of Prenzlau; finally east of the Mittelmark on the Oder and Warthe was the Neumark, with only one significant urban centre, the fortress-town of Kostrzyn/Küstrin. The whole electorate was landlocked and lacked defensible, natural frontiers. It was also very flat and the soil poor and sandy, leading to its nickname of the 'sandbox' of Germany. Although cereal crops were grown (rye rather than wheat) and cattle raised, large areas had been turned over to sheep. Much of the countryside was moorland and there were also vast dense forests of birch and fir. Both the Elbe and Oder, two of Germany's major rivers, which eventually discharged into the North Sea and Baltic, flowed through Brandenburg, and there were also several meandering, sluggish streams, such as the Havel and Spree, as well as many lakes and extensive fenland. The countryside was dominated by the Lutheran nobility, while the towns, including Berlin-Cölln, were small and unimportant, isolated from the major German trade routes and commercial centres.

The natural poverty of their possessions had meant that the Hohenzollerns, who had ruled Brandenburg since the beginning of the fifteenth century, were only important in the Empire immediately before Imperial elections since they were traditionally the most senior of the seven Imperial electors. The Hohenzollerns were overshadowed politically by their Wettin neighbours in Saxony. Because of this, it is perhaps surprising that Lutheranism, very much a homegrown Saxon product, came comparatively late to Brandenburg. It was really only under Elector John George (1571–98) that the dynasty and its subjects finally abandoned Catholicism.[8] In doing so, however, Brandenburg adopted a rigid Lutheran orthodoxy on the Saxon model, and there was no enthusiasm among the clergy or nobility for further religious change. It was to be the Hohenzollern dynasty itself which was to want a 'second reformation' in the Calvinist mould. This began very cautiously under Elector Joachim

Frederick (1598–1608) and then gathered pace under his successor, John Sigismund (1608–19), grandfather of the Great Elector.

Elector John Sigismund eventually announced his conversion to Calvinism on Christmas Day 1613, and he was joined by his heir, George William, and some of his closest councillors. He seems to have acted from genuine conviction and undoubtedly hoped that his subjects would follow suit.[9] At the same time he hoped to be able to align Brandenburg with the Calvinist bloc around Frederick of the Palatinate and the Dutch Republic and to play an active role in the Empire. The electoral prince, and heir, George William, was already betrothed to the Elector Palatine's sister, Elizabeth Charlotte (1597–1660), and the two married in 1616. As Elizabeth Charlotte's maternal grandfather had been William the Silent, Stadtholder and architect of Dutch independence from Habsburg Spain, the marriage also brought a dynastic connection with the Dutch house of Orange. Unfortunately, Elector John Sigismund had miscalculated badly: his conversion produced uproar within Brandenburg, and even his wife, Anna of Prussia, sided with the Lutheran opposition. It soon became clear that the clergy, the nobility and the noble-dominated Estates would not abandon their faith, so that Calvinism remained confined to the narrow circle of the court. The dynasty itself, which was already less powerful than its Estates and depended on them for taxation, was weakened further. Consequently, to associate openly with the Calvinists in Heidelberg and The Hague would have been far too dangerous. Before he died in 1619, Elector John Sigismund could do no more than observe the growing crisis within Germany from the sidelines. His death brought to the throne the Great Elector's father, George William, a man totally unfitted for the challenges ahead.

Within a year of Elector George William's accession (b. 1595, ruled 1619–40), his brother-in-law, Frederick of the Palatinate, had to flee from Bohemia, and the Calvinist political and military position in the Empire collapsed. As a Calvinist, without the security afforded Lutheran rulers by the Peace of Augsburg, the Elector of Brandenburg's own throne could all too easily have been threatened by the triumphant Emperor Ferdinand II and his allies. It made sense, therefore, for the politically and militarily weak young ruler to distance himself from his rebellious in-laws and to assert his loyalty to the Emperor. In 1620, under pressure from his fiercely Lutheran mother, he also had to allow his younger sister to marry the Lutheran Gustavus Adolphus of Sweden rather than a Calvinist.

During the next few years George William did his best to keep out of the Thirty Years War, which continued in a series of minor campaigns in Germany.

The Elector in any case had problems enough in trying to rule the possessions left him by his father. These were far more than just the electorate of Brandenburg. George William's maternal grandfather, Duke Albert Frederick (1553–1618) of Prussia (East Prussia), was a member of another branch of the Hohenzollern family. His duchy on the shores of the Baltic to the east of Brandenburg was surrounded by Polish territory. Settled mainly by Germans and ruled by the Teutonic Knights till it was secularised in 1525, Prussia was outside the Holy Roman Empire and had long been a fief of the Catholic kingdom of Poland.[10] Although Duke Albert Frederick ruled in name till his death in 1618, he was insane, and King Sigismund III of Poland (1587–1632) had allowed first Elector Joachim Frederick (from 1605) and then Elector John Sigismund, who was married to the Duke's daughter, Anna, to act as regent. In 1623 King Sigismund formally invested George William with Prussia. This dynastic good luck brought together what became the core territories of Brandenburg-Prussia, which were to be ruled by the Hohenzollerns until the fall of the dynasty itself at the end of the First World War. Their new acquisition, however, gave the electors no immediate advantage and weakened their own position even further. Their hold on Prussia was to be very tenuous. The German-speaking nobility and the diet it controlled were all-powerful, fervently Lutheran and hostile to their foreign Calvinist rulers. At the same time the duchy was separated physically from Brandenburg by 200 kilometres of Polish territory, and the Polish king as overlord was able to insist on investing every new duke. Possession of Prussia also threatened to draw the Hohenzollern rulers into the existing dynastic and territorial conflict between Catholic Poland and Lutheran Sweden. In the years 1625–9 George William could only look on helplessly as Sigismund III and Gustavus Adolphus waged war against each other, largely in Polish Royal Prussia which lay between Brandenburg and ducal Prussia. The truce of Altmark (1629) left the Swedes in control of the two East Prussian ports of Pillau/Baltiysk and Memel/Klaipeda and of all access to the duchy by sea, including to its main port and capital of Königsberg/Kaliningrad.[11]

In addition to Prussia and Brandenburg, George William ruled over a third territory, where he faced different, but equally daunting, problems. This was the duchy of Cleves/Kleve and the county of Mark, hundreds of kilometres to the west in the Rhineland and separated from Brandenburg by the lands of several German princes. Until 1609 Cleves and Mark, together with the duchies of Jülich and Berg, had been ruled by yet another insane prince, Duke John William (ruled 1575–1609).[12] His death, without direct heirs, led to a dispute as complicated, persistent and engrossing for the seventeenth and eighteenth centuries as that of Schleswig-Holstein for the nineteenth.[13] The nearest claimants to this bundle of lands, which were among the most prosperous in Germany and very different economically and socially from Brandenburg and Prussia, were Elector John Sigismund of Brandenburg (through his wife Anna of Prussia) and the Duke of Pfalz-Neuburg, both of whom at this time were Lutherans. They agreed initially to rule the whole jointly, but this arrangement collapsed in 1613, when the Elector declared himself a Calvinist and Duke Wolfgang William (ruled 1609–1653) became a Catholic. Given the mutual hostility of the Protestant Union and the Catholic League and the position of Cleves-Jülich on the Lower Rhine, an area of strategic importance for the Dutch and their Spanish enemy in the Southern Netherlands, conflict seemed inevitable, and both Dutch and Spanish troops did occupy several fortresses there. Fortunately, diplomatic intervention by the French and English defused the crisis by the Truce of Xanten in 1614, and this provisionally assigned the mainly Catholic duchies of Jülich and Berg to Wolfgang William and the mainly Lutheran and Calvinist Cleves and Mark, with the small county of Ravensberg, to John Sigismund. The power of the local Estates, and the continuing presence of Dutch garrisons, meant that Hohenzollern control of their new Rhenish lands was initially no more profitable or secure than that of Prussia. Although these gains in the Rhineland and Prussia doubled the size of the possessions of the electors of Brandenburg in the decade before the Thirty Years War, the territories stretched in three discrete and extremely vulnerable blocks across northern Germany and Poland from the Rhine to the Niemen/Nemunas. Not only were they vulnerable to potential predators but they were also in strategically important areas in the conflicts between the European and German powers. The Hohenzollern rulers were far weaker than those of the leading German states of Saxony and Bavaria and even of medium-sized ones like Hesse or Württemberg. Moreover, the new acquisitions had further complicated the dynasty's religious problems: urbanised Cleves and Mark contained many Catholics as well as Calvinists and Lutherans, while in predominantly Lutheran East Prussia there was also a sizeable Catholic minority, protected by the Polish crown.

Elector George William succeeded to the Brandenburg throne on 23 December 1619, old style, or 2 January 1620, new style,[14] just a month before the birth of his son, Frederick William, the Great Elector. Although George William was only twenty-five and had been physically active and healthy, within a year of his accession he had a crippling fall. A wound on his thigh failed to heal, and a few years later the other leg gave way, making walking so difficult that he had to be carried everywhere in a chair or litter. This disability, together with a natural diffidence, made him a weak and timid ruler, looking for someone stronger to lean on. He found this for most of his reign in Count Adam von Schwarzenberg (1583–1641), a Catholic from Jülich, who was both capable and domineering. Although George William, his court and most of his ministers were Calvinist, Schwarzenberg's Catholicism did not prove a drawback: it actually helped make the Elector more acceptable to Emperor Ferdinand II, while the Brandenburg Lutheran Estates initially preferred him to Calvinist ministers. In any case, for most of the 1620s, George William's policies, guided by Schwarzenberg, were neutralist, largely loyal to the Emperor and accepting of the increase of Imperial and Catholic power. These policies were similar to those pursued by the Lutheran Elector of Saxony and could be justified as safeguarding the Hohenzollern dynasty from the Emperor's hostility. Moreover, they helped persuade the Catholic Sigismund III of Poland to invest George William as duke of Prussia. The pro-Imperial policies were also welcomed by the Elector's Lutheran Estates, as they made an army unnecessary and Brandenburg could keep out of the sporadic warfare between sundry supporters of Frederick of the Palatinate and the Emperor. However, the entry of King Christian IV of Denmark (ruled 1588–1648) into the Thirty Years War in 1625 and its focusing the struggle on northern Germany were to change matters fatally for Brandenburg and to push her towards the abyss.

George William's electorate immediately became a battleground for the Danes and their German allies on the one hand and for the Catholic League and Emperor Ferdinand's new army under the successful adventurer, Albrecht von Wallenstein (1583–1634), on the other. Wallenstein's army was to stay in Brandenburg after the defeat of the Danish King in 1626, and the Elector, with no army of his own, had to declare his complete loyalty to the Emperor. This was a prudent move at a time when the dukes of Mecklenburg, who had supported the Danes, were deposed by Ferdinand and their duchy given to the increasingly ambitious Wallenstein. But it meant effectively handing over the unarmed electorate to the Imperialists, who quartered their troops there, seized supplies and raised war taxation, known as contributions, at will. By May 1629 George William was complaining to the Emperor: 'I see nothing before my eyes but the ruin and devastation of my poor innocent country . . . [and] no one . . . would believe that there is still an elector [here].' Yet far worse was to come. In February 1630, as Wallenstein passed through the Brandenburg capital of Berlin, he warned Schwarzenberg, 'if the Swede comes with an army, it will be worse. This will be the seat of the war: Pomerania, the Mark [Brandenburg] and Mecklenburg will go to the wall.'[15]

King Gustavus Adolphus and his Swedes did come to Germany, on what soon became an anti-Habsburg and anti-Papal crusade, in July 1630, and Wallenstein's warning proved all too true. The Swedish invasion put Elector George William in an impossible position. With Brandenburg occupied in all but name by Imperial troops, the electorate was bound to be the main victim of a Swedish–Imperial war. The Lutheran Swedish King, who was of course George William's brother-in-law, put it brutally to a Brandenburg envoy:

I don't want to know or hear anything about neutrality. My Cousin has to be friend or foe. When I come to his borders, then he must declare himself cold or warm. God and the devil are at war. If My Cousin wants to side with God, then he has to join me; if he prefers to side with the devil, then indeed he must fight me; there is no third way.[16]

This threat led to the collapse of the Habsburg faction in Berlin, and Schwarzenberg had to retire to Cleves. The powerful Brandenburg Estates, who held the purse strings in the electorate, also identified with the Swedish King, as a fellow Lutheran, hoping he would free the country from the extortions of the Imperial troops. For a time, the Calvinist Chancellor Sigismund von Götzen and other ministers who had close ties with the Estates came to the fore. Although George William still hesitated, the arrival of the whole Swedish army in Brandenburg in spring 1631 concentrated his mind: he quickly agreed to an alliance with Gustavus Adolphus, which Saxony also joined. The King's victories kept both Protestant states on Sweden's side, even after his death in 1632. At first the regency in Stockholm for the child Queen Christina (ruled 1632–54) seemed to be as successful militarily. But the shattering, joint Spanish and Imperial victory over the Swedes at Nördlingen in 1634, followed by the Peace of Prague between the Emperor and Saxony (1635), was to bring George William back to his old allegiance.

Although this pro-Habsburg policy accorded with the Elector's own personal loyalty to the Emperor and Empire, it could also be justified in that safety for his militarily helpless state lay with the winning side, which in the late 1630s was once more the Emperor's. As Imperial troops moved into the electorate, the pro-Swedish councillors in Berlin were overruled, Schwarzenberg returned and an alliance was formed in 1636 with the Emperor and Saxony against Sweden. The Elector and Schwarzenberg now went beyond passive support for the Imperialists and in 1637–8 tried to raise an army to help the new emperor, Ferdinand III (1637–57). The spur to this military adventure was the large neighbouring Baltic duchy of Pomerania, where Duke Bogislav XIV died in 1637 without immediate heirs, but naming the Hohenzollerns as his successors. As the Swedes were occupying Pomerania and using its ports as their gateway to Germany, George William hoped an Imperial victory would bring him possession. Unfortunately, the campaign went horribly wrong: raising a Brandenburg army proved a disaster, the electorate was devastated by both sides, especially by the Imperialists and Saxons, and in 1638 George William and his court were forced to take refuge in Prussia. He left Schwarzenberg to represent him as his stadtholder or viceroy in Berlin, and the minister in effect turned over the electorate and its resources to the Imperial war machine. Had the Imperialists triumphed, the horror might have soon been over for Brandenburg and its population. However, Swedish recovery and their military successes and that of their Dutch and Hessian allies, together with the crucial entry of France into the conflict against the Spanish and Austrian Habsburgs in 1635, meant a further decade of war, with Brandenburg apparently tied to the losing side. Emperor Ferdinand III was powerless to defend Brandenburg from the Swedes, who soon occupied almost all the electorate as well as Pomerania. Schwarzenberg, who had been given absolute powers and was ignoring the Privy Council (*Geheimer Rat*) and the Estates, controlled only a few fortresses. Devastation and defeat were to be the legacies of George William's reign. At his death in December 1640 one of his councillors in Berlin wrote: 'We could end up having a master without any lands to rule over . . . Pomerania is lost, Jülich [Cleves] is lost; we are holding on to Prussia by its tail like an eel; and as to the Marks [Brandenburg], there is talk of a deal over them.'[17]

. . .

FREDERICK WILLIAM'S CHILDHOOD

Frederick William was born on 6/16 February 1620, a month after his father became elector, and he was the only son to survive infancy. His first years were spent close to his mother, Elizabeth Charlotte of the Palatinate, and his maternal grandmother, Louise Juliana of Orange (1576–1644). Both were strong Calvinists and partisan supporters of their unfortunate brother and son, Frederick V of the Palatinate. It was probably as much to remove Frederick William from their influence, as well as to have him in a place of comparative safety as the Thirty Years War spread to Brandenburg, that he was sent east at the age of seven to the gloomy fortress of Kostrzyn on the River Oder. Here he was brought up by his tutor, Johann Friedrich von Leuchtmar, a Calvinist from Berg. Religious instruction from Calvinist clerics bulked as large in his education as the subjects conventionally taught to a young prince: mathematics, drawing, geometry, studying fortifications, history and languages. He absorbed his Calvinist faith naturally and confidently, with no room for doubt or speculation. In addition to German, Latin and French, he was also taught some Polish. But he was keenest on the more practical subjects and was certainly no scholar. He was also encouraged to ride, to hunt and to hawk: an essential part of the upbringing of all princes and nobles, providing both recreation and an introduction to the skills needed for war. As with most of his princely contemporaries, the chase was to become part of his daily routine throughout his life.

The isolation at Kostrzyn was occasionally relieved: there were a few trips to Berlin, a visit to his aunt, the Swedish Queen, in Pomerania, then a further visit there to pay respects to the dead Gustavus Adolphus, as his body was taken back to Sweden after the fatal battle of Lützen. Finally at the turn of the year 1633–4 he spent a few months in Szczecin/Stettin at the court of the last Pomeranian duke, Bogislav XIV. But when Frederick William was fourteen, his father decided to widen his horizons. The grand tour of European courts, enjoyed by many princely contemporaries,

Fw highly influenced by Dutch

was impracticable because of the war and the empty Brandenburg treasury. Given George William's temporary commitment to the anti-Habsburg side, and the undoubted pressure from his wife and mother-in-law, it was decided in spring 1634 to send Frederick William and Leuchtmar to stay in the Dutch Republic. Living in a Calvinist country would reinforce his faith, his Orange relatives there could introduce him to a more refined court life, and he would be safe from the war, which had hardly troubled the flourishing Dutch cities.

In summer 1634 Frederick William and Leuchtmar established themselves at Leiden. At this time the Northern Netherlands were the most dynamic economic, scientific and cultural region of Christian Europe, and the university in Leiden was the most popular on the continent for Protestant scholars and students. Although the young prince attended only the odd lecture there, he received private instruction in philosophy, religion, history and politics. How much he understood is a different matter. Yet he does seem, like so many of his Orange relatives and his own ministers later, to have been affected by the fashionable ideas of neo-stoicism, propounded in Leiden. While these had much in common with the Calvinist ideals of thrift, modesty and correct behaviour towards one's fellow men, the neo-stoicists also stressed the duties of princes to rule the state for the benefit of their subjects. And of particular significance, in this era of marauding and mutinous armies, was their belief that an army with 'tight military discipline constituted a benefit for society and a strengthening of the state and its capacity successfully to regulate relations between military and civil society, minimising disruption'.[18] In Frederick William's case, however, these ideas were adopted, like his Calvinism, as part of his natural beliefs rather than as a subject for academic study. He was undoubtedly even more impressed by the outward signs of Dutch economic success: a prosperous population, the largest navy and commercial fleet in western Europe, and hegemony over European and world trade and finance. The Dutch, of course, also boasted the most advanced agriculture, many of the most developed industries, and the most impressive military engineers and infantry drill masters. Frederick William discovered all this for himself through visits to the great Dutch cities and also to The Hague where the Dutch Stadtholder, Prince Frederick Henry of Orange, was establishing an impressive court in the 1630s.[19] Frederick Henry (Stadtholder 1625–47), who later became Frederick William's father-in-law, also invited him to visit the

Dutch army which was investing the Spanish-Netherlands fortress of Breda. Although the seventeen-year-old spent only a very short time at the siege in summer 1637, Dutch military as well economic success was to have a lasting influence on him, much the same as on the young Peter the Great at the end of the century.

Frederick William's stay in Holland, and his closeness to both the Orange court and that of the exiled Palatinate family at Rhenen, was to prove an increasing embarrassment to his father, as the latter moved back fully into the Imperial camp in 1636. The Elector and Schwarzenberg soon began to press Frederick William to return to Berlin. For over a year the young prince tried to postpone this with a string of excuses about how war and plague made it dangerous to cross Germany and how travelling by ship made him seasick. There were two reasons for this procrastination. First, he feared that Schwarzenberg was working to marry him into the Austrian Habsburg family; and second, he hoped to persuade his father to give him a semi-independent position as stadtholder of Cleves. As George William would not hear of the latter and insisted on his return, Frederick William became convinced that Schwarzenberg was to blame and he came to hate the chief minister. At last in May 1638, with all his excuses exhausted and financial support from Berlin cut off, Frederick William, now eighteen and evidently having found his sea legs, finally sailed from Amsterdam to Hamburg and then continued by land.

Frederick William reached Berlin in summer 1638 at the height of the devastation and disappointment caused by Schwarzenberg's military alliance with the Emperor against Sweden. The Prince's hatred of Schwarzenberg immediately became even fiercer: after a banquet given by the Catholic minister to welcome his return, Frederick William developed a rash and fever. Although it was measles, he was convinced till the end of his life that Schwarzenberg had tried to poison him.[20] During the next two years, while Schwarzenberg ruled in Brandenburg, George William and his family, including the Prince, sheltered in the safety of the ducal castle in Königsberg in Prussia. Relations between father and son were poor, and the Elector was suspicious of the anti-Habsburg views of both Frederick William and his mother and grandmother. Consequently, despite his health collapsing, George William excluded his heir completely from government and, in the Prince's own words, 'kept [him] out of all deliberations', treating him as a 'complete stranger'.[21] Frederick William believed later, as he wrote in his *Political Testament* for his own son, that if he had been given some responsibilities then 'my own government would not have been so difficult at the beginning'.[22] His exclusion was to continue till George William died from pneumonia in December 1640, aged forty-five.

. . .

NOTES AND REFERENCES

1 F.L. Carsten, 'The Great Elector', *History Today* (1960), p. 83. Later he felt it more prudent to call him merely 'the most important of the Hohenzollern rulers'. F.L. Carsten, ed., *The New Cambridge Modern History, Vol. 5, The Ascendancy of France, 1648–88* (Cambridge, 1961), p. 545.

2 P. Schröder, 'The Constitution of the Holy Roman Empire after 1648: Samuel Pufendorf's assessment in his *Monzambano*', *Historical Journal*, 42 (1999), p. 966. The article is very important for its discussion of sovereignty within the Empire.

3 See V. Press, *Kriege und Krisen: Deutschland, 1600–1715* (Munich, 1991). In English by far the best guide is now P.H. Wilson, *The Holy Roman Empire, 1495–1806* (Basingstoke, 1999).

4 For international relations before the Thirty Years War see M.S. Anderson, *The Origins of the Modern European State System, 1494–1618* (London, 1998); N.M. Sutherland, 'The origins of the Thirty Years War and the structure of European politics', *English Historical Review*, 107 (1992); and G. Parker, ed., *The Thirty Years' War*, 2nd edn (London, 1987).

5 The best accounts in English of the internal German conflict are R.G. Asch, *The Thirty Years War: The Holy Roman Empire and Europe, 1618–48* (Basingstoke, 1997), ch. 1, and G. Parker, ed., *The Thirty Years' War*, ch. 1. But also see C.-P. Clasen, *The Palatinate in European History, 1555–1618* (Oxford, 1966).

6 For the Lutherans' attitude see Asch, *Thirty Years War*, pp. 18ff.

7 Berlin-Cöln were twin towns much like London-Westminster.

8 See B. Nischan, *Prince, People and Confession: The Second Reformation in Brandenburg* (Philadelphia, 1994), passim.

9 See ibid., pp. 81ff.; and the same author's 'Confessionalism and absolutism: the case of Brandenburg', in A. Pettegree, A. Duke and G. Lewis, eds, *Calvinism in Europe, 1540–1620* (Cambridge, 1994), pp. 181ff.).

10 In 1466 the Teutonic Knights were forced to cede the western part (Royal Prussia) of their Prussian lands to the Polish crown and only kept the rest (East Prussia or the duchy of Prussia) by swearing fealty to the Polish king as their sovereign.

11 East-European place-names are a political minefield for the unwary, and the wary. Generally, I have kept English usage for places such as Warsaw and Vienna but have tried to use present-day national ones for the rest. By this token Königsberg should be Kaliningrad, but it seems only a matter of time before this former Soviet president becomes another geographical non-person.

12 For the phenomenon of insanity among German princes in the late sixteenth century, with chapters on the Prussian and Cleves variety, see H.C.E. Midelfort, *Mad Princes of Renaissance Germany* (Charlotteville and London, 1994).

13 Fairly painless accounts are Asch, *Thirty Years War*, pp. 29ff., and Parker, *Thirty Years War*, pp. 36ff.

14 Protestant states, including Brandenburg and England, still used the old calendar, which was ten days behind the reformed one adopted by the Papacy and Catholic Europe after 1582. Single dates in the text are new style.

15 Both quotes from L. Hüttl, *Friedrich Wilhelm von Brandenburg, der Große Kurfürst* (Munich, 1981), pp. 37f.

16 Ibid., p. 39.

17 O. Meinardus, ed., *Protokolle und Relationen des Brandenburgischen Geheimen Rathes aus der Zeit des Kurfürsten Friedrich Wilhelm* (Leipzig, 1889–1919), I, pp. 44f.

18 J.I. Israel, *The Dutch Republic: Its Rise, Greatness, and Fall, 1477–1806* (Oxford, 1995), p. 269. For neo-stoicism see particularly G. Oestreich, *Neostoicism and the Early Modern State* (Cambridge, 1982), and R. Tuck, *Philosophy and Government, 1572–1651* (Cambridge, 1993), ch. 2. It is often forgotten that these ideas also affected Catholic rulers, such as Maximilian of Bavaria and Emperor Ferdinand II, as well as Calvinist ones.

19 For this see J. Israel, 'The Court of the House of Orange, c.1580–1795', in J. Adamson, ed., *The Princely Courts of Europe: Ritual, Politics and Culture under the Ancien Régime, 1500–1750* (London, 1999), pp. 126f.

20 See 11/21 May 1680, R. Southwell to Secretary Jenkins, P[ublic] R[ecord] O[ffice], S[tate] P[apers] 81/82. Frederick William told the English envoy, Southwell, 'he had been poysoned when young by a Favorite of his Father's'. He implied Austria was involved, because he was 'an Heretick, and it appeared as an old grudge, wch still sticks fast. He said he kept his bed eighteen months after it before he could recover.'

21 M. Philippson, *Der Große Kurfürst Friedrich Wilhelm von Brandenburg*, 3 vols (Berlin, 1897–1903), I, p. 20.

22 Hüttl, p. 67.

Chapter 2

THE BEGGARLY ELECTOR, 1640–1648

. . .

FREDERICK WILLIAM ASSUMES POWER

The accession of Frederick William was to transform the destinies of both Brandenburg-Prussia and its ruling dynasty. It would be absurd to claim his reign and his achievements were the catalyst which ensured Bismarck's united Germany and the Second Empire, but it is impossible to see how Hohenzollern Prussia could have risen to the heights it did over the next centuries if Frederick William had not rescued his lands and dynasty from the position of impotence and even irrelevance he inherited. By his death he had made the Hohenzollerns a permanent and increasingly influential factor in both Germany and northern Europe. To use the essential cliché of the historical profession, Brandenburg-Prussia had become 'a force to be reckoned with'!

All this was very much in the unimaginable future: the first essential was mere survival. Frederick William's youthful energy and resilience were in marked contrast to his wretched father. He was also undoubtedly astute, even canny. Although this trait developed with age, it was shown from the very beginning in how he went about isolating Schwarzenberg. Immediately on his accession Frederick William set out to destroy the hated first minister, to regain control of his electorate and to make peace with the Swedes who occupied two-thirds of it. From the security of the castle at Königsberg in distant Prussia, he worked to create an electoral party from Schwarzenberg's many enemies. But, to head off any outright opposition, he immediately assured the Stadtholder of his complete confidence.

A couple of months short of his twenty-first birthday and leaning heavily on the advice of his mother, grandmother and his former tutor, Leuchtmar, he quickly summoned to Königsberg the elderly Chancellor, Götzen, and other councillors ousted by Schwarzenberg when he had suspended the hostile Brandenburg Privy Council in 1638. Most, like the Chancellor, were Calvinists and opposed to the war and the alliance with the Emperor. Once Götzen arrived in Prussia in February 1641, it was mainly his advice the Elector followed over the next year. At the same time, to restore direct control over the troops in the electorate, he gave orders that colonels known to be loyal were to obey him alone. The most important of these was the Calvinist commander at Kostrzyn, Konrad von Burgsdorff (1595–1652). Although an enemy of Schwarzenberg and of the war against Sweden, he had managed to stay friends with both George William and his son. This friendship must have infuriated Schwarzenberg, who had maligned him as 'the child of corruption', claiming that sending him money was like giving 'the cat the cheese' and comparing his troops with the biblical cattle 'who devoured all but stayed lean'.[2] For his part Burgsdorff warned Frederick William 'to be very careful of the people around you and also what you eat and drink'.[3]

In late January 1641, to undermine Schwarzenberg's authority, Frederick William re-established the Privy Council in Berlin and insisted the Stadtholder obey it. At the same time, he ordered him to end hostilities and disband the 4,000–5,000 army which was mostly made up of mercenaries. The Elector felt the war was 'pointless' and merely leading to 'the destruction and burning of one place after another',[4] and he was convinced Brandenburg's lawless army had 'cost the country a great deal and done much wanton damage. The enemy could not have done worse. . . . Therefore we have resolved to keep only what is necessary as a garrison for our fortresses.'[5]

There was a danger that Schwarzenberg would call on the Brandenburg regiments to resist. Many of the mercenary colonels and their officers were mutinous, refusing to swear allegiance to the new elector and insisting they were in Imperial service, since their troops had sworn to serve both Ferdinand III and George William. In the event, the increasingly ailing Schwarzenberg held back, and in late March 1641 he died of a stroke, brought on, according to his doctors, by 'depression and anxiety'.[6] Because of the chaos in the electorate and because he still had to be invested by the Polish King as duke of Prussia, Frederick William decided to stay in Königsberg and send his dependable second cousin and heir, Margrave Ernst of Jägerndorf, to Berlin as new stadtholder. Ernst was a year older

Fred. Will. didn't get along w/ Schwarzenberg + distrusted him

than the Elector and engaged to his sister. The real power, however, was to be in other hands, since Burgsdorff was to accompany him: he was appointed to the Privy Council and given command of all the Brandenburg fortresses as well as the highest court office, Lord High Chamberlain (*Oberkammerherr*). At the same time Burgsdorff was also gradually becoming Frederick William's most influential minister. The Elector came to trust the blunt and pragmatic approach of this energetic and coarse soldier and was ready to put up with his arrogance, drinking and greed. None the less, despite Frederick William's youth and inexperience, there was really no 'Burgsdorff era', especially as the new *Oberkammerherr* was incapable of pursuing systematic policies. The Elector always consulted other ministers, usually following the advice of the majority. Götzen continued as chancellor and was invaluable, shouldering the main burden of routine administration, first in Königsberg and later in Berlin. Moreover, soon after his accession Frederick William became the 'driving force'[7] behind policies.

In his confrontation with Schwarzenberg, Frederick William had enjoyed the full support of the Brandenburg Estates. Until the 1630s these had been the dominant political force in the country, effectively sharing most decision-making with the electors. Controlled by the nobility, they held the whip hand in matters of taxation. Schwarzenberg, however, in the last years of George William's reign, had managed to use the emergency of the war and the threat of his mercenary army to ignore the Estates and impose taxes at will, although even he did not challenge the nobles' own exemption from paying these. His arbitrary actions had led to repeated protests from the Estates, who accused him, in December 1640, of leading the country to 'total ruin' and demanded Brandenburg should leave the war, especially as the electorate was having to pay taxes to the occupying Swedes as well.[8] At George William's death the Estates immediately appealed to his son to free them from Schwarzenberg's tyrannical government and urged him not to make further alliances 'without their advice and approval'.[9] They complained more about the behaviour of the troops of Schwarzenberg's allies, the Emperor and the Elector of Saxony, than about the Swedes.[10] Frederick William responded readily, hoping to rebuild the traditional relationship with the Estates shattered by Schwarzenberg. Control of taxation and of raising troops was therefore immediately restored to them. Then, after Schwarzenberg's death, Margrave Ernst and Burgsdorff worked closely with the Estates' representatives, leading

FW can't control army so he disbands them

the late Stadtholder's son to remark that the Elector 'wants to consult the Estates before undertaking or concluding anything of importance'.[11] Yet Frederick William's hopes that the Estates would also play an active advisory role were unfulfilled; they were 'above all apolitical', wrapped up in their local interests.[12] The electoral government, moreover, still had less direct impact on most of his subjects than the Swedish and Imperialist military. In early June 1641 the Privy Council informed Königsberg that even in the Altmark they had hardly any power since the Swedes had almost 'formed a state' there.[13]

By autumn 1641 Margrave Ernst and Burgsdorff had managed to cut back the Brandenburg army to 2,000 foot and a single company of 125 horse, encouraging the rest to join Imperial service. This went some way to reduce the financial and material burden on the country. The remaining infantry was to garrison the few fortresses in electoral hands, and the cavalry company, which the Elector insisted carry carbines like the Dutch army, was given the hopeless task of protecting the countryside and small towns. The inhabitants of these continued to judge it safer to flee with their possessions into the fortresses or woods if any troops approached.[14] As late as November 1641, some electoral troops sent to protect the town of Brandenburg 'smashed up all the household utensils, chests, cupboards, doors and windows, knocked down the walls of the few houses standing, tore out the lintels and beams, ripped up the floors, burnt the timber . . . , drove their horses into the gardens and vineyards'.[15]

This dissolution of the Brandenburg army did nothing in itself to rid the electorate of the Swedes and Imperialists or their depredations. Frederick William had hoped to achieve this by simultaneously making a truce with the Swedes and signing agreements with them and the Imperialists for both sides to withdraw. Given Sweden's proximity and continuing military successes, relations had to be regularised with her above all. Consequently, Frederick William and his ministers worked hard to accommodate the Swedes, and in any case many Brandenburg Lutherans still considered them a natural ally. The younger Schwarzenberg had noted in May 1641 that 'the Estates are almost all friends of Sweden and enemies of the Emperor'.[16] Eventually a two-year truce was signed in July 1641, and this was to last tacitly till the end of the Thirty Years War in 1648. But harsh terms had to be agreed: the Swedes kept fortresses throughout Brandenburg, could cross it at will and continue to recruit men and impose heavy taxation there. While the truce and

20 — attempts to lighten financial burden + drive out Swedes + Imperialists

withdrawal from the war freed the Elector from depending politically on the Emperor and from direct Swedish attack, it did not free
the population from the effects of the war itself. Swedish troops
remained and the Imperialists were to return when it suited them,
both sides seizing what they wanted. The problem was largely in-
soluble: if Swedes and Emperor continued to fight, geography dictated they would do so, at some time, on Brandenburg soil and at
her expense, unless Frederick William was strong enough to keep
them out. As he had dissolved the rabble he had inherited and could
not afford to raise a proper army, the devastation of his lands inevitably continued. In January 1643 the Privy Council wrote to the
Elector that the Swedes were taking so much in manpower, forage,
grain and cash, that 'nothing is left for the electoral troops'.[17] This
looting probably had a political motive, since early in 1642 the
Swedish general Lilljehöök told a Brandenburg officer that 'the Elector should not be allowed to recover'.[18] The Swedes certainly saw
little reason to accommodate Brandenburg by disciplining their
troops, who in any case were largely a law to themselves.

. . .

FREDERICK WILLIAM AND PRUSSIA

The general devastation in Brandenburg and in particular the dilapidated state of the electoral palace at Cölln, the old island heart
of Berlin in the middle of the River Spree, made it too risky for
Frederick William to leave the safety of Königsberg prematurely.
Here his court was comparatively lavish, with 400 persons as well as
a troop of 20 apes.[19] Although the revenues he could draw on from
Prussia were scanty enough, they were nonetheless essential. Chancellor Götzen told an English envoy there, in May 1642, that his
master 'had scarce any where means for his sustenance and support,
but out of . . . Prussia [sic]'.[20] Frederick William also had to remain
in the duchy to have his sovereignty confirmed by the Polish crown.
Because Prussia was a Polish fief, his father's death gave him no
rights there until the Polish King Władysław IV (1632–48) invested
him as duke. This had seemed problematic at first, since Władysław
wanted to use the change of ruler to assert more direct control: he
even tried, unsuccessfully, to appoint the highest officials in the
Prussian government. Frederick William, however, played on the
King's own financial desperation. He offered to pay the customary

tribute of 300,000 crowns at once and promised, like his father, to share the toll receipts from his Prussian ports. These offers had the desired effect. But Frederick William had to agree as well to continue to exclude all but native Lutherans and Catholics from office. Church services were also restricted to these two faiths, while those of others, including his fellow Calvinists, were forbidden.[21] Władysław moreover insisted that the new duke come to Warsaw in person to be invested. In October 1641, therefore, Frederick William had to kneel before the Polish King and swear allegiance in return for the duchy. However, he ignored strong hints that he might marry Władysław's sister. At a reception in Warsaw:

> the princess danced a graceful ballet to give him pleasure. But the Elector appeared in dirty neckband and boots all worn on one side and muddy half way up the leg, and altogether dressed with such negligence that the least observant could easily see that he had little heart for dancing in that company.[22]

Although the investiture confirmed that ultimate sovereignty lay in Warsaw, Władysław was to interfere very little in Prussia. In 1645 he accepted 4,000 thalers from Frederick William to allow Calvinist services to be held in Königsberg castle during the Duke's absence: beforehand these could only take place while he was there in person. Then in 1646 Frederick William reduced the rates on the tolls at the Prussian ports and refused to make further payments to Władysław. He had found it difficult to pay these, especially as the toll revenues had declined: shipping had moved to the Polish ports of Elbląg/Elbing and Gdańsk/Danzig, where rates were lower. Although Władysław blustered, he did nothing, having too many problems of his own. He was about to embark on war with the Turks and was also soon immersed in the massive Cossack revolt of Bohdan Khmel'nitsky in the Polish Ukraine. When Władysław died in 1648 and his brother, John Casimir, was elected Polish king (1648–68), relations became easier. Frederick William's support for his election, and a hefty cash gift, persuaded John Casimir to concede that the dukes of Prussia need not come in person to Warsaw to be reinvested with the duchy at the accession of a new king. During the election Frederick William had raised troops in Prussia in case John Casimir needed them. But his own Prussian government and diet refused to pay for these, arguing it was his own affair if he wanted to help the King. It was clear from this episode that Frederick

William would not be able to pursue a foreign policy in north-eastern Europe requiring troops without his Prussian subjects' consent. His relations with Władysław and John Casimir at the beginning of his reign also showed that Polish sovereignty was a live issue and constant irritant.

The duchy of Prussia was slightly smaller than Brandenburg. It lay further north, on the Baltic, and had an odd-shaped sandy coast, with two large lagoons. But it had much in common with the electorate: both were flat, with huge forests and many sluggish, boggy watercourses, although Prussia had more lakes. The duchy's soil was largely difficult clay, with a short growing season, but it was more fertile than Brandenburg's sandy heaths. In both countries agriculture was heavily dependent on servile peasant labour (see pp. 118–22). With a population of around a quarter of a million,[23] Prussia as a whole was prosperous, having been free of warfare since 1629. Its wealth was built on amber collected from the seashore, cereals, timber products and hides, most exported through the main port and capital of Königsberg on the River Pregel/Prege. This city was four times the size of Berlin and almost as large as Polish Gdańsk, and with a university boasting more students than Leipzig. Königsberg, like Gdańsk, also exported the raw materials of the Polish and Lithuanian hinterlands and imported western European and colonial goods. These were carried by Dutch and English merchantmen and little of Königsberg's wealth, or that of the rest of the country, came the duke's way. Prussia's rulers, moreover, were feeble political figures. Long before the Brandenburg Hohenzollerns succeeded in the early seventeenth century, the dukes had become political captives of the Estates. The latter met frequently as a full diet (*Landtag*) in Königsberg and effectively controlled the central and local government, finances and militia. All important posts, laws, taxes and foreign treaties had to be approved by them, and the collection of taxation was in their hands.[24] Although the duke had the right to summon and dissolve the diet, he was too weak to take advantage of this. The ultimate guardian of the Estates' privileges was the Polish crown, and the Estates insisted that the Prussian constitution did not rest on agreements between them and their dukes but on those made in previous centuries by Polish kings, Estates and dukes. These agreements meant Prussia enjoyed 'a special three-cornered relationship'.[25] Many Prussian nobles also had lands in Poland and, despite being mainly German-speaking, felt no affinity with Frederick William's German territories.

The Prussian diet was made up of three houses or estates. The first was the twelve *Landräte* (provincial councillors), nobles appointed for life to administer the largest Prussian districts (*Ämter*, singular *Amt*); the second was all the nobility (usually known as the Junkers); and the third was the towns. The second house was really the most important, since it effectively nominated the members of the first and the other major officials. Although there were a few great nobles in Prussia (the *Herren*), the Junkers were much smaller fry, petty nobles, but as insistent on their rights and independence as the Polish magnates. By the mid-seventeenth century most of their peasants, many Polish- or Lithuanian-speaking, had been reduced to what amounted to serfdom. About 15 per cent of the population, however, were prosperous and free land-owning peasants, called *Kölmer*. While these *Kölmer* were not represented in the main diet, they did attend provincial ones (*Amtstage*) till 1686,[26] where delegates were chosen for the diet and grievances were aired. Both nobles and *Kölmer* paid some taxation, but only that approved by the diet.

The towns were the third estate in the diet, although Königsberg's size and wealth meant it dwarfed the rest. The city was really three towns, Altstadt, Kneiphof and Löbenicht, each with a mayor and council, where guilds and citizens still played an active role. The three towns usually presented a united front in the diet. Given the chance, Königsberg would undoubtedly have liked to copy the semi-republican Imperial free cities in Germany or Gdańsk in Poland. As it was, it considered itself a match for the duke or even the noble estate, and it did exert some restraint on the latter. It was probably because of Königsberg's influence that Prussia had not become a noble republic like Poland.[27]

Despite Königsberg's power and pretensions, the chief officials and the central and local administrators of the duchy were always nobles. At the top were the four *Oberräte* (superior councillors). These were nominated by the *Landräte*, who administered the larger districts. All had to be native Lutheran or Catholic nobles (under a privilege called the *Indigenatsrecht*, which the Polish crown guaranteed) and they were effectively nominees of their peers. Leading officeholders swore allegiance to the diet as well as to the duke. When the full diet or *Landtag* was not sitting, its role was filled by the *Consilium*, an executive committee made up of the four *Oberräte*, four of the *Landräte*, and the three mayors of Königsberg. As the mayors could be outvoted, they were no threat to noble monopoly on power. In this system the ruling duke was an unequal partner with the *Oberräte*, who would quickly appeal to Warsaw if he stepped out of line. The *Oberräte* also controlled the Chamber (*Kammer*) in Königsberg, which collected the duke's own revenues. The latter came from the ducal domains, the tolls, monopolies such as the amber trade, and some indirect taxes. Very few of these revenues reached the duke himself. Although he had vast domains (from the secularisation of church lands at the Reformation), about two-fifths of Prussia, the *Oberräte* administered these, leasing or mortgaging them to fellow nobles. In 1649 the *Oberräte* claimed the total income from the ducal domains was a mere 6,000 thalers,[28] and the situation had hardly improved by the start of the War of the North in 1655.[29] Not surprisingly Frederick William's government in Prussia was heavily in debt throughout the 1640s.

Elector George William had enjoyed easy relations with his Prussian subjects. He had deliberately downplayed his own religion so as not to offend their Lutheranism and he had also cooperated with the diet and Polish crown on most issues.[30] At first Frederick William did much the same. He immediately confirmed the *Indigenatsrecht* and soon had to reaffirm his father's ban on Calvinist services outside the court. At his accession he had already been fiercely attacked by the diet for having two instead of one Calvinist pastor there. By August he agreed to get rid of the second one and promised to take the other with him when he left Königsberg. All this was a 'deep humiliation for him both as a Calvinist and as a ruler'.[31] It meant that Calvinism was limited to the court, the odd noble family such as the Dohnas, and small communities in the ports for foreign merchants, effectively protected by the Dutch Republic. In spring 1642 Frederick William even had to beg Władysław IV to persuade the Königsberg Lutherans to let a Calvinist cleric take his father's burial service – the body had been kept embalmed till then.[32] Even so, the funeral provoked rowdy protests from the Lutheran clergy, and there were similar protests three years later when Władysław agreed Calvinist services could be held in the castle even if Frederick William were away. But these were mere hiccups in his early relations with his Prussian subjects. When he left the duchy for Brandenburg early in 1643, his absence made little difference. The duchy remained in the hands of its real masters, the *Oberräte* and *Landräte*. Though they were told not to call a diet without his approval and to refer 'matters of importance' to him, everyone knew this was for form's sake.[33] And for the rest of the 1640s and early 1650s Frederick

25

William was not to challenge 'his' government or the privileges of the Estates.

. . .

RETURN TO BRANDENBURG

Frederick William entered Brandenburg for the first time as elector in March 1643, to find conditions had hardly improved since his accession. His cousin, Margrave Ernst, had spent eighteen desperate months as stadtholder, trying to govern from the shambles of Berlin. He and Burgsdorff had been effectively ignored by both Swedes and Imperialists as both powers continued to use Brandenburg as a battleground and to draw on it as an increasingly empty storehouse in their war for control of north and central Germany. Without an army behind him, Ernst found it difficult even to feed himself and his own servants. In May 1641 he was already writing in despair that 'the cart has sunk so deep . . . in the mire, that it will need singular help from the Almighty to drag it out'.[34] The situation proved beyond him and Burgsdorff, and Ernst grew increasingly depressed. He refused to eat and began to lose his mind: he became convinced, 'if he heard the slightest noise of knocking, that people were trying to wall him up'.[35] In October 1642 he collapsed and died, and Frederick William realised at once that he would have to go to Berlin himself. He nonetheless put off doing so till the winter was over.

On returning to Brandenburg the young ruler – he was just twenty-three – made a determined effort to rule through his Privy Council and to cooperate with the Estates.[36] He quickly established a routine of working with half a dozen councillors two or three days a week, usually following their advice on a range of foreign and domestic issues.[37] At this point in the reign most privy councillors were drawn from the Brandenburg nobility. Although the more important ones, such as Götzen, Burgsdorff and the *Hofmarschall*, Putlitz, were Calvinists, they still had close family and social ties with the Lutheran noble Estates. While Prussian and Cleves matters were discussed in the Privy Council, its authority was limited to Brandenburg, and the governments of Frederick William's other lands would have ignored any instructions from it. It should be stressed that Frederick William ruled essentially over a composite realm of separate territories with very little in common except his own person.

Cooperation with the Brandenburg nobility and Estates, however, did not entail calling a full diet or *Landtag*, with its two houses – one house for the whole nobility and one for the towns. Meetings of all the members of the diet – there were actually two, one for the original electorate of Brandenburg (*Kurbrandenburg*) and another for the more easterly Neumark, usually meeting in different rooms of the Cölln palace – were a rare event and had last taken place in 1615.[38] As in many German states, the Estates were represented by periodic temporary meetings, deputation diets (*Deputationstage*), of between forty and sixty noble and urban deputies, called for a specific purpose, and by a small permanent committee of twenty deputies (the *Ausschuß*), which met for a couple of weeks every June and December to oversee existing taxes and government loans.[39] And it was both groups of deputies whom Frederick William and his privy councillors, in direct contrast to Schwarzenberg's practice, frequently consulted on foreign as well as domestic problems. The deputies seemed to want this, having pressed Frederick William from his accession to consult them before deciding on 'important matters affecting the country's prosperity'.[40] But as the months passed, it became clear that the deputies were uninterested in playing an active and continuous political role, and their advice never usually rose above platitudes. They were essentially concerned with defending their privileges and with ending the war and its miseries, and they showed no interest in events beyond their own borders.

The Estates' main value for the crown, of course, had been as a source of taxation. In the sixteenth century their representatives had periodically agreed to pay off electors' debts by providing occasional taxes. These were collected by the Estates themselves and imposed on the peasantry and the towns but not on the nobility. As the crown became dependent financially on the Estates, it also allowed them to administer its own lands and control the tolls and minting of coin.[41] In this way the Estates, particularly the dominant nobility, assumed the leading political role in Brandenburg. During the Thirty Years War, however, the presence of foreign and electoral troops had forced the Estates to vote regular taxes, called contributions (*Kontributionen*), to support these. In 1643 Götzen persuaded the deputies in the permanent committee to agree to further contributions of 118,000 thalers a year to support the Elector's garrisons and his diplomatic representatives at any future peace talks. This sum was in addition to the annual 120,000 thalers in contributions and 12,000 bushels of corn being paid to the Swedes, as well as many more times that in unofficial exactions. Fortunately there were three successive good harvests from summer 1643, which made the burden on the peasantry less, but still horrendous. Just as badly affected, possibly worse, were the towns: these, despite their decreasing economic as well as political importance, were already paying two-thirds of the contributions. Even Frederick William and his councillors recognised this was too much, and they managed, after much negotiating, to persuade the Estates to adjust the proportion slightly to 59 and 41 per cent. At this stage in their relationship, especially because of their experience with Schwarzenberg and the war situation, the Estates seem to have accepted that the Elector's 'demands were really for the common interest'.[42]

While the Estates' horizons were limited to Brandenburg, Frederick William had to take a wider view. Besides safeguarding Brandenburg from the combatants in the continuing German conflict, he also had to consider his other dynastic possessions, in the Rhineland and on the Baltic. Within a year of returning to Berlin, he seems to have realised that, if he were to have any role in Germany or influence on an eventual peace settlement to the Thirty Years War, he would need more than a few garrison troops. Some twenty years later, in his *Political Testament*, he advised his successor that other rulers would only respect him if he had a strong army, adding: 'I always regret that at the beginning of my reign I let myself, to my very great disadvantage and against my will, be misled and follow contrary advice.'[43] Yet this was distorting the facts, since he had been just as responsible as his ministers for disbanding Schwarzenberg's army because of its dangerous condition and divided loyalties. Any new force would have to be very different, tightly disciplined and paid properly. As Brandenburg herself could clearly not pay for more troops, in January 1644 Burgsdorff was sent to Königsberg on a dual mission. His main purpose was to obtain 'butter, tallow, wax and some carcasses' for the electoral court, and by March he managed to load and dispatch six waggons to Berlin. His secondary aim was to raise cash to pay for troops to be recruited in Brandenburg. Inevitably he found the *Oberräte* and the *Consilium* unsympathetic, especially as they did not regard Brandenburg's concerns to be those of Prussia, and on his return he brought a trifling 10,000 thalers, much of it from loans and mortgaging more ducal land.[44]

When the Brandenburg Privy Council discussed raising the troops at the end of June, there was fierce disagreement. Götzen and some older members, such as Putlitz, who were in tune with the Estates' views, knew only too well the disasters Schwarzenberg's army had caused. Mindful also of Burgsdorff's failure in Prussia, they insisted that Brandenburg could not afford more troops as it was already 4 million thalers in debt. Burgsdorff, however, would not listen and argued that it was 'better to mortgage a quarter of the country than to live in fear of losing all'.[45] He was supported by Leuchtmar, who pointed out how such minor German rulers as the Landgrave of Hesse and Dukes of Brunswick had disproportionate influence in the Empire through their armies. While Frederick William shared Burgsdorff's and Leuchtmar's views, he bowed to the majority's advice that the country could afford only its 2,000 or so garrison troops. Instead, he was to be forced to look elsewhere, to his territories in the Rhineland (see pp. 33–4).

. . .

THE SWEDISH MATCH

Frederick William's tentative moves to raise an army tied in with his efforts to take part in the negotiations to end the Thirty Years War, begun hesitantly in the Westphalian city of Münster during 1643. His failure to assemble more than a token force inevitably meant that he had a very weak diplomatic hand. It was especially important, therefore, to have the protection of one of the major powers, although he was determined this would not entail the kind of strings which had destroyed his father. The obvious choice of protector was Sweden, because of her repeated military successes, his own ministers' pro-Swedish past and the hostility of the Emperor over Frederick William's desertion in 1641. Consequently, the Privy Council decided in April 1643 to begin negotiations with the Regency for Queen Christina in Stockholm. They hoped to avoid a military alliance but to conclude a treaty of friendship which would persuade the Swedes to withdraw completely from Brandenburg and to hand over the neighbouring Baltic duchy of Pomerania, occupied by them now for over a decade. The Hohenzollerns had the best dynastic claim to this and had been recognised as such by the Pomeranian Estates after the death of the childless Duke Bogislav in 1637. Brandenburg's offer of a treaty was also to be accompanied by broad hints that Frederick William wanted to marry his cousin, the seventeen-year-old Queen Christina. Now without a direct heir after Margrave Ernst's death, the Elector realised he had to think seriously about his own succession. Those closest to him were pressing this, and in December 1642 the Prussian *Oberräte* had written, urging him to marry.[46] Circumstances had clearly changed from just after his accession, when he had declared he 'did not want a wife yet . . . it was difficult enough to cope with himself during these hard times'.[47]

In diplomatic circles there had been talk of an Austrian, French, Dutch, Polish and even Russian bride, leading Frederick William himself to remark that 'they will soon be suggesting a Tartar match'.[48] But he and his ministers had their sights on Christina, despite her reputation as a headstrong bluestocking. This marriage would have immediately solved his Brandenburg and Pomeranian problems and made him the strongest ruler in northern Europe. Unfortunately the Swedes were never keen, and it is surprising that the Brandenburgers persisted, especially as rumours of it upset the Habsburgs and Poles. Christina did not want to marry anyone, while her all-powerful Chancellor, Axel Oxenstierna, had no intention of sharing power with a royal husband. Yet the Swedes did not refuse outright and strung the suitor along with excuses about the Queen's youth and the Elector's Calvinist religion. They were especially encouraging from spring 1644, when they became involved in a short conflict with Denmark while still at war with the Imperialists. In June 1644 they even handed over a few Brandenburg fortresses, although insisting the electorate continue to pay its annual tributes of cash and grain. But in 1645, once Sweden had re-established her military dominance in north Germany by forcing the Danes to an ignominious peace and by smashing the Imperialists at the battle of Jankau/Jankov in Bohemia, her troops reappeared in Brandenburg in plundering strength. Nonetheless, throughout 1645 the Swedish marriage still remained 'the pivot of Brandenburg policy'.[49] In February, to bring matters to a head and be in easier reach of Stockholm, Frederick William returned to Königsberg for a year, negotiating from there as well as through his Council in Berlin. Moving to Königsberg also lifted the burden of supporting the court in Berlin. In February 1645 one of his ministers, Arnim, complained they were desperately short of provisions at court, with 'not even a mouthful of wine', because the food allowance had been used to pay the garrison.[50] But the stay in Prussia had no effect on the match, and by the end of 1645 Frederick William accepted he had been led a dance. The failure also meant that no treaty had been concluded with Sweden, and her troops remained in Brandenburg and Pomerania. In this final decade of the Thirty Years War, therefore, Brandenburg continued to be at the mercy of the Imperialist and Swedish combatants.

The collapse of the Swedish marriage inevitably led to an urgent search elsewhere by Frederick William, who was twenty-six in 1646. While there were plenty of German princesses, including Calvinists, to choose from, he was already showing himself a prince with wider political ambitions and was determined on a wife who would bring maximum advantage. He therefore now looked to a daughter of his Calvinist relative and Stadtholder of the Dutch Republic, Prince Frederick Henry. This was encouraged by his mother, Elizabeth Charlotte – her own mother, Louise Juliana, who died in 1644, had been an Orange princess and Frederick Henry's half sister. While family sentiment therefore played a part in this new match, just as important was the support it might bring in the peace negotiations in Westphalia and in strengthening Frederick William's hand in his own territories in the Rhineland.

. . .

FREDERICK WILLIAM AND CLEVES-MARK

Frederick William had not visited his isolated possessions in west Germany since his accession in 1640. The most important was the duchy of Cleves, which was cut in two by the Rhine. Close by, to the south-east in what later became the industrial Ruhr, was the larger county of Mark, while further north was the tiny county of Ravensberg. These lands, especially Cleves, were urbanised and had close political and economic ties with their Dutch neighbours. The population density was three times that of the electorate, and by the end of the reign Cleves and Mark had about 140,000 inhabitants. The crown itself possessed few lands there and those of the nobility were small and scattered. Town and countryside overlapped, with burghers owning many estates. Most farms were leased to prosperous free peasants, on what amounted to hereditary tenure. The towns, particularly those on the right bank of the Rhine in Cleves, were wealthy: they manufactured textiles and were part of the Dutch trading network in western Germany. Real power lay with the urban oligarchs rather than the nobility, who actually paid some taxation. Even in the countryside the nobles' influence was limited

by having to cooperate with peasants' deputies in local representative bodies (*Erbentage*), which allotted and collected taxes.

The Hohenzollern dynasty exercised even less political power in
its Rhenish lands than in Prussia and of course held them under
different titles as duke of Cleves and count of Mark and of
Ravensberg. Both Cleves and Mark had their own Estates, usually
meeting in separate diets but occasionally together. Both diets had
two houses, the first for the nobility and the second for the towns,
the second being far more important. Permanent committees had
not developed, as the full diet (*Landtag*) met regularly, not needing
to be summoned by the ruler. The diet largely chose the governing
council (*Regierungsrat*), insisting on the *Indigenatsrecht* that restricted
office to natives of Cleves and Mark. Taxation had to be approved
by the diet and was administered by its officials. The bulk was paid
by the countryside: for every 5 thalers paid by the rich burghers, the
peasants paid 70–80 and smallholders paid 15.

During the sixteenth century the weak dukes of Cleves-Jülich had
allowed their Estates a predominant role in government and had
also failed to stem the growth of Protestantism. By the 1600s Catholics, Lutherans and Calvinists coexisted everywhere,[51] and to ensure
his succession there Elector John Sigismund had promised to tolerate all three. The division of the duchies between the Hohenzollern
and Pfalz-Neuburg families after 1609 hardly changed the situation,
although the urban elites in Cleves-Mark were largely Calvinist
and several nobles had remained Catholic. The division had also
probably even increased the power of the Estates, especially as the
Hohenzollern rulers' position was insecure because no definitive
treaty had been made with their Pfalz-Neuburg rivals. Legally Cleves-
Mark and Jülich-Berg were still united and both families claimed
each other's share. As ultimate overlord, the emperor was able to
use this disputed succession as an excuse to interfere, especially as
the territories still had the right to appeal to Imperial law courts.[52]
Much more dangerous for the Hohenzollern ruler was that the
Cleves-Mark Estates and the urban oligarchs, particularly in the
most important town of Wesel in Cleves, looked to the Dutch Republic for protection against both foreign enemies and their own
prince. The arrival of Dutch garrisons in the Cleves towns after
1614 brought resident guardians. Estates power and the distance
from Berlin meant that for most of the early seventeenth century
the Hohenzollerns left their Rhenish subjects to rule themselves.
Control also became impossible in any case during the Thirty Years

War when foreign armies overran the duchies. The county of Mark was occupied by Hessians and Imperialists, who levied contributions there, while the Dutch stationed more troops in Cleves. Although they imposed contributions as well, there was little hostility towards the Dutch because they brought political protection and commercial advantages, and their garrisons remained till the 1670s. On the whole these Rhenish lands escaped the Thirty Years War lightly: they could afford to pay their occupiers to act with some restraint.

The absentee Frederick William's government in Cleves and Mark was heavily in debt at his accession. Insignificant revenues were collected and his officials, tied to the urban oligarchs, wanted to keep it that way. There was little he could do about this, given the facts of geography and his own military weakness. To change matters, he really needed to be there in person to assert his authority (he did not go there till 1646) and at least to persuade the occupying forces to leave and to try to raise his own troops. During 1644 and 1645 an opportunity arose for the latter because the Hessians and the Dutch, for their own strategic reasons, began to withdraw troops. With only a few garrison troops in Brandenburg and Prussia, Frederick William was to seize the chance to raise a sizeable and flexible force in the Rhineland. Unfortunately this was inevitably to bring him up against the Cleves-Mark Estates, and over the first two decades of his reign he was to wage an intermittent struggle with these for control of his own government and revenues. For most of the time the Estates had the upper hand and considered their ruler an irritant rather than a real threat, especially as he was usually absent and they knew they could always appeal to the Dutch or the Emperor for protection. The Estates even had their own permanent representative at The Hague till 1660. A republican government on the Dutch model, or even union with the United Provinces, was openly discussed in the Cleves towns. It was these, especially Wesel, Emmerich and Rees on the right bank of the Rhine, which were to cause Frederick William most trouble. Consequently, it was a high-risk strategy for him to raise troops in Cleves-Mark from 1644. While the force was mainly intended to improve the Elector's standing within Germany, Burgsdorff's remarks in the Privy Council in June 1644 show they were also an attempt to assert ducal power in Cleves-Mark. He pointed out that Frederick William's 'authority [had] considerably declined there' and needed to be 'established through the sword'.[53]

Between 1644 and 1646 Frederick William's Stadtholder in the Rhenish lands, Johann von Norprath, mustered around 4,000 troops. He did this in the smaller towns away from the Dutch garrisons, and he used his own military commissioners (*Kriegskommissare*) instead of following the normal practice of subcontracting to mercenary colonels. The small army, however, always existed on a knife-edge and would have been difficult to deploy. Opposition came, inevitably, from the Estates, who had not been consulted, continually pressed for its removal and refused to pay for it. Norprath therefore had to squeeze what he could from the ducal domains and the customs. Throughout 1645 and 1646 the Estates would not grant any taxation and insisted they were 'exempt from all contributions and taxes . . . unless they had freely consented to them'. This led to Frederick William's warning in vain through Norprath in 1646 that if the Estates did not pay for the troops, 'he must permit the occurrence of disorder and military executions' to impose taxation. However, when Norprath's commissioners tried to collect taxes in July, they met widespread resistance. The Dutch garrisons protected the rich cities in Cleves and even posted up the Estates' decrees forbidding payment. In the autumn the Dutch States General urged Frederick William 'to remove and do away with the troops recruited in the land of Cleves or brought there from outside' and ordered their own garrisons to prevent 'any military execution . . . within the range of the[ir] cannon'.[54]

. . .

THE DUTCH MARRIAGE

These first tentative moves to raise his own army produced little benefit for Frederick William. The major powers were not impressed, and when they did begin to withdraw from Brandenburg and Cleves-Mark it was for other reasons. His lands would remain vulnerable until the Thirty Years War ended in Germany, their fate determined by the belligerents. This was why he and his ministers, even during the negotiations with Stockholm, had cast their nets wider. By summer 1644 it had become clear that they ought to look to Sweden's allies, the Dutch Republic and France, for protection and help in the peace talks in Westphalia. Even the pro-Swedish Leuchtmar had declared in the Privy Council in May that they were 'on the edge of the abyss: only foreign help can bring recovery.

Poland would seize Prussia if it were strong enough; Pomerania is subject to the Swedes and Cleves to the [Dutch] States General. All the lands are in danger. Besides the States General, I can only see France as the best candidate for Your Highness.'[55]

The French proved the more receptive. They had intervened in the Thirty Years War to undermine the power of both Spanish and Austrian Habsburgs, and they were keen to sign up as many states in Germany as possible to use as their clients. Cardinal Mazarin, chief minister of the French Regent Anne of Austria (her husband Louis XIII had died in 1643, leaving a minor, Louis XIV), had already been urging the Elector to send a representative to the Westphalian peace negotiations. These talks were progressing very slowly and enthusiasm for peace on both sides fluctuated with their success in the war. As a servant of the French representative d'Avaux put it: 'The peace always warms up in winter and cools down in spring' when a new campaigning season began.[56] None the less, the French began to take Frederick William's part and by the end of 1644 d'Avaux had secured the neutrality of Cleves. Then at the beginning of 1645 France proposed an alliance. This was a clear offer for Frederick William to join France's other clients such as Hesse and to enter the war as a French mercenary: the Elector would surrender his independence for protection, subsidies and territorial gains at the peace. The offer led to two years of tedious and fruitless negotiations. The French wanted clear commitments, which would have meant war with the Emperor, while the Brandenburgers wanted more positive support over Pomerania, which the French could not give because of their Swedish allies. Although Frederick William never rejected the offers outright, fear of being reduced to a dependant like his father stopped him from committing himself. The French eventually decided the talks were intended 'more as a compliment than as real'.[57] None the less, relations between the two states remained cordial, if not intimate, and would bring Brandenburg further advantages in the Westphalian negotiations.

Frederick William probably felt he need not take up French offers because of brighter prospects elsewhere. In spring 1646, just after the final collapse of the Swedish match, he responded to his mother's suggestions of a marriage with the Dutch Stadtholder Frederick Henry's eldest daughter, nineteen-year-old Louise Henrietta. The Orange family itself was eager, but because of Frederick Henry's poor health his wife Amelia von Solms took the lead. Frederick William himself had been an enthusiast of most things Dutch since his stay in the Republic as a teenager, and Louise Henrietta had the obvious advantage of being a Calvinist. Frederick William could also hope that the Stadtholder would curtail Dutch support for the Cleves Estates and help in his dynastic quarrels over the Rhenish lands with the pro-Spanish Catholic Duke of Pfalz-Neuburg (see pp. 8, 37–8). There was also the chance that the Dutch might back Hohenzollern claims to Pomerania, especially as Sweden's recent victories over Denmark threatened the Republic's naval and commercial supremacy in the Baltic. One of Frederick William's councillors, the Prussian Calvinist Fabian von Dohna, summed up the diplomatic advantages: 'I . . . can see no state which can serve Your Electoral Highness more because of its great power on land and especially at sea, because it is so close to Your . . . Jülich [sic] and Cleves lands and because it might give considerable naval help over Pomerania and Prussia.'[58] What could not be foreseen, however, was that Orange power in the Republic would soon collapse and that Frederick William's Orangist connections would prove a dangerous liability there.

Negotiations for the marriage from spring 1646 were completely successful. Although Louise Henrietta was in love with a French Huguenot noble in Dutch service, her mother gave him his marching orders. The girl bowed to her parents' wishes, and by early October Frederick William could announce his forthcoming marriage to his Privy Council. The next month he was in Holland and on 23 November he drove in procession with thirty carriages to address the States General in The Hague. Clearly hoping for close relations, he asked for their support against Sweden in Pomerania and help in his dynastic quarrel with the Duke of Pfalz-Neuburg, a quarrel which had just developed into war (see pp. 38–40). A dinner followed with Frederick Henry and some of the deputies, where the Elector made the mistake of telling them he believed princes should be directly involved in conducting their own affairs. When some of his privy councillors, including Burgsdorff, suggested an alliance with the States General, they were rebuffed. The deputies had no wish to shore up a prince with such obvious ambitions in the Rhineland, particularly one marrying into the Orange family.

Because Frederick Henry's health deteriorated alarmingly, the marriage was celebrated hurriedly and quietly on 7 December 1646 in a small room in the palace at The Hague. The bride wore a gold-brocade dress, covered in pearls, her long train carried by nine counts. Frederick William was equally glittering in a black and white satin suit, set off with diamonds and gold embroidery. The couple were together only a few weeks before he had to leave for Cleves to deal with what was becoming a humiliating war with the Duke of Pfalz-Neuburg. Louise Henrietta followed in March 1647 when her father died. A petite, delicate and even-tempered woman, with long chestnut hair, the new Electress only learned German slowly and often had to fall back on Dutch in conversation. On the other hand, as Frederick William's spoken French was poor, she sometimes translated for him with non-German visitors. She shared her husband's strong religious piety and fatalism, and this gave a solid, if rather serious, basis to their twenty years together. Louise Henrietta was described by a close observer in 1657 as 'of a melancholic temperament, who has little to say but does so to effect. She has little time for trivia and believes women should be involved in [public] business.'[59] Their first child, a boy, was born in May 1648 but died an infant. Another son followed in 1655 and survived. As Louise Henrietta believed (wrongly) she could not have more children, she offered to let Frederick William divorce her. He refused, and, unlike most contemporary princes, he never seems to have had a mistress or strayed outside marriage. He also soon came to value Louise Henrietta's political sense. The French Secretary for Foreign Affairs, Lionne, described her role aptly in 1666 just before her death: 'The Electress, by her gentle suggestions rather than the qualities of her mind, has great influence over her husband.'[60] Soon after their marriage she took a strong dislike to Burgsdorff and his raucous ways, and she came to depend on a young privy councillor, Otto von Schwerin, who was *Hofmeister* (steward) of her household, actively fostering his growing influence with Frederick William.

. . .

THE FIRST BERG WAR

The Elector's marriage coincided with an attempt to resolve the Cleves-Jülich succession issue by force. From the beginning of his reign Frederick William had been as set on pursuing his dynastic claims against the Duke of Pfalz-Neuburg as those against the Swedes in Pomerania. As we have seen, the problem went back more than a generation. The provisional division of the territories in 1614 had given the Hohenzollerns Cleves and Mark, while Wolfgang William of Pfalz-Neuburg acquired the larger Jülich and Berg. Both sides had continued to claim the whole succession, but in 1629 Elector George William had concluded a further provisional treaty, drawn up by Schwarzenberg, which confirmed the existing division. The isolated county of Ravensberg on the River Weser was also to be held jointly, but the Hohenzollerns were to administer only a quarter of it. As Wolfgang William now enjoyed two-thirds of the revenues of the former united duchies, he was widely believed to have bribed George William's Catholic first minister.

Wolfgang William had become a very zealous Catholic after his conversion, but throughout his long reign (1609–53) he always tried to compromise with Brandenburg. Frederick William almost from his succession, however, was determined to change the 1629 settlement, believing it unfair and another of Schwarzenberg's crimes. The appointment of Norprath as stadtholder of Cleves in September 1643 clearly showed the new ruler's intentions: Norprath had previously served Wolfgang William, bore him a grudge and quickly became 'the driving force' behind a new aggressive policy.[61] By December 1643 Frederick William was already agreeing with him that the Duke's 'breaches' of the 1629 treaty justified 'attacking the places held' by him.[62] Both men recognised they would need an army for this, and the small force created in the Rhineland was at least 'partly intended for the war against Neuburg'.[63]

Open conflict developed only slowly, but in the last months of 1645 Norprath pressed for immediate war or at least the seizure of Wolfgang William's share of Ravensberg and the imposition of contributions there. He had urgent grounds for this: the hostility of the Cleves Estates made it difficult to find the 12,000 thalers a month necessary for his troops. However, when Frederick William, who was in Königsberg, wrote to his Privy Council in Berlin, asking if he should 'break' with the Catholic Duke,[64] Götzen and his supporters, who had never wanted troops raised in Cleves, urged restraint. They insisted the force was untrained and lacked artillery; and they did not underestimate Wolfgang William himself, 'an old hard-working and experienced ruler',[65] who could expect help from his fellow Catholic Spaniards and Imperialists. Pointing out that the Elector had no alliances with the anti-Habsburg powers, they warned that the whole Empire wanted an end to the existing war in Germany and would blame him for delaying it. Conflict with Pfalz-Neuburg might spread to Frederick William's own lands and turn his subjects against him. The councillors then went on to lecture their 25-year-old ruler, claiming it was essential to see the end result: before beginning something, special attention should be paid to why ... it had been begun and if the means were available to carry it out ... For if blood is to be shed and the people put in danger, want and misery, and even himself and the state endangered, then there had to be great and important reasons for doing so.[66]

Faced with this outright opposition, Frederick William backed off. For almost another year he bided his time, waging a pamphlet war against Wolfgang William and accusing him of ill-treating his Protestant subjects. During this time his Estates in Cleves and elsewhere were pressing him to disband his small army, and it was proving impossible to raise enough taxes to maintain it. There was an obvious solution: other powers had shown how troops could be kept at a neighbour's expense and were still doing so in his own electorate. The opportunity seemed finally to arrive in autumn 1646 with his marriage to Louise Henrietta. When he stopped at Cleves on his way to Holland in October, he came free of the restraints of the Privy Council in Berlin. With the bellicose Burgsdorff and Norprath for advisers, Frederick William was now determined to seize at least some of Berg and the rest of Ravensberg. Burgsdorff above all was confident of success, contemptuously dismissing Wolfgang William as someone 'the Jesuits have in a vice like a schoolmaster with his schoolboys'.[67] He was also convinced that there would be little resistance, since the Duke's own Estates in Jülich-Berg were proving even more awkward than the Elector's in Cleves. Consequently, in mid-November Frederick William sent 1,800 troops into Berg, with orders to treat the population well and avoid unnecessary fighting. Unfortunately, as the army advanced across the open countryside, the peasants fled with their belongings and animals into the fortified towns. Without artillery, it was impossible to attack these, and in the wintry weather the troops found little to eat except turnips still left in the fields.

While Frederick William had miscalculated badly, his opponent acted sensibly. Wolfgang William refused to negotiate, realising hunger and pressure from the other powers would soon drive out the invaders. The Emperor Ferdinand and the Spanish government in the Southern Netherlands were quick to demand Frederick William's troops leave, while the French also condemned him. Far worse, his attempt to play the Protestant card and use his marriage and visit to the Dutch Republic to get support from the States General failed miserably. After a month he had to send orders from

The Hague for his troops to withdraw. Having rushed impetuously into the adventure, he at least showed good sense in escaping it as quickly as possible. During February 1647 Burgsdorff was sent to negotiate in Berg, and a treaty was eventually signed in April. Given Frederick William's ambitions, this settlement was a defeat for him, and his impatience to revise it shows he felt this. None the less, he did receive the whole of Ravensberg. The old Duke, after a night spent worrying that he had lost his soul to the devil, also agreed to restore the religious position in Jülich-Berg to that of 1609 and to return some churches to his Protestant subjects. He could afford to do so because he knew that the approaching settlement of the Thirty Years War in Westphalia would reverse this.

. . .

BRANDENBURG AND THE PEACE
OF WESTPHALIA

The major European powers decided the outcome of the Berg adventure and they inevitably did so as well over what Frederick William gained at the end of the Thirty Years War. What he wanted, of course, was Brandenburg's northern neighbour, Pomerania. The fate of this Baltic duchy, with its excellent port of Szczecin at the mouth of the River Oder, was to be an open sore throughout his long reign. His dynastic claim to the whole territory was indisputable; the Pomeranian Estates, though they were Lutheran, also wanted him to succeed and had refused to recognise Queen Christina and her military administration there. But the Swedes had begun to dig themselves in, handing out land to their generals as if the country was theirs. They needed Pomerania as an open door into Germany for their armies and also to make themselves members of the Empire with a seat in the Imperial Diet. The duchy furthermore extended their political and economic control of the southern shores of the Baltic Sea. In 1643 the Chancellor, Oxenstierna, declared to the Swedish Council: 'Pomerania is a rampart of Sweden, a naval base against Denmark, a troop base against Poland, and a defensive point to secure the link between Kalmar [in Sweden proper] and Narva [in Swedish Estonia].'[68]

Given his own political and military weakness and the failure of negotiations for a marriage to Queen Christina, Frederick William could realistically only hope to force the Swedes from Pomerania with the help of the other powers. At the peace talks in Westphalia, therefore, the Elector had to try to use the latter's differences to his own advantage. In the event his gains there were won largely through the goodwill of the French, who were emerging as the real victors of the Thirty Years War. Cardinal Mazarin hoped to fit Brandenburg into his policy of using the German princes as counterweights to the Habsburg Emperor. The electorate would also be useful to balance Sweden, whose hegemony in the north was beginning to worry her allies in Paris as well as in The Hague.

The peace negotiations got under way seriously in the Westphalian cities of Münster and Osnabrück in 1645, and almost from the start Frederick William tried unrealistically to claim all Pomerania, to the derision of the other participants. After Sweden's recent crushing defeats of both the Imperialists and the Danes, she was in no mood to put up with this nonsense. Her representative at Osnabrück, Salvius, warned bluntly in October that Frederick William would be attacked if he tried to dislodge her from Pomerania, adding 'Sweden wants Pomerania as her satisfaction [for participating in the war], and his Electoral Highness ought to realise this and reflect on it, . . . since we will not budge'.[69] No one was impressed by the Elector's ordering his representative, Wittgenstein, to insist that the duchy was an essential 'outer wall' for his electorate and 'link with my territories in Prussia'.[70] The French would not break with their Swedish ally for his sake, especially as he was refusing to become one of their German dependants. The Emperor Ferdinand III had not forgiven him for ending George William's Imperial alliance and he preferred the Swedes, whose troops had invaded Bohemia, to find territorial satisfaction in distant Pomerania instead of further south, particularly in Habsburg Silesia. By 30 January 1646, at least the Brandenburg Privy Council had begun to live in the real world. They nervously pressed their master, at this time in far-off Königsberg, to settle with the Swedes, so that the other powers would not sacrifice him and follow the high priest Caiaphas in proclaiming, 'better that one should perish than all'.[71] But Frederick William stood his ground, to the fury of the Imperialists. Emperor Ferdinand's representative at Münster, Trautmannsdorf, declared the Elector would not get 'a hair' in compensation.[72] His hands and lips trembling with rage, the minister accused the Elector of obstructing the whole peace settlement, warning he would be on his own if the Swedes attacked.

On 1 June 1646 Frederick William met his Privy Council at Kostrzyn on his return from Prussia. Led by Götzen, it urged him to be satisfied with part of Pomerania and to seek compensation for the rest elsewhere. Frederick William himself now realised he had to make some concessions, and in August he abandoned the crucial claim to Szczecin and offered to make do with East Pomerania (Hinterpommern), free navigation of the Oder and the port of Wolgast in West Pomerania (Vorpommern). But as compensation he demanded Halberstadt, Minden, Hildesheim, Osnabrück, Münster, Bremen, Magdeburg, all Jülich-Berg and a clutch of minor territories in Habsburg Silesia! These demands, and his attack on Pfalz-Neuburg in the autumn, show that Frederick William had still not grasped European realities. His attitude was to exasperate the other states, who saw him as a persistent and annoying obstacle to the general peace. In France Mazarin wanted to be rid of the German war to concentrate on that with Spain, while Emperor Ferdinand just wanted peace.

On 12 December 1646, a few days after his marriage, Frederick William was handed an ultimatum by the Imperial minister in The Hague, threatening to sign peace without him if he did not accept Sweden's terms. The following month his Privy Council in Berlin, fearing a Swedish attack, pleaded with him to settle at any price. On 13 January 1647, therefore, he ordered Wittgenstein in Westphalia to surrender West Pomerania and the right bank of the Oder, but to demand 120,000 thalers for Szczecin and compensation in Magdeburg, Halberstadt, Minden and either Osnabrück or Glogow/ Glogau and Żagań/Sagan in Silesia. Despite the extravagance of these demands, the French representative in Westphalia, d'Avaux, largely on his own initiative, achieved a compromise.[73] He persuaded the two Swedish representatives to soften their terms, and had Frederick William promise them 25,000 thalers each as well as presents to other Swedish generals and diplomats. In February 1647 the Swedes signed a preliminary treaty, giving Brandenburg East Pomerania without the right bank of the Oder, the exact boundaries to be settled later. Frederick William immediately accepted. With his Berg adventure in ruins (see pp. 39–40) and his hopes of Dutch support disappointed, he was finally confronting reality. By March the French and Swedes had also got the Emperor to agree that Brandenburg should have the more limited compensation of the former bishoprics of Halberstadt, Minden and the expectancy of Magdeburg when its incumbent Administrator, a Saxon prince, died.

All these gains were to be confirmed by the final peace of Westphalia, which ended the Thirty Years War in Germany the following year, 1648.

Compared with other German princes, including actual combatants, Brandenburg did very well out of the peace settlement. It has been argued[74] that this was because of Frederick William's obstinate and exorbitant demands and his efforts after 1644 to play an independent role in European politics, one made possible by raising an army. His pigheadedness in the negotiations may indeed have exasperated the powers into offering him more, but it was a high-risk strategy, and, given his trifling forces and wretched performance in Berg, his gains probably owed most to the powers' calculations of their own interests. In Frederick William's eyes, of course, the settlement was far from satisfactory since the Swedes had robbed him of the richer half of his Pomeranian inheritance, together with control of the Oder. As East Pomerania had no significant towns or adequate harbour, this thwarted his evolving ambitions to turn Brandenburg itself into a commercial power. It also led to a feeling of righteous outrage, which influenced his foreign policy till his death. In reality the territorial compensation for West Pomerania more than made up for it: the revenues alone were three times as great.[75] With the addition of Magdeburg, Halberstadt and Minden, which set Brandenburg squarely in central as well as north-eastern Germany, she was now larger than neighbouring Saxony and second in size in the Empire to the Austrian Habsburgs. When Magdeburg was finally absorbed in 1680, Hohenzollern territory stretched in an unbroken line westwards from the Altmark to the rich secularised bishopric of Halberstadt. Although Minden was much poorer[76] than the latter and far to the west on the River Weser, it bordered directly on the Hohenzollern possession of Ravensberg.

The German religious and constitutional settlements at Westphalia were also to affect Brandenburg. The provisions of the Augsburg peace of 1555 were now extended to include Frederick William's fellow Calvinists together with the Lutherans. This legitimised Calvinist rulers within the Empire, and it had been opposed less by the Emperor and the Catholics than by such fanatical Lutheran princes as Elector John George I of Saxony. Joint efforts during the peace negotiations by Frederick William and by the militarily powerful Calvinist Hessians, who were supported strongly by their Swedish allies, proved successful. This recognition of his own faith as a legitimate religion naturally improved his own standing with his

subjects in Brandenburg. The settlement also brought limited toleration within the German states, since rulers had to allow those
Catholic, Lutheran and Calvinist communities existing in 1624
to continue. They could still expel dissidents without this previous right of worship, but they had to do so within five years of
the peace. This limited toleration within the Empire also actually
included the right 'to attend their devotions in their houses and
in private'.[77] But this inevitably depended a good deal on the whims
of individual rulers, and the Habsburg emperors refused to accept
that it applied to any of their hereditary lands, except Silesia.

The Westphalian settlement was important in limiting the power
of the emperor and increasing that of the princes within Germany.
The guaranteeing of the settlement by the two foreign and anti-
Habsburg powers, France and Sweden, and their entry into the
Imperial Diet through their territorial gains of parts of Alsace on
the one hand and Bremen, Verden, Wismar and West Pomerania
on the other, provided a practical restraint on Imperial power. The
settlement also destroyed the emperor's claim to be the only sovereign power in the Empire by granting the princes what the French
called 'droit de souveraineté'.[78] Sovereignty was now effectively
divided between emperor and princes, and his powers to interfere in
their internal affairs were also reduced. This strengthened the princes'
domestic position vis-à-vis their Estates and made it easier for some
to establish more absolute forms of government. Moreover, to prevent a return to the era of his father, Emperor Ferdinand III had to
accept that the Imperial Diet had to approve all Imperial laws, taxes,
armies, alliances, declarations of war and signatures of peace. At the
same time the princes were now allowed legally, instead of tacitly,
to ally with non-German rulers, with the untenable rider that no
treaty should harm Empire or emperor. While France and Sweden
had certainly intended the settlement to undermine the emperor's
power, the German princes were not trying to destroy the Empire
itself. They wanted to tip the balance of power within it their way,
and they managed to do this. It is a mistake, however, to underestimate the strength of the emperors after 1648. While their
constitutional rights were more circumscribed, on occasion their
political and military power was to rival that of Ferdinand II. For
example, in the 1690s and 1700s Leopold I and then Joseph I managed to deploy most of the resources of the Holy Roman Empire, as
well as their own hereditary lands, against the Ottoman Turks and
Louis XIV.[79]

· · ·

NOTES AND REFERENCES

1 See J. Vahtola, *Brandenburgs Annäherung an Schweden zu Beginn der Regierungszeit Kurfürst Friedrich Wilhelms, 1640–1641* (Helsinki, 1984), p. 59.

2 J. Schultze, *Die Mark Brandenburg* (Berlin, 1964–9), IV, p. 269.

3 *Urk[unden] u[nd] Akt[enstücke zur Geschichte der inneren Politik des Kurfürsten Friedrich Wilhelm von Brandenburg]*, ed. Preußischen Kommission bei der Preußischen Akademie der Wissenschaften, 23 vols (Berlin, 1864–1930), I, p. 422, Burgsdorff to Frederick William, Cüstrin, 5 February 1641 (old style).

4 Meinardus, *Protokolle*, I, p. 121.

5 S.B. Fay, 'The beginnings of the standing army in Prussia', *American Historical Review*, 22 (1917), p. 767.

6 A. Waddington, *Le Grand Électeur Frédéric Guillaume de Brandebourg. Sa politique extérieur*, 2 vols (Paris, 1905–7), I, p. 63.

7 E. Opgenoorth, *Friedrich Wilhelm, der Große Kurfürst von Brandenburg. Eine politische Biographie*, 2 vols (Göttingen, 1971–8), I, p. 151.

8 Schultze, *Brandenburg*, IV, p. 284.

9 C. Fürbringer, *Necessitas und Libertas. Staatsbildung und Landstände im 17. Jahrhundert in Brandenburg* (Frankfurt am Main, 1985), p. 58. See Fürbringer, passim, for the Estates in general.

10 *Urk. u. Akt.*, X, p. 79, Deputies to Frederick William, Berlin, 8 January 1641 (old style).

11 J.G. Droysen, *Geschichte der Preußischen Politik*, 5 parts (Berlin, 1855–86), part 3, I, p. 167.

12 Opgenoorth, *Friedrich Wilhelm*, I, p. 93.

13 Meinardus, *Protokolle*, I, p. 490.

14 Ibid., I, pp. 371, 505, 513.

15 Droysen, part 3, I, p. 277.

16 Ibid., p. 167.

17 Meinardus, *Protokolle*, I, p. 584.

18 Philippson, I, pp. 41f.

19 B. Beuys, *Der Große Kurfürst. Der Mann, der Preußen schuf* (Reinbek bei Hamburg, 1979), pp. 75f.

20 W.F. Reddaway, 'The advent of the Great Elector', *Transactions of the Royal Historical Society*, new series, 15 (1900), p. 166.

21 For religious restrictions, see M. Lackner, *Die Kirchenpolitik des Großen Kurfürsten* (Witten, 1973), pp. 155f.

22 Report of French minister, d'Avaugour, in Reddaway, p. 158.

23 S.B. Fay, *The Rise of Brandenburg-Prussia to 1786*, 2nd edn (New York, 1974), pp. 43f. This figure, and a similar one of 250,000 for Brandenburg, and of Cleves/Mark, at 100,000, can only be a very rough estimate.

24 See especially H. Wischhöfer, *Die Ostpreußischen Stände im letzten Jahrzehnt vor dem Regierungsantritt des Großen Kurfürsten* (Göttingen, 1958), passim, and W. Neugebauer, *Politische Wandel im Osten: Ost- und Westpreußen von der alten Ständen zum Konstitutionalismus* (Stuttgart, 1992), pp. 35ff.

25 A. Nachama, *Ersatzbürger und Staatsbildung: zur Zerstörung des Bürgertums in Brandenburg-Preußen* (Frankfurt am Main, 1984), p. 54.

26 Frederick William then explicitly excluded them. Neugebauer, p. 40.

27 F.L. Carsten, *The Origins of Prussia* (Oxford, 1954), p. 205.

28 Droysen, part 3, II, p. 516.

29 R. Gothelf, 'Absolutism in action: Frederick William I and the government of East Prussia, 1709–30', Ph.D. thesis, St Andrews, 1998, p. 54.

30 See Wischhöfer, passim.

31 Lackner, pp. 155f.

32 H. Rachel, *Der Große Kurfürst und die ostpreußischen Stände, 1640–1688* (Leipzig, 1905), p. 23.

33 J. Jacoby, *Boguslaus Radziwill, der Statthalter des Großen Kurfürsten in Ostpreußen* (Marburg, 1959), p. 44.

34 Hüttl, p. 89.

35 Meinardus, I, p. 525.

36 See especially, Nachama, pp. 43f., 72.

37 Meinardus, I, pp. lvi, lxxxv.

38 Previous ones had been in 1602, 1572 and 1565, and the next one was in 1652.

39 See *Urk. u. Akt.*, X, pp. 48f., and *Acta Borussica* (Berlin, 1894 onwards), *Behördenorganisation: Die Behördenorganisation und die allgemeine Staatsverwaltung Preußens im 18. Jahrhundert*, ed. G. Schmoller and O. Hintze, VI (1901), p. 351.

40 Fürbringer, p. 57.

41 The Estates were probably not quite as dominant as used to be thought, since they still tended to allow the ruler to legislate himself. See U. Lange, 'Der ständische Dualismus – Bemerkungen zu einem Problem der deutschen Verfassungsgeschichte', *Blätter für deutsche Landesgeschichte*, 117 (1981), pp. 324–6, and P. Baumgart, 'Zur Geschichte der kurmärkischen Stände in 17. und 18. Jahrhundert', in D. Gerhard, ed., *Ständische Vertretungen in Europa im 17. und 18. Jahrhundert* (Göttingen, 1969), pp. 131ff.

42 Opgenoorth, *Friedrich Wilhelm*, I, p. 132.

43 R. Dietrich, ed., *Die politischen Testamente der Hohenzollern* (Cologne, 1986), p. 192.

44 K. Spannagel, *Konrad von Burgsdorff. Ein brandenburgischer Kriegs- und Staatsmann aus der Zeit der Kurfürsten Georg Wilhelm und Friedrich Wilhelm* (Berlin, 1903), pp. 256ff.

45 Hüttl, p. 101; and see Spannagel, *Burgsdorff*, p. 248.

46 Meinardus, I, p. 571.

47 Opgenoorth, *Friedrich Wilhelm*, I, p. 120.

48 B. Erdmannsdörffer, *Deutsche Geschichte vom Westfälischen Frieden bis zum Regierungsantritt Friedrichs des Großen, 1648–1740* (Leipzig, 1892), I, p. 96.

49 O. Meinardus, 'Kurfürst Friedrich Wilhelms Bemühungen um die pölnische Königskrone', *Historische Zeitschrift*, 72 (1894), p. 62.

50 W. Ribbe, ed., *Geschichte Berlins* (Munich, 1987), I, p. 343.

51 See A. Holenstein, 'Formen politischen Handelns der Kleve-Märkischen Landstände, 1640–1660', *Parliaments, Estates and Representation*, 5 (1985), part 1; F.L. Carsten, *Princes and Parliaments in Germany from the Fifteenth to the Eighteenth Century* (Oxford, 1959), pp. 269ff.

52 In Brandenburg itself there was no right of appeal to the Imperial courts, but the other Hohenzollern lands outside Prussia had this right till 1701.

53 Fürbringer, p. 71.

54 F.L. Carsten, *Essays in German History* (London, 1985), p. 82.

55 Philippson, I, pp. 56f.

56 Waddington, *Le Grand Électeur*, I, p. 195.

57 Philippson, I, p. 164.

58 Hüttl, p. 119.

59 P. des Noyers, *Lettres de Philippe des Noyers, secrétaire de la reine de Pologne, Marie-Louise de Gonzague ... de 1655 à 1659*, ed. E. Rykaczewski (Berlin, 1859), p. 355.

60 Waddington, *Le Grand Électeur*, I, p. 253.

61 Opgenoorth, *Friedrich Wilhelm*, I, p. 140.

62 Philippson, I, p. 77.

63 H. Schmidt, *Philipp Wilhelm von Pfalz-Neuburg (1615–90) als Gestalt der deutschen europäischen Politik des 17. Jahrhunderts* (Düsseldorf, 1973), I (1615–58), p. 31. This is by far the best discussion of the whole issue.

64 Hüttl, p. 13.

65 Opgenoorth, *Friedrich Wilhelm*, I, p. 141.

66 Hüttl, pp. 132f.

67 Spannagel, *Burgsdorff*, p. 277.

68 F. Dickman, *Der Westfälische Frieden* (Münster, 1949), p. 220. Two years later a Swedish peace negotiator at Westphalia made its importance even clearer: 'the Baltic Sea will be the ditch, Pomerania and Mecklenburg will serve as counterscarps, and the other Imperial estates will be, so to speak, the outer works'. See D. Croxton, 'The peace of Westphalia of 1648 and the origins of sovereignty', *International History Review*, 21 (1999), p. 589.

69 Philippson, I, p. 89.

70 Droysen, part 3, I, p. 282.

71 Waddington, *Le Grand Électeur*, I, p. 177.

72 M. Hein, *Otto von Schwerin. Der Oberpräsident des Großen Kurfürsten* (Königsberg, 1929), p. 23.

73 At this time a privy councillor, Loeben, wrote to Burgsdorff: 'We do not have a single friend and [can] only trust d'Avaux'. Hein, p. 24.

74 Opgenoorth, *Friedrich Wilhelm*, I, p. 264.

75 A. Osiander, *The States System of Europe, 1640–1990: Peacemaking and the Conditions of International Stability* (Oxford, 1994), p. 65, note 134.

76 The Stadtholder of Minden, Wittgenstein, reported in 1651: 'The principality is in a desperate state. Most subjects have neither bread nor seedcorn.' K. Spannagel, *Minden und Ravensberg unter brandenburgisch-preußischer Herrschaft von 1648 bis 1719* (Hanover, 1894), p. 83.

77 C. Parry, ed., *Consolidated Treaty Series* (Dobbs Ferry, New York, 1969), I, p. 229. The religious provisions are set out best in J. Whaley, *Religious Toleration and Social Change in Hamburg, 1529–1815* (Cambridge, 1985), p. 5.

78 See R. Braun, 'Taxation, socio-political structure, and state building: Great Britain and Brandenburg-Prussia', in C. Tilly, ed., *The Formation of National States in Western Europe* (Princeton, 1975), p. 249. Croxton, p. 589, points out that in the settlement there was no idea of creating an international system of sovereign independent states, as is often claimed.

79 See in English D. McKay, *Prince Eugene of Savoy* (London, 1977); C. Ingrao, *In Quest and Crisis: Emperor Joseph I and the Habsburg Monarchy* (West Lafayette, IN, 1978); and Wilson, *Holy Roman Empire*, pp. 28ff.

Chapter 3

FREDERICK WILLIAM'S ATTEMPT TO ESTABLISH HIS AUTHORITY

. . .

CONDITION OF BRANDENBURG AT THE END OF THE THIRTY YEARS WAR

Germany was devastated by the Thirty Years War. At the close her population had shrunk by at least a third, possibly more, from around 18 million to 12 million. These losses were not made good till the next century,[1] and they were greatest in the north-east, east and south-west, where the war had been its most unremitting. Worst hit was Mecklenburg, which a Swedish general admitted in 1638 was 'nothing but sand and air'.[2] Pomerania suffered almost as badly, especially the east, with population cut to under a third of its pre-war level. Brandenburg, which was a part of the same campaigning area, was close behind: in the electorate as a whole the population sank to under a half.[3] In the northern Prignitz, which bordered Mecklenburg, losses may have reached 90 per cent, while in the Altmark they ranged from 60 per cent east of the Elbe to only 20 per cent west of the river. Far to the west in Minden and the county of Mark they were under 10 per cent. The worst affected parts of the electorate were usually the open countryside and the unfortified small towns. There were some dramatic losses in these towns – the population of Belitz fell from 1,000 to 50, that of Prenzlau from 9,000 to 600, and that of Osterburg, though it was in the Altmark west of the Elbe, from 2,500 to 125. But even the large towns of Frankfurt an der Oder and Brandenburg, which were bigger than Berlin before the war, lost two-thirds of their population – the town of Brandenburg collapsed from 12,000 to 2,500 inhabitants. Despite its walls, the capital of Berlin-Cölln suffered a 40 per cent loss, its population falling to 6,000.

The German demographic disaster was not directly caused by battles, massacres or even famine, although these were real enough. The relentless passage of troops, seizing or destroying homes, crops and animals, forced peasants and townspeople to flee constantly with their belongings by cart or on foot. The greatest killer was disease. Shifting masses of troops and refugees brought epidemics to the malnourished population. At this time plague, now increasingly an urban contagion, was also reappearing more frequently throughout Europe as well as in Germany. Outbreaks struck Berlin in 1631 and again in 1637–8, causing most of its overall population loss; and that in Frankfurt an der Oder in summer 1631 carried off a third of the town. Yet just as devastating could be dysentery, typhus and influenza. Added to these ravages of disease, births fell sharply as marriages were delayed and fertility declined.

Because the Swedes, Imperialists and other German troops received little cash and few supplies from home, they took what they needed where they campaigned in summer and quartered in winter. Plundering was of two kinds. First, the armies imposed continual war taxes, the contributions, on enemy, neutral or even friendly states. These should not have been too destructive, given a fair allotment and orderly collection. Inevitably there was neither. Moreover, the rulers and Estates still tried to collect their own taxation, the nobles their rents and dues and the churches their tithes. Added to this was the second form of plundering, the direct seizure of recruits, food, fodder and draught animals. This went together with the destruction of homes, crops, beasts and tools to deny them to the enemy. One of the leading mercenary generals, Mansfeld, was quite matter of fact about these tactics in 1626 early in the war: 'when soldiers are not paid, they cannot be kept under any war discipline. They and their horses cannot live on air.'[4] Twenty years later, a Swedish observer described what his own army and others had done to Germany:

> How wretched the great towns are now! Where once there were thousands of streets, there are now only hundreds . . . The small towns . . . lie burnt, turned into stables and homes for sutlers[5] . . . You can wander for ten miles without seeing man or beast . . . In all the villages the houses are full of bodies and carcasses, a man, his wife, their children, servants, horses, swine, cattle and oxen, all lying side by side, killed by hunger and plague . . . , eaten by wolves, dogs, crows and ravens, because no one is left to bury them . . .'[6]

The late 1630s saw the worst exactions in Brandenburg, but it had been a combat zone since 1626. Some idea of the desperate situation is evident from a report at the end of George William's reign from the Ruppin district in the northern Mittelmark: 'Throughout the country it is impossible to buy a bushel of rye. The poor have to bake acorns. The dead lie on the roads and in the hedgerows, and those half alive cry: bread, bread.' There were accounts of people being forced to cannibalism in the Uckermark in 1638 and in Ruppin the following year,[7] and in May 1641 the magistrates of the small town of Strassburg, also in the Uckermark, reported: 'To survive, the inhabitants had to eat cats and dogs, and then one another.'[8] The historian of Brandenburg, Johann Schultze, is amazed that the troops found anything left to seize after their repeated onslaughts. What is perhaps as surprising was the lack of local resistance, although exceptionally peasants in the Altmark in 1639 did attack marauders, forcing Imperial troops to leave briefly.[9]

In Brandenburg, as in so much of Germany, the war was accompanied by economic ruin. There is considerable debate about German decline before the war, but there can be none about its condition afterwards. Only sutlers and higher officers benefited from it materially. Except in north-west Germany, trade and industry went into steep decline, although the most dramatic effects were in agriculture. Almost everywhere in the Empire 'the Thirty Years War brought farming to a complete collapse'.[10] Armies plundered, peasants fled to escape and there was no incentive to sow for others to harvest. In Brandenburg as a whole perhaps half the farms and plots of peasants and cottagers (*Kossätten*) were waste or deserted, especially east of the Elbe. On an estate belonging to the rich Arnim family at Boitzenburg in the Uckermark only a tenth of the farms was being worked at the end of the war.[11] Four years after the Peace of Westphalia, when some recovery might have been expected, a report on the Elector's own manors in Brandenburg found only half the peasant and cottager holdings occupied. At the same time 60 per cent of those in the Ruppin district were waste, and even by 1687 over 13 per cent were still unoccupied. Much the same pattern of ruin was found in the towns: 'In 1660 half the towns in the Neumark, east of the Oder, stood empty.'[12] And even in Berlin-Cölln a quarter of the houses was unoccupied in 1654.[13]

Any recovery was bound to be slow in the countryside. Unlike after such natural disasters as failed harvests or plague, peasants also had to cope with the loss of stock, buildings and tools. Consequently, during and immediately after the war farming was reduced to subsistence level and below. The Uckermark deputies reported in despair in 1643 that nothing was being sown or grown.[14] There was also little point in producing anything to sell: while grain prices were high during the 1630s, by the early 1640s these had collapsed and remained depressed till the 1680s.[15] Nobles as well as peasants were affected by the war and the collapse in prices: their incomes fell and they were desperately short of labour to work their estates. At the return of peace the revenues from the Elector's own manors had declined by two-thirds and those of the nobles may have suffered more. Some Junker nobles, such as those in Saxon Lower Lusatia, bordering the Mittelmark, underwent the ultimate indignity: 'many . . . because they can no longer afford servants, work the land themselves. With their children, their ploughs and harrows they scrape a bare existence with their own hands, pushing wheelbarrows, making their own bread and fetching their own water.'[16]

Times were hard + comeback was slow.

. . .

CONFLICT WITH THE CLEVES-MARK ESTATES

We do not know Frederick William's own feelings about the plight of his subjects, although he probably shared other contemporary rulers' fatalistic indifference. He was certainly very aware of the scale of the material disaster, and the ruin in Berlin and the electorate was one reason why he did not return there at once with his new wife and growing court. Except for an extended stay in Berlin for most of April 1650 to April 1651, he was to remain from 1647 to 1652 in the ducal palace in Cleves, where the physical conditions were far more congenial. There were other reasons as well: he hoped to tap the wealth of Cleves-Mark, which had emerged relatively unscathed from the war, and also to resolve the Jülich-Berg dispute. Both hopes were to be disappointed, and his time in Cleves brought almost continual political problems, as he tried to assert his authority there.

The failure of the first invasion of Berg in December 1646 was followed by similar frustrations in Frederick William's relations with the Estates of Cleves and Mark. As his troops returned there from Berg, he was faced with the unresolved and now even more pressing need to pay them. In January 1647 the diet contemptuously dismissed 'as frivolous, impertinent and puerile' his claim that he had not 'meant to diminish their privileges' by raising the troops,[17] and the deputies continued to refuse him money. They cannot have been reassured by the presence of his Brandenburg privy councillors around him. Frederick William also did himself no good by blustering to some Cleves deputies that his princely office was bestowed by God and that he would not allow 'the introduction of a condominium and a division of power'.[18] By March he was complaining privately that 'this diet is composed of really evil people, who stick to their views like a buck to its horns'.[19] The main opposition was coming from the towns rather than from the nobility, and he was clearly rattled by the urban deputies, many of whom were lawyers and were often officials in his own government. The next month he angrily interrupted one of these, Dr Isinck, in the diet and declared: 'the learned doctors were all scoundrels and (pointing to the noble deputies) if His Electoral Highness only had to work with gentlemen everything would be settled soon'.[20] Frederick William immediately realised he had gone too far. He sent his most conciliatory Brandenburg privy councillor, Schwerin, to explain 'his anger had got the better of him', and he then drank Isinck's health at table.[21]

It was clearly time for a major concession, and in April Frederick William sacked his stadtholder, Norprath, who had been closely associated with the abortive invasion of Berg. A few months later he replaced him with Prince Johann Moritz of Nassau (1604–79), a relative and personal friend. Although not a native, the Prince was acceptable to the Estates because he had commanded the Dutch garrison in Wesel. At the same time, as a member of the Calvinist Orange-Nassau family, and a successful former governor of Dutch Brazil, his prestige made him more than a mere electoral servant and he provided a credible substitute for Frederick William when he was absent.[22] Given the disparate nature of Frederick William's territories, stadtholders, especially such Calvinist relatives as Johann Moritz, were essential to provide the 'political loyalty', which at this time 'was attached to persons' rather than to 'the abstract authority of institutions'.[23] Johann Moritz was to remain stadtholder till his death in 1679 and became indispensable. His stature, tact and common sense also made him popular in Cleves and Mark.

The change of stadtholder, while welcomed, was not enough to persuade the diet to pay for the troops. In desperation, therefore, Frederick William allowed the army to levy contributions in areas well away from the centres of political opposition, the Cleves towns with their Dutch garrisons. Almost inevitably the troops plundered and burned farms and villages. The Estates responded by appealing to the Dutch Republic to press the Elector to restore 'their free status and old liberties from the state of suppression and intolerable slavery'.[24] Frederick William then changed tack on the advice of the adroit Schwerin: the army was spread out more thinly over the countryside, and money was borrowed, offices sold and the few taxation rights farmed out to pay for it. Schwerin also worked patiently over the summer to reach an agreement with the diet. By November 1647, in return for the confirmation of their privileges, the deputies voted taxes of 50,000 thalers a year to clear Frederick William's debts in the duchies. Although they still refused to pay for the troops, it must have been obvious where some of the money would go.

This agreement was followed by a year of comparative political peace. It was not to last, for in April 1649 the Cleves diet assembled in an angry mood. Its grievances were the same as ever – Frederick William still had troops in the duchies and was breaking the *Indigenatsrecht* by employing outsiders. Subsidies were refused and months of wrangling ensued till Schwerin persuaded the Elector to sign an agreement (*Rezess*) in October, giving way completely. In return for subsidies and the acceptance of Johann Moritz as stadtholder, he promised to dismiss all other 'foreigners'; the diet could assemble when it wished; it had to be consulted about the appointment of councillors and even stadtholders, who would have to swear to uphold its privileges. Finally, Frederick William had to promise not to impose taxes without its consent and to remove his troops, except for a personal guard of 300 men.

The Estates seemed to have won hands down and a peaceful year followed while Frederick William was absent in Berlin, but this settlement was no more stable than earlier ones. Despite his promises, troops remained, and so the subsidies were not paid. When he returned to Cleves in April 1651, he also came intent on a further expedition against Jülich-Berg. This meant raising even more troops and illegal taxes and led inevitably to a further confrontation. The second invasion of Berg, the so-called 'Cow War' (see pp. 81–3), in June, produced uproar in the Cleves diet. Much of its past hostility to a standing army had come from fear of becoming involved in just this kind of foreign adventure. Retaliatory raids by Pfalz-Neuburg troops on Mark over the summer increased the anger, and in July the Cleves-Mark deputies joined those of Jülich-Berg in dissociating themselves from their rulers' quarrels and forbidding the payment of taxes. Frederick William denounced this 'Godless, frivolous and insolent' behaviour and justified his demands for money to the Cleves diet the next month on the grounds of political 'necessity'.[25] But his position was being effectively undermined by the failure of the 'Cow War'. In late summer the Estates appealed to the Emperor and the Dutch, and both responded with angry and repeated diplomatic pressure. Isolated and unable to pay his troops, in October 1651 Frederick William had to make another humiliating accommodation and agree once more to remove his army from the duchies.

By late 1651 Frederick William's position was so weak that the Estates could probably have overthrown him, had they wanted. There were examples close at hand in the triumph of English republicanism over the Stuarts in 1649 and of the Dutch States party over the house of Orange in 1650. The diets' annual meetings and right to assemble without a summons from the ruler were particularly dangerous, since these gave them permanence, the first step to a parliament on the English and Dutch model. Yet the majority of the deputies, like those in other German states, do not appear to have wanted to go down the republican road, and Frederick William's continual retreats made this unnecessary. But the disputes were to fester because Frederick William still hoped to wriggle out of his promises. Over the next months, till he left the duchies for Berlin once more in September 1652, he managed to keep some troops by using his toll revenues, which had more than trebled since his accession, especially since the end of the Thirty Years War. The Stadtholder, Johann Moritz, was ordered to continue this policy after Frederick William had left. Inevitably the Estates objected, and in August 1653 they sent a delegation to Vienna, urging Ferdinand III to force their absentee ruler to honour his promises to remove his troops. The driving force behind the mission was both the rich Calvinist towns in Cleves and the minority Catholic nobles there. The latter championed the independence of the diet, because being members gave them the right to claim Catholic benefices elsewhere in Germany for their children.[26] On the other hand the smaller towns and the Calvinist nobility in Cleves, as well as almost all parties in Mark, were becoming more accommodating. This was an effect of Frederick William's policy from the late 1640s of appointing Protestant nobles to the administration in the duchies.[27]

The appeal to the Emperor seemed likely to force the squabble to a head, but once more autumn brought compromise. In October

1653 the Stadtholder cut the ground from under the feet of the delegation in Vienna by confirming the *Rezess* of 1649. Yet this also meant the Estates had won again and seemed even stronger after a decade of disputes. Further conflict was inevitable: the Elector still intended to hold on to his troops, some remaining garrisoned in Mark, while the Estates were equally determined not to grant taxation till these left. The Estates could only have finally settled the whole quarrel by deposing Frederick William, which they were still reluctant to do.

In July 1654 Frederick William decided on a show of strength, especially as the administration was grinding to a halt, with officials as well as troops going unpaid. He now felt stronger: in May Ferdinand III had been forced by the Imperial Diet to accept a resolution (*Reichsabschied*), permitting the German princes to demand taxation from their Estates to maintain garrisons and fortresses. Probably on Johann Moritz's advice, the Elector struck at one individual rather than the whole Estates. His troops seized his most intractable opponent, a Catholic noble, Wilich zu Winnenthal, accusing him of stirring up conflict between ruler and Estates.[28] Inevitably Wesel and the major Cleves towns, as well as the Catholic nobles, reacted noisily, especially as Wilich had been carted off to Berlin. Frederick William stood his ground and events seemed to move his way. Most Calvinist nobles and all groups in Mark refused to become involved; even the Cleves diet began to retreat by the end of 1654, when Johann Moritz made great play of Wilich's Catholicism and his supposed contacts with Catholic powers. Wilich himself destroyed his own case, tacitly admitting his guilt by asking for a pardon. The opposition now quietened down, but there was no solution to the political deadlock before the outbreak of war around the Baltic in summer 1655. It was this war (see pp. 85–105 for War of the North) which was to resolve matters far more in the Elector's favour.

The War of the North was hardly one which concerned his Rhenish lands but Frederick William was determined to squeeze as much as possible from them. At the start his troops imposed taxes and seized animals and goods from those who refused. This led the Estates in June 1655 to complain in both The Hague and Vienna that their ruler was treating them like 'open enemies', claiming he had raised more than 300,000 thalers illegally so far that year. Unfortunately for them, neither the Dutch nor the Emperor wished to risk offending Frederick William at this point, wanting him to help

Poland resist the Swedes. With enough troops on foot, the Elector therefore could take what he wanted, and in February 1656 he wrote from Königsberg to Johann Moritz that the war emergency meant he would 'consider neither friend, nor enemy, nor Estates'. Accordingly the impositions and recruiting continued at a high level throughout the war, despite the repeated protests of the Estates that the conflict had nothing to do with them or the Empire. The level of the exactions was high enough (17,000 thalers a month in taxes) to worry Frederick William's own administration in Cleves, which warned him in December 1656 of 'more complications, if not a general uprising of desperate subjects'.[29] Continual appeals from them and Johann Moritz eventually persuaded Frederick William to reduce his monthly demands to 12,000 thalers in summer 1658. But during the six years of the war he wrested 1.5 million thalers, as well as food, forage and animals, from Cleves and Mark. The heavy military presence meant there was no open revolt.

RELATIONS WITH THE BRANDENBURG ESTATES BEFORE THE WAR OF THE NORTH

During the first decade of the reign Frederick William and the Brandenburg Estates worked well together, with mutual goodwill replacing the bitterness of the Schwarzenberg era. The new ruler had been encouraged in this by his Privy Council, most of whom had ties with the Estates, especially his Chancellor Götzen. The deputies had cooperated in raising the contributions and grain demanded by Sweden during the 1640s, and in May 1648 six of them accompanied Götzen and Leuchtmar to Szczecin to discuss the final withdrawal of Swedish troops. Yet Frederick William's cooperation with the Estates was inevitably limited because their provincial horizons were even narrower than those of such advisers as Götzen. This became clear in the early 1650s, when strains began to develop. Difficulties arose because of Frederick William's wish to raise more than garrison troops and ambitions to pursue an active dynastic policy over Pomerania and Jülich-Berg. Although these policies, especially raising what amounted to a standing army, had a whiff of absolutism about them, the Elector does not seem to have wanted the troops in order to intimidate his Estates and impose arbitrary rule. He had no programme for suppressing the Estates and was always hoping for a compromise which would give him greater control over the finances, army and administration.[30] The Estates, however, inevitably sensed both a threat to their traditional privileges and the danger of further war. At first they were more concerned about the latter and were openly opposed to the two adventures in Berg. Their hostility to these was shared of course by the older members of the Privy Council, and it is perhaps no coincidence that relations deteriorated soon after Götzen died in December 1650. As chancellor, he, together with such councillors as Putlitz and Thomas von dem Knesebeck, basically shared the Estates' traditional and limited view of the world. They all wanted to follow a passive foreign policy, just as the Estates had demanded in the 1630s. The horrors of the Thirty Years War seemed to prove the dangers of not keeping their heads down.

Although Frederick William throughout his life was to be keen on an active, and even interventionist, foreign policy, when he returned to Brandenburg temporarily in 1650–1 he was faced by a problem not of his making: how to secure the share of Pomerania ceded to him at the peace. Diplomatic efforts failed to persuade the Swedes to leave, and the only solution seemed military action. In September 1650, therefore, he asked the Estates' representatives in Berlin for higher taxes to recruit more men. Here he once more came upon the problem of the personal nature of his rule in territories traditionally separate from each other. The representatives were not sympathetic, insisting Pomerania was a 'foreign' land.[31] Instead they demanded the contribution taxes be cut, claiming these were ruining the country and were even higher than when the Swedes had occupied Brandenburg. With their recent experience of Schwarzenberg in mind, they went on to accuse the Elector of undermining their privileges and treating them 'harshly',[32] warning that keeping troops permanently could lead to 'absolute rule'. This roused Frederick William to respond with an argument that reflected his own dilemma as a ruler of a composite state but was completely alien to their thinking: 'both the duchy of East Pomerania and the electorate belong to a legitimate and God-given ruler, and these lands are like limbs with a single head; Pomerania has to be supported as if it were part of the electorate'.[33] As the Estates would not budge, he continued to collect contributions, even though they had not been approved. Possibly emboldened by his departure for Cleves in April 1651 (he was to stay there a year), in the following month the Estates insisted that in a 'Christian government' 'in matters affecting the country's prosperity or ruin, nothing should be decided without the advice and general consent of the Estates'.[34] At the same time a brother of the Privy Councillor Knesebeck acted on his own authority as director (*Kreiskommissar*) of the Altmark provincial Estates[35] to call a local diet.[36] This similarly demanded an end of taxes not approved by the Estates and a reduction of the troops. Then in late July the Brandenburg permanent committee openly criticised the invasion of Berg, claiming Frederick William had acted illegally in waging 'a bloody, religious war' he could not afford.[37] By September the Privy Council itself, which clearly shared their views, was sending similar complaints to the Elector in Cleves. The failure of the Berg adventure and a bad harvest encouraged the Estates to continue their opposition into the autumn.

The Estates, and their Privy-Council sympathisers, were determined not to surrender their traditional fiscal powers or pay for policies which they considered personal to the Elector as ruler of Cleves or Pomerania. Given the limited revenues from his own domain lands after the Thirty Years War, Frederick William was in a cleft stick: an effective foreign policy required him to resolve his financial difficulties with his Estates. As he had no intention of abolishing their taxation privileges, he had to go on trying to persuade them that the troops were needed for their mutual benefit or, as a last resort, he had to circumvent the Estates. Consequently at the end of 1651, while still in Cleves, he took the highly unusual step of summoning a full diet (*Landtag*) of the Brandenburg Estates to meet in Berlin, in the hope that this would be more compliant than the usual permanent committees (*Ausschüße*) or representative diets (*Deputationstage*). The *Landtag* was the first to meet since 1615 and the only one of his reign. Now all the Junkers could attend as members of the first house of the *Landtag* and the towns in the second house.[38]

During the year or so that the diet met,[39] Frederick William was away in Cleves. The discussions were therefore conducted by three privy councillors, Joachim von Blumenthal and Thomas von dem Knesebeck, who were both Brandenburg Junkers, and Dr Johann Tornow, a lawyer. These involved numerous written proposals and counterproposals, as well as consultations with the Elector in Cleves, and they dragged on for most of 1652 with breaks for the deputies to return home. Although the diet proved far less militant than those in Cleves and Prussia, it was almost as obstinate. The main issue was the Elector's request to be allowed to raise troops by continuing the wartime contribution and introducing a Dutch-style excise on agricultural and industrial goods. His privy councillors argued the Elector had brought peace to Brandenburg largely by using revenues from his own domain lands and this peace would not be safe while the Swedes were in Pomerania. The suggestion of an excise immediately upset the Junker deputies, since it would threaten their own tax exemptions. Claiming it would drag them down to the level of commoners, they demanded the confirmation of their own privileges as an Estate. Their objections were shared by Knesebeck himself, despite his role in the discussions, and by two other noble privy councillors, Putlitz and Platen. In June 1652 these councillors actually wrote to the Elector, urging him to accommodate the diet and reduce his troops. The commoner Tornow pointedly dissociated himself from them.

Frederick William was determined not to back down, and he was encouraged by the ministers with him in Cleves, especially the new and increasingly influential Waldeck (for him see pp. 65–72). When he returned to Berlin in autumn 1652, he quickly concluded that calling the full *Landtag* had been a blunder, dissolved it and the following May summoned a routine representative diet (*Deputationstag*). As this proved no more compliant, the Elector, who could now see the opposition at first hand, decided to call it a day. In July 1653 a settlement was made fairly quickly with both the Brandenburg and Neumark Estates.[40] This agreement (*Landtagsrezess*) was not the significant victory for the Elector which many historians have claimed.[41] It was rather an attempt to return to the old working relationship, and 'the year 1653 represents one of the highpoints of Estate power'.[42] Like earlier recesses, this one was a kind of constitutional agreement, setting out the privileges of the Estates, which effectively meant those of the Junker nobility.

The agreement did not call on Frederick William to disband his troops, and the Estates tacitly accepted they would pay for them, in return for his abandoning the proposed excise: they promised to impose contributions of 530,000 thalers over six years to support the troops and to pay off his debts. The longer period was agreed, instead of the usual annual grant, in the hope that it would deter him from levying further illegal taxes. The sum, however, was less than that being currently raised, and the Estates therefore promised an additional tax of 20,000 thalers a year for the 'better upkeep' of the troops and fortresses.[43] In accepting the money the Elector had effectively conceded the Estates' right to vote taxation, but by the same token they had agreed to support at least some of his troops.

The remainder of the agreement was a detailed confirmation of the Estates' privileges. Although Frederick William did not specifically promise to consult before imposing taxation, he repeated the traditional formula to 'make no decisions nor take steps in important questions crucial for the welfare of the country, or its reverse, ... and ... also conclude no alliances ... without the advice and consent of the Estates'. The Estates had shown in the past that they did not intend to scrutinise his policies in detail, but they wanted to prevent these getting out of control. Certainly more important to them were clauses confirming the Junkers' social and economic supremacy. These were perfectly acceptable to the Elector, who knew his own authority rested on the existing social hierarchy. The list was extensive, essentially repeating earlier agreements and confirming established privileges. It began by affirming the general principle of the *Indigenatsrecht*, although Frederick William reserved his right to employ commoners and 'non-natives ... who have rendered ... good services to the country'. A further clause prohibited commoners' buying lands, but the Elector could give his own 'to servants of ours'.[44] (This hardly affected the principle as these servants were almost invariably ennobled.) Just as important in safeguarding Junker interests was a clause allowing them to export abroad goods from their own estates and to import ones for their personal use, free of all tolls.

The *Landtagsrezess* dealt at length with the Junkers' relations with their peasants (for this see section on peasantry, pp. 120–1) and also had something to say about religion. It was one of the periodic attempts made by the Calvinist Hohenzollerns to pacify their predominantly Lutheran nobility and clergy. Assuring them 'We have never thought to claim dominion over consciences', Frederick William guaranteed their religious freedom and patronage rights over churches and schools.[45] He also continued the century-old ban on Jews except at a few markets, and he conceded the Estates' demand to prohibit 'the practice of their religion, publicly or privately, to Papists, Arians [sic], ... Anabaptists', and other Protestant sects.[46] This clause of course contradicted the vague promise in the Westphalian settlement allowing Catholics, Lutherans and Calvinists to worship in private.

This agreement with the Brandenburg Estates in 1653 was not a final political settlement or a blueprint for the rest of the reign,

Big Problem: ~~tha~~ Various Estates do not see
themselves as connected in a single
THE GREAT ELECTOR *power*

since important changes were to follow which altered the balance of
political power. It essentially set out the privileges of the nobility
and reflected the relations of ruler and Estates in the first decade or
so of Frederick William's rule. Above all it had not solved the basic
financial problem, and the taxation guaranteed was too little to support an army of any size. Six months later the Elector had only a
derisory 1,800 troops in Brandenburg. With the accession of the
bellicose Charles X of Sweden in 1654 and the danger of almost
immediate war between him and Poland (see pp. 85–6), Frederick
William was to need many more troops merely to protect
Brandenburg, let alone Prussia. Consequently, in autumn 1654, only
a year after their agreement, he had to turn yet again to the Estates'
permanent committee for more money. As in Cleves, he now had a
stronger hand, because of the Imperial Diet's decree of the previous
May that 'every freeholder, subject and burgher of an Elector or
Estate is obliged obediently to give the necessary assistance to their
Princes, Lords and Commanders for the support and occupation
of . . . fortified places and garrisons'.[47] The Elector had been an
enthusiastic supporter of this decree, which has been called the
'Magna Carta of absolutism'.[48] He made sure the Estates knew
about it, and at the end of December he insisted that 'the military
force of a country must be organized in accordance with the danger
and the necessity'. The representatives none the less would not budge
from the agreement of the year before, stressing that Prussia, not
Brandenburg, was in danger and that the duchy was not their responsibility. After more negotiations over the winter, the permanent committee did agree to pay a small sum. Inevitably, as the danger
of a Swedish–Polish conflict became more acute, in July 1655
Frederick William had to come back yet again, telling them: 'The
military preparations of all our neighbours compel us to follow their
example. And since this army is for the benefit not simply of one,
but of all my lands, I deem it proper that the cost and maintenance
of the troops must be borne by all.' The Estates were unmoved,
insisting in true Lutheran fashion that they should 'trust in God and
wait patiently upon events'. Frederick William therefore ignored
them, imposing further contributions on the electorate under threat
of force. The permanent committee responded by referring to the
1653 agreement and complaining that his action was 'contrary to
the constitutional laws . . . and . . . recent promises of the Elector. It
was taking without consent and by force a greater and more unbear-
able amount in four months than even an irate enemy had ever

demanded in a whole year.'[49] But these complaints went unheard. Given his own involvement in the Swedish–Polish conflict later in 1655, one which developed into the wider War of the North, Frederick William had no option while it lasted, but to enforce mounting taxation.

The war resolved Frederick William's problem of funding a modest, permanent army, and there is little doubt that his new minister Georg Friedrich von Waldeck pointed the way. Waldeck admired the French monarchy and 'its countless means [i.e. including direct taxes] for obtaining money because of its absolute power', and he exploited the Imperial decree of 1654 to raise a hundred men in his own tiny German principality of Waldeck. He had little patience with Estates, telling the Privy Council in November 1654 that 'the Prince is not obliged to risk his state because of privileges'.[50] Once the War of the North began it was his views which prevailed. In the first two years of the conflict, till May 1657, Frederick William was to levy contributions in Brandenburg of 750,000 thalers, far above the annual sum agreed by the Estates in 1653. In addition supplies in kind, possibly worth as much again, were demanded from the peasantry. Complaints by the Estates' representatives were ignored: in July 1656 they protested that their 'miserable' land had 'been forced to contribute . . . to the limit' illegal taxes for a foreign war.[51] Frederick William's other important minister, Schwerin, who had returned to Berlin from the campaign in Prussia in spring 1656, was alarmed about this. He was always a man to prefer conciliation to confrontation, and he wrote to Waldeck: 'I am very afraid that one day the Elector will blame us for not having told him clearly enough how impossible it is to fulfil his demands. The Estates are complaining noisily that the demands for contributions fly in the face of custom. We are doing our best to pacify them to carry out the Elector's orders.'[52]

The nobles, of course, were not required to pay the taxes: roughly two-thirds of the contributions fell as usual on the poverty-stricken towns, while the peasants paid the other third as well as providing food, fodder and draught animals. Once again peasants began to abandon their farms, and in the Prignitz there were serious disturbances for some months in 1656. The following year the Privy Council feared the continuing heavy contributions, usually needing force to collect, would soon depopulate the towns. But Frederick William, campaigning first in Prussia and then in Denmark and Pomerania, was deaf to all this: he was determined that the separate

Imperial Decree of 1654 most importa— than Estates Agreement of 1653

parts of his territories should contribute to his personal dynastic objectives. In January 1657 he insisted to the Privy Council that 'defence of the country authorised him to decide himself what needed to be spent and how, whatever the Estates wanted'.[53] Throughout the war he merely informed the Brandenburg Estates' committee of his demands, justifying his actions on the grounds of 'necessity' and the Imperial decree of 1654.[54] It was this practice of the War of the North, following on the Imperial decree, not the agreement with the Estates of 1653, which eventually allowed him to resolve his financial problems. 'Consent' of the Estates to taxation was coming increasingly to mean grudging acceptance after the event. The large number of troops in Brandenburg throughout the war ensured they had no real option. At least in these years, unlike during the Schwarzenberg era, payment of heavy taxation did ensure Brandenburg had freedom from invasion by foreign troops and their exactions.

. . .

CHANGE OF MINISTERS AND FIRST ATTEMPTS AT GOVERNMENTAL AND FINANCIAL REFORM

Frederick William's failure in the 'Cow War' of 1651, the second military and diplomatic humiliation in the Rhineland in four years, led to a shake-up in his ministers and government. He felt let down, and the obvious scapegoat was his old comrade Burgsdorff, who had been an enthusiast for these adventures. While Götzen carried out most of the routine administrative work in Berlin till his death in 1650, ultimate responsibility over the past decade, particularly for the army and finances, had belonged to Burgsdorff. Unfortunately he had shown no talent for government and had been clearly negligent. The revenues had hardly increased, especially those from the Elector's domain lands in Brandenburg, which yielded a mere 50,000 thalers a year in 1650. His mismanagement was pointed out in 1651 by Johann Tornow, the commoner appointed to the Privy Council for his legal and financial expertise.

Even stronger criticism, tinged with personal rancour, came from Otto von Schwerin (1616–79), who had been an increasingly reliable councillor since 1644. He had taken on much of the workload from the ageing Götzen in Berlin and had accompanied the Elector to Cleves, conducting many of the discussions with the Estates there.

He was soon to become invaluable for his diplomatic skills, frustrating foreign envoys who found it 'impossible to discover his own views'.[55] Schwerin was a Pomeranian noble, who had converted to Calvinism and travelled widely in western Europe, including England. A particular confidant of Electress Louise Henrietta, he wrote hymns and poetry. His piety did not stop his enriching himself through presents from the electoral couple and 'compliments' from foreign princes,[56] and by 1650 he already had a fine estate close to Berlin. While he wanted to be rid of Burgsdorff because of personal ambition and frustration at having to sort out difficulties created by him, he lacked the clout to destroy him. More instrumental in this were the Electress herself and two rising stars, Joachim von Blumenthal and Georg Friedrich, Count [later Prince] von Waldeck. They convinced Frederick William that Burgsdorff was to blame for the second shambles in Berg and the truculence of the Brandenburg Estates. The Elector probably needed little prompting: Burgsdorff's earlier energetic and plain-speaking approach to problems had degenerated with age into rude bullying and outbursts of temper. This, and his coarseness, had especially offended the young Electress and her widowed mother, Princess Amelia, who had also settled at the electoral court. Louise Henrietta was set on his dismissal, even saying she did not want children while he was around.[57] In February 1651 Frederick William criticised Burgsdorff openly in the Privy Council, telling him angrily: 'You can never admit or even see, that everything is going to the devil.'[58] During the year he was eased out, being ordered back to Berlin from Cleves in September and then dismissed the following January. He took it badly: Tornow reported that he 'cried and clawed wildly at his hair'.[59] This brutal dismissal of his Falstaffian servant was out of character for Frederick William, but he told people that he had no choice because Burgsdorff lacked respect for him and his position.[60]

During the next year the most important minister was Blumenthal. 1652 A native Brandenburg Junker, who had served the Emperor, he entered Frederick William's employ in 1650 and soon impressed him with his administrative ability. Like Götzen before, he wanted to cooperate with the Estates and was chiefly responsible for the agreement of 1653. He also urged the Elector to manage from the income of his domain lands and other personal revenues and to avoid asking the Estates for more. This traditionalist approach would have entailed following the kind of passive foreign policy urged by the Estates. While this fitted in with Frederick William's subdued mood immediately after the Cow War, it was unlikely to appeal for long. In any case Blumenthal was soon to be eclipsed by the other newcomer, the far more dynamic Waldeck.[61] The same age as Frederick William, Count Waldeck (1620–92) was the Calvinist ruler of a minor principality in Westphalia. He had married Prince Johann Moritz's sister and like him had served in the Dutch army. This connection had led the Elector to give Waldeck command of the cavalry during the second Berg war. His military advice was already so trusted by December 1651 that Frederick William laid down that 'all things concerning the military that we alone [the Elector] need to carry out and decide in secret, are the responsibility of Count Waldeck'.[62] In employing this newcomer, Frederick William had acquired more than a general. Waldeck himself boasted in 1652: 'My nature pushes me to bold actions and enterprises, which will bring me honour; I crave for great adventures.'[63] He certainly had enough ambition to become another Richelieu: when the court returned to Berlin in autumn 1652, Waldeck needed forty-five trunks, ten more than Frederick William himself.[64] He also did not come cheap, being paid 4,000 thalers a year, four times the usual salary for a privy councillor.[65] A tempestuous man, who later served both Charles X of Sweden and the Dutch William III, he was bubbling with ideas, often verging on the fanciful. A contemporary diplomat, Wicquefort, observed acidly that he was 'more capable of talking about war than waging it'.[66] But Waldeck's shortcomings were not immediately apparent, and his polish and energy helped his rapid rise in the increasingly refined and cosmopolitan Hohenzollern court. After having helped to destroy Burgsdorff, he then worked to be rid of Blumenthal, whose conservatism he despised. When Blumenthal went to the Imperial Diet in summer 1653, Frederick William was persuaded to leave him there. Waldeck now became the most important minister, and he did much to restore the Elector's confidence after the Cow War, providing the kind of emotional crutch Burgsdorff had once offered. But Frederick William was never to give him full control and always listened to other ministers, especially Schwerin, who was soon to replace him (see pp. 64–5, 68–9).

Waldeck's influence had already been evident in the last months of 1651 while the court was still in Cleves. He was mainly responsible for persuading his new master to overhaul the government, claiming that 'things at this court are everywhere in such a bad state, that only a proper repair will prevent total ruin'.[67] What needed tackling above all were the workings of the Privy Council and the conduct of the finances, both areas where Burgsdorff had brought confusion. In December 1651 Frederick William issued an ordinance to reorganise the Council, since it functioned 'awkwardly and slowly . . ., many things . . . not being discharged properly' and the work 'not being shared out'.[68] The existing practice was the usual German one, where about ten councillors dealt with everything. This had been followed since the Privy Council had been set up in 1604 by the Elector Joachim Frederick. He had wanted a personal dynastic body, independent of the Brandenburg Estates, for advice over the Prussian and Cleves-Jülich successions. However, under John Sigismund and George William, the nobles and Estates had exerted their influence, and its role shrank to 'a local council for the Brandenburg Mark'.[69] When Frederick William revived it in 1641, after its eclipse under Schwarzenberg, he appointed mainly Calvinist Brandenburg and Pomeranian nobles, and over the next decade outsiders and commoners were the exception.[70] On his return to Berlin in 1643, the Council was held twice or more a week and he usually followed its advice on domestic and foreign issues, including ones relating to Prussia and Cleves. But its administrative and judicial authority was limited to Brandenburg where it was the pivot of government for the electorate.[71] As Frederick William was very much a peripatetic ruler and absent from Berlin for most of the first dozen years of his rule,[72] he took some of the members of the Council with him, and these tended to deal with the affairs of the dynasty as a whole. The Chancellor, Götzen, as the most experienced member, was usually left behind to look after Brandenburg concerns. His death in 1650, and then the fall of the most powerful Privy Councillor, Burgsdorff, a year later, made reform of the whole Council easier.

On Waldeck's advice,[73] Frederick William split up the Council's business into nineteen areas. These were largely territorial categories and were clearly intended at this stage to bring some supervision from Berlin to all the Hohenzollern lands. And over the coming years the introduction of more non-Brandenburgers and commoners tended to sever the previous close ties between the Council and the Brandenburg Estates. J. Schultze has argued that this ordinance of 1651 provided the germ of the later unitary state (*Gesamtstaat*) of Prussia: 'through this it [Privy Council] began to function as a central administrative organ for all the territories . . . where not only Brandenburg but also Rhenish-Westphalian and Prussian affairs were discussed and presented to the Elector for his decision'.[74] However, the various territorial governments in Cleves, Prussia and elsewhere

Privy Council foundation of centralized

Prussian Bureaucracy

were to escape real subordination to the reformed Privy Council under Frederick William, and he was largely to respect their insistence on the appointment of native officeholders. Moreover, proper discrete departments with their own staff, as in Louis XIV's France, did not develop out of the Council and its reform. Real departmentalisation, especially for foreign affairs, the military and finances, was to grow out of institutions which appeared separately from the Council later in the reign and were to marginalise it (see pp. 159–69). Moreover, these new bodies, such as the General War Commissariat, rather than the reformed Privy Council, were also to be the main instruments in creating the eventual unitary Hohenzollern state.

Responsibilities in the new Council were shared among ten men, none with overall control of foreign or domestic policy. For example Waldeck dealt with relations with France and Denmark, Blumenthal with the Emperor, and Schwerin with the Dutch. Most duties were still shouldered by two workhorses – Tornow was involved in ten areas and Schwerin in as many, including the secret correspondence, Prussia, Pomerania, Jews, the post, coinage and salt monopoly. Although there does seem to have been some immediate improvement in the Council's workings, the system remained fairly fluid and could be rather chaotic, with councillors being 'continuously transferred from one task to another'.[75] Just as damaging were regular disputes between the noble and non-noble members, who usually had a legal background. Waldeck was particularly cavalier towards the commoners and dismissed them in a letter to a friend in 1653 as 'the doctors'.[76] In 1655 the two factions quarrelled openly over a further attempt by the commoners to introduce an excise tax in Brandenburg. Accused of being 'nobles' foes',[77] they began to band together in self-defence. In January 1656 Tornow confided to his fellow lawyer and commoner on the Council, Friedrich Jena (1620–82): 'I am sorry to see that they [noble privy councillors], privately and publicly, want to stifle, insult and destroy the commoners' estate; . . . therefore I . . . should like the non-noble councillors to work together as well.'[78] These disputes, and the long absences of the Elector from Berlin during the War of the North, led, according to Schwerin in January 1658, to 'frightful confusion' and 'unheard of licence' in the Council.[79] This was probably why Schwerin, who became the leading minister when Waldeck left Frederick William's service, was appointed President of the Privy Council in August 1658, an office he held till his death in 1679. In effect he was filling the role in abeyance since Götzen died. The document appointing him stressed that someone was needed to oversee business and chair the Council when the Elector was away.[80] But even with this new post and the return of Frederick William in the 1660s, problems continued.

The old quarrels between nobles and commoners soon resurfaced. After 1662 the noble faction was led by Schwerin and the other side first by Friedrich Jena and then by Franz Meinders (1630–95), who was from Minden and had come to the court as Waldeck's secretary. Schwerin was to complain strongly to the Elector in 1663 that Jena was telling people that the post of president was unnecessary and that he could do the work instead.[81] The quarrels and bad feeling went on for more than a decade. The differences seem to have been largely over the commoners' wanting to be tougher with the noble-dominated Estates and, as we will see, it was their approach which was really adopted. None the less, nobles always filled the higher offices of state, and the Elector himself wrote to the Pomeranian Estates in 1654: 'it is the custom throughout the world, for the nobility to be given preference before the non-noble estate, [which fills the positions of] secretaries, recorders, notaries . . . , tax collectors . . . , toll collectors'.[82] However, he clearly recognised he needed the legal expertise and professionalism of such commoners as Tornow, Jena, Meinders and, finally, the Pomeranian Fuchs, a Calvinist convert and a lawyer. After 1651 they always made up about a quarter of the Privy Council, although the Elector usually gave them lands and secured titles for them from the Emperor,[83] allowing their families to merge into the established nobility.

The reorganisation of the Privy Council in 1651 was accompanied by the development of an inner council or quasi-cabinet round Frederick William, and by the 1670s this became the more important body.[84] The Elector gradually reserved the most sensitive business, particularly foreign affairs, for private discussions with about four favoured ministers, in this way showing how individuals were still more important than institutions. Although the Privy Council still functioned and discussed issues and Frederick William continued to attend it till his death, he tended to take the real decisions outside it, with this inner group. This meant more speed and secrecy, and it developed from the advice he gave his successor in his *Political Testament* of 1667, to decide very important issues, which had been discussed in the Council, later with one or two councillors and a secretary: 'Do as the bees, which suck the best juice from the flowers.'[85] This inner group was later to develop into a more formal cabinet, operating side by side with the Privy Council. Schwerin's great influence from 1651, and that of Meinders and Fuchs later, was to be based on being Frederick William's *de facto* secretary, charged with dealing with his correspondence in this cabinet. The Elector himself was essentially to fill the coordinating role of chief minister from the 1650s. Schwerin summed up the ruler–minister relationship, when he told the French envoy Blondel in December 1667: 'The Elector asks us . . . but he acts in the end according to his own judgement.'[86] While Frederick William was certainly not as keen on the bureaucratic routine as his younger contemporary Louis XIV of France, he did not shirk the work and took the final decisions. In 1657 the Polish Queen's secretary observed that the Elector 'discusses business well and understands it',[87] and some years later the Imperial envoy Goess reported home that Frederick William was 'very busy and hardworking, sleeps little and always rises early . . . he has a good and exact knowledge of all his business; very little occurs that he is ignorant about'.[88]

The Privy Council was never to regain the influence over military and foreign affairs it had enjoyed in the 1640s. While foreign affairs were passing to the inner cabinet, military matters were eventually to pass under the direction of the later General War Commissariat (see pp. 165–9). Even within Brandenburg itself, during the War of the North, the Council's influence was being undermined. While the Elector was mostly out of the electorate, military matters were largely dealt with by a stadtholder, Count Dohna, a Prussian Calvinist, and the Council complained in 1657 that Dohna dictated to them.[89] A similar decline in the Council's influence was to take place in the financial sphere.

In 1651 the first serious attempt in the reign was made to grapple with the finances. At his accession Frederick William had found he was in debt throughout his possessions, and since then he had still had to live largely hand to mouth. It was once again probably through Waldeck's influence that he set up a committee of his senior ministers – Waldeck himself, Blumenthal, Schwerin and Tornow – to repair 'our finances, which have rather deteriorated'.[90] This committee's importance, however, can be exaggerated:[91] it was limited to overseeing the finances of Brandenburg alone, and its chance of success was reduced by its members' other duties. In the event the necessary reforms were not carried out, primarily because of the complexity of the existing system. The electorate had been burdened since the sixteenth century with a jumble of financial institutions. The revenues from the contribution, which the Estates voted and collected, were handled by their own treasury, the *Kreditwerk*. Separate from this were three overlapping treasuries, belonging to the electors themselves – the *Hofrentei* (Electoral Treasury), the *Amtskammer* (Exchequer) and the *Schatulle* (Privy Purse).[92] The *Hofrentei* collected the revenues from the Brandenburg tolls and monopolies and used them to pay officials' salaries and court expenses. The *Amtskammer* was the main administering organ as well as treasury for the electors' domain lands, forests, mines and mint. Revenues from these arrived in both kind and cash. They were then handed over to the *Schatulle*, which paid for the electors' personal expenses, especially hunting. Since the 1610s the *Hofrentei* and *Amtskammer* had been overseen by the same official, the President of the Chamber (or Exchequer), *Kammerpräsident*, but none of the presidents had coped well: revenues had stagnated or fallen and no proper budget had been drawn up. Large deductions were made and spent locally, and revenues were also often committed in advance, such as those of the electoral lands of Oschersleben in Halberstadt, which paid for the court musicians.

The finance committee's main tasks in 1651 were to work out an annual budget of income and expenditure, to recommend savings and to overhaul the finances of the domains. Frederick William had been as much to blame as anyone for overspending. Even in the desperate years at the beginning of his reign, he had spent extraordinary sums in Prussia on luxuries – 6,000 thalers on jewels in 1641; 5,000 for a diamond ring, 1,285 for jewels and gold and amber ornaments in 1643; 3,333 for another diamond ring and 3,500 for jewellery in 1644; 7,047 for gold and silver objects and 3,044 for tapestries and silks in 1645; and 9,339 marks for jewellery, gold and silver in 1646. During these six years only 23 thalers were spent on books![93] It seems unlikely that he acted differently when he was in Cleves or Brandenburg. Although the committee did manage to establish a budget, it only had minor success in reducing court expenses by sacking petty officials and cancelling doubtful debts. The court musicians also had to take on extra duties by playing in the cathedral twice a week. As to the domains, an effort was made to lease them all out and to insist on payment in cash not kind. But this failed: there was no rush to take up leases, given the shortage of capital and glut of land after the Thirty Years War and also because of the poor state of many electoral lands – although extensive, large tracts were fenland, moors and forests, suitable only for hunting. Over the next seven years the Brandenburg domain revenues actually fell from 50,000 to 43,000 thalers. A novel expedient proposed by the committee for an excise tax on trade and manufactures had to be abandoned because of opposition from the Estates' representatives and from within the Privy Council.

In August 1652, even while the committee was still operating, Schwerin wrote to Waldeck: 'I must try to get money from Amsterdam [i.e. a loan]. You would not believe how little money there is where we should expect to find it. I am quite desperate.'[94] Above all the problems arising from having three (four, with the *Kreditwerk*) overlapping treasuries in Berlin had not been tackled. Furthermore the Elector himself did little to ensure the committee succeeded: he probably looked on it merely as a temporary expedient to solve the immediate problems after the Cow War. Neither he, nor most of the ministers closest to him at this stage, had the taste or aptitude for the mechanics of finances. Waldeck, in an autobiographical fragment, written in 1652, commented that the Elector rapidly lost interest 'in the new plans'.[95] The committee itself disappeared within a year, and from 1652 to 1655 Schwerin was burdened with overseeing the three treasuries. He was given the title *Kammerdirektor* in 1654, but the outbreak of the War of the North the next year and his involvement in its diplomacy meant he could not exercise real overall financial control. In February 1655 he and Waldeck quarrelled fiercely in front of the Elector. Schwerin accused Waldeck of wanting to run everything and causing chaos by interfering, and Waldeck countered by criticising the other's management of the finances. Waldeck above all wanted to increase the revenues by reforming the domains, which he blamed Schwerin for neglecting, while Schwerin wanted to spend less, especially on the military. Frederick William tried to reconcile them, but the attack had struck home and Schwerin soon lost control of finances.[96] In August 1655 a new *Kammerdirektor*, supposed to have some financial expertise, was appointed, the Westphalian Raban von Canstein (see pp. 159–60).

! 1655- War of the North begins

· · ·

THE CREATION OF A COURT

Before his marriage Frederick William had few interests outside his official duties. He showed little taste for the arts, except the military

72

ones. In his twenties, first in Prussia and then in Brandenburg and Cleves, he spent most of his spare time hunting. Like most of his aristocratic contemporaries, he hunted obsessively, and did so for the rest of his life: in 1680 an English envoy noted, 'This Elector has been lately at the hunting, or rather in deed the carnage of his stags'.[97] Almost every afternoon he was out on horseback, wherever he happened to be. His favourite hunting grounds were the Grunewald pine forests south-west of Berlin and other forests and heaths on the Neumark–Polish frontier, where he usually spent six weeks in late summer and early autumn.[98] Here his quarry were mainly deer and boar, but in Prussia there were wolves, bears and elk. Inevitably life at what passed for his court was rather boorish and spartan, reflecting the influence of such men as Burgsdorff, although Berlin had never been an important cultural centre and had always been overshadowed by the Saxon court. Even the fabric of the Hohenzollern palaces in Königsberg, Cleves and Berlin-Cölln was in an obvious state of disrepair. These buildings, which also housed the records and administrative offices, were still very much hangovers from the gaunt medieval castle, the typical German *Schloß*. There were spots of refinement, however, in the private rooms of Frederick William's mother Elizabeth Charlotte, his sisters and aunts. There was also a court painter in Berlin, the Czech Matthias Czwiczek (1601–54), who produced stylised portraits of the electoral family between 1643 and 1649; and in Berlin and Königsberg there was a small band of musicians, some of whom accompanied Frederick William to Holland for his marriage.[99]

The whole tone of the Berlin court was to change with the arrival of the young Dutch Electress Louise Henrietta in 1647 and then of more cosmopolitan figures such as Waldeck. During 1647 repairs were carried out on all the palaces. The Berlin-Cölln *Schloß* was in a particularly poor condition: roof, stairs and stonework had to be renewed. Although it was difficult to find the money, some bare walls were decorated with pictures and drapes. Some of the funds for this early renovation had to be borrowed in 1650 from one of those who had gained from the Thirty Years War, the commander of the Spandau garrison, von Ribbeck.[100] Before Johann Memhardt (1615–78), a Protestant refugee from Austria and trained in Holland as a military architect, was called to Berlin in 1650, the court had no architect or even a proper stone-mason.[101] Little more was done to the *Schloß* in the 1650s, and the French envoy, de Lesseins, described it in 1662 as 'the most ruined that I have seen in Germany'.[102] It was

not till the next decade that Memhardt and the Piedmontese architect Philippe de Chièze (1629–73) did some rebuilding. It is clear
that Frederick William was largely immune to the compulsion felt
by many seventeenth-century rulers to build and build, although, of
course, he never really had the money to do so. On the other hand,
he did make surprising impulse buys: as well as the large quantity
of jewellery in the 1640s, in December 1648 he had a rare jasper
drinking vessel bought in Warsaw for 150,000 Polish gulden, which
was more than the Prussian Estates voted in taxes that year![103] In
1661 he held a birthday banquet at Cleves for his mother-in-law,
Princess Amelia, giving her a diamond ring worth 8,000 Dutch
gulden and all the court servants presents of silver plate.[104]

Another area where he spent freely was his gardens, which became a life-long passion. Just after his accession he had begun an
ornamental garden (*Lustgarten*) in Königsberg, and by the end of
1645 the wild boggy ground between the Berlin-Cölln *Schloß* and
the River Spree was cleared, planted up and tulips ordered from
Hamburg. Between 1647 and 1652 limes and walnuts were planted,
fountains and ponds were added with oriental water fowl, and a hot-
house built for citrus trees. The obvious intention was to reproduce
the formal geometrical gardens of his Dutch relatives, and he also
relied on the advice of Prince Johann Moritz, who was establishing
his own gardens in Cleves.[105] Even during the War of the North,
the Elector found time to appoint Sigismund Elsholtz court bot-
anist, encouraging him to set up a herbarium and list the plants in
the garden. The Elector's *Lustgarten* at the Berlin *Schloß* provided
him with continual pleasure, although his militarist grandson,
Frederick William I, was to turn it into a parade ground!

The young Frederick William and Louise Henrietta's court in
Berlin was as strongly influenced by Dutch models as their gardens.
They almost had to create the court from scratch, taking their
ceremonial from the Orange one and dressing in the same style.
A celebrated Dutch portraitist, Wilhelm Honthorst (1604–66), was
engaged in 1647 and paid the same salary as a councillor; and paintings were regularly ordered from Dutch and Flemish artists, some
of whom came to decorate the ceilings of the *Schloß*. Paintings and
hangings of the usual classical scenes were bought by the metre. No
works of real value, or by the great masters, seem to have been
acquired, but the Elector was the first of his dynasty to have what
could be called a picture collection, his personal preference being
still lifes of flowers. He also followed the fashion of accumulating

hunting, jewelry, gardens

large collections of *objets d'art*, many of them Chinese and Japanese, coins, medals and natural curiosities, setting a room aside in the *Schloß* to display them all. As Prussia was the main source of Baltic amber, it is not surprising that he also had a magnificent collection of amber artefacts.

The Berlin *Schloß* was also to house a sizeable library of books and manuscripts, acquired haphazardly from the 1650s. Frederick William himself bought many volumes on war, engineering and architecture, as well as others on travel and Oriental languages which he felt would be useful for developing trade. Several volumes, especially on geography and natural history, were sent by Prince Johann Moritz, and various scholars contributed their works to try to curry favour. Books from church libraries in Brandenburg were also simply removed and added to the collection. The volumes were shelved, with various manuscripts, in a library room, with a reading room next door. By his death there were 20,000 printed works in 90,000 volumes as well as 1,600 manuscripts. From 1661 high officials and men of standing could consult the books and even borrow volumes to read at home. Unfortunately a history of the Hohenzollern dynasty was not among them, although Frederick William had made various half-hearted attempts to have one written since the 1650s. In 1686 Meinders and Fuchs, both former academics, were keen to have a history of the Great Elector's reign written. They were aware of the abilities of Samuel von Pufendorf, who was at the Swedish court and had already written a life of Charles X. They therefore got Frederick William to press him to come to Berlin. When Pufendorf eventually arrived in the last months of the Elector's life, he set to work immediately on his famous *De rebus gestis Friderici Wilhelmi Magni electoris Brandenburgici.* This was published in Latin, to reach a wider European reading public, in 1695, a year after Pufendorf's own death.

During the 1670s and 1680s, as Frederick William became a figure of obvious European importance, his court became a focus of attention for other rulers. Their ambassadors, including the French, Dutch and Imperial ones, were now fixtures, and the Berlin court began to take on a much grander tone, although it was still one of the smaller European courts and the Elector's own entourage was modest. There was extensive internal decoration of the *Schloß*, with fine gilding, sculptures, carpets, furniture and tapestries. For the first time the actual façade was refashioned and a new wing constructed along the Spree by Johann Nehring. Little was now left

*culture
brought w/ Louise
Henrietta*

of the old *Schloß*, and several new rooms, with an impressive large reception hall, the *Alabastersaal*, brought Frederick William's main residence more in keeping with the better German ones. On the other hand the palaces at Cleves and Königsberg, favoured in the 1640s and 1650s, were now neglected. In 1669 the Elector remarked that it was so cold in the one at Cleves that 'I must write with gloves on; the ink is freezing'.[106] A few years later an English minister remarked that the palace there 'is not at all magnificent'.[107]

. . .

NOTES AND REFERENCES

1 Figures vary, depending on which borders of Germany are used, although the trends are the same. See above all Asch, *Thirty Years War*, pp. 185ff.; Press, *Kriege und Krisen*, pp. 31, 270; and C. Dipper, *Deutsche Geschichte, 1648–1789* (Frankfurt am Main, 1991), p. 45. Confusion has arisen through the uncritical acceptance of S.H. Steinberg's absurd claim, in his popular *The Thirty Years' War* (London, 1966), p. 107, of a 'total population of about 15 to 17 million in 1600 and about 16 million to 18 million in 1650'!

2 R. Vierhaus, *Staaten und Stände: Vom Westfälischen bis zum Humbertusbergischer Frieden, 1648 bis 1763* (Berlin, 1984), p. 57.

3 Schultze, *Brandenburg*, IV, p. 287, puts the decline even steeper. Besides Schultze, the obvious authority is still G. Franz, *Der Dreißigjährige Krieg und das deutsche Volk: Untersuchungen zur Bevölkerungs- und Agrargeschichte*, 4th edn (Stuttgart, 1979), passim. Surveys of 1643 and 1652 provide most of the firm evidence.

4 F.W. Henning, *Handbuch der Wirtschaft- und Sozialgeschichte* (Paderborn, 1991), I, p. 241.

5 Sutlers were camp followers who sold troops provisions. A famous, if rather unsuccessful one was Brecht's Mother Courage.

6 Hüttl, p. 158.

7 Schultze, *Brandenburg*, IV, p. 270.

8 Meinardus, I, p. 253.

9 Schultze, *Brandenburg*, IV, p. 270.

10 W. Abel, *Agricultural Fluctuations in Europe from the late 13th to the 20th Centuries* (London, 1980), p. 151.

11 J. Gagliardo, *Germany under the Old Regime, 1600–1790* (London, 1991), p. 226.

12 W.W. Hagen, 'Seventeenth-century crisis in Brandenburg: the Thirty Years War, the destabilisation of serfdom, and the rise of absolutism', *American Historical Review*, 94 (1989), p. 315.

13 Hüttl, p. 70.

14 Philippson, I, 28.
15 H. Kellenbenz, *The Rise of the European Economy* (New York, 1976), p. 324.
16 Abel, *Agricultural*, p. 155.
17 Carsten, *Essays*, p. 83.
18 Opgenoorth, *Friedrich Wilhelm*, I, p. 165.
19 Hüttl, p. 174.
20 F.L. Carsten, 'The resistance of Cleves and Mark to the despotic policy of the Great Elector', *English Historical Review*, 66 (1951), p. 225.
21 Hein, pp. 27f.
22 For him see E. van den Boogart, ed., *Johan Mauritz van Nassau-Siegen, 1604–1679: A Humanist Prince in Europe and Brazil* (The Hague, 1979). Johann Moritz was a count until 1652, when the Emperor made him a prince.
23 E. Opgenoorth, 'Johan Maurits as the stadtholder of Cleves under the Elector of Brandenburg', in van den Boogart, pp. 43, 46.
24 Carsten, *Essays*, p. 84.
25 Opgenoorth, *Friedrich Wilhelm*, I, p. 222.
26 See R.G. Asch, 'Estates and princes after 1648: the consequences of the Thirty Years War', *German History*, 6 (1988), pp. 113ff.
27 Carsten, *Origins*, pp. 235ff.; and especially J. Kloosteruis, 'Fürsten, Räte, Untertanen: Die Graftschaft Mark, ihre lokalen Verwaltungsorgane und die Regierung zu Kleve', *Der Märker*, 35 (1986), p. 107.
28 For the episode see Opgenoorth, 'Johan Maurits', p. 50, and his ' "Nervus rerum", die Auseinandersetzung mit den Ständen um die Staatsfinanzierung', in G. Heinrich, ed., *Ein sonderbares Licht in Teutschland: Beiträge zur Geschichte des Großen Kurfürsten von Brandenburg, 1640–88* (Berlin, 1990), p. 102.
29 Carsten, *Origins*, pp. 243f.
30 See especially P. Baumgart, 'Der Große Kurfürst': Staatsdenken und Staatsarbeit eines europäischen Dynasten', in Heinrich, ed., *Ein sonderbares Licht*, pp. 40ff.
31 A. Waddington, *Histoire de Prusse* (Paris, 1911), I, p. 272.
32 Fürbringer, p. 85.
33 Philippson, I, pp. 137f.
34 Fürbringer, p. 85.
35 Altmark, Prignitz, Uckermark and the district circles of the larger Mittelmark all had a local diet (*Kreistag*). Together they made up the general diet (*Landtag*) of the electorate.
36 For the local diets see especially, P.-M. Hahn, 'Landesstaat und Ständetum im Kurfürstentum Brandenburg während des 16. und 17. Jahrhunderts', in P. Baumgart, ed., *Ständetum und Staatsbildung in Brandenburg-Preußen* (Berlin, 1983).
37 Philippson, I, p. 158.

38 The Neumark had a separate diet and this was now called and met apart. See Hagen, 'Seventeenth century crisis', p. 319. Even in the permanent committees and deputation diets the Neumark deputies met separately from those of the rest of the electorate (*Kurmark*) till the early 1680s. See Hahn, 'Landesstaat und Ständetum', p. 55.

39 For it see especially Carsten, *Origins*, pp. 185ff., and Fürbringer, pp. 128ff.

40 For extracts from the text in English, see C.A. Macartney, *The Habsburg and Hohenzollern Dynasties in the Seventeenth and Eighteenth Centuries* (London, 1970), pp. 228ff.

41 Philippson, I, p. 388, and H. Rosenberg, 'The rise of the Junkers in Brandenburg-Prussia', *American Historical Review*, 49 (1943), p. 240.

42 Nachama, p. 43.

43 Hüttl, p. 193.

44 All quotes are from Macartney, pp. 232–7.

45 Lackner, p. 112.

46 Macartney, p. 231.

47 W. Jannen, ' "Das Liebe Teutschland" in the seventeenth century – Count George Frederick von Waldeck', *European Studies Review*, 6 (1976), p. 191.

48 V. Press, 'Vom Ständestaat zum Absolutismus: 50 Thesen zur Entwicklung des Ständewesens in Deutschland', in Baumgart, ed., *Ständetum*, p. 324. At the election of Emperor Leopold I in 1658 Frederick William and his fellow electors forced him to confirm the decree. See Press, *Kriege und Krisen*, p. 333. Limits were placed on the right of Estates in the Empire to assemble without being called by their ruler, although those with established precedents (as in Cleves-Mark) were usually to ignore this. In 1669–71 Frederick William also supported unsuccessful attempts to extend the terms of the Imperial decree, see A. Schindling, 'Kurbrandenburg im System des Reiches während der zweiten Hälfte des 17 Jahrunderts', in O. Hauser, ed., *Preußen, Europa und das Reich* (Cologne, 1987), p. 41.

49 Fay, 'The beginnings', pp. 770f.

50 Jannen, p. 176.

51 Philippson, I, p. 243.

52 Hein, p. 86.

53 Waddington, *Prusse*, I, p. 272.

54 Nachama, p. 84.

55 *Urk. u. Akt.*, II, p. 407, Colbert de Croissy to Louis XIV, 19 April 1666.

56 See the biography by Hein and comments by Opgenoorth, *Friedrich Wilhelm*, I, pp. 126f.

57 B. Erdmannsdörffer, *Graf Georg Friedrich von Waldeck. Ein preußischer Staatsmann im 17. Jahrhundert* (Berlin, 1869), p. 56.

58 Beuys, p. 146.

59 Erdmannsdörffer, *Waldeck*, p. 57.

60 Spannagel, *Burgsdorff*, p. 342.

61 The recent biography by G. Menk, *Georg Friedrich von Waldeck (1620–92)* (Arolsen, 1992), is less useful for his years in Brandenburg service than Erdmannsdörffer's older work.

62 Droysen, part 3, II, pp. 55f.

63 Erdmannsdörffer, *Waldeck*, pp. 12f.

64 Opgenoorth, *Friedrich Wilhelm*, I, p. 236.

65 Jannen, p. 188.

66 Droysen, part 3, II, p. 4.

67 Spannagel, *Burgsdorff*, p. 431.

68 Hüttl, p. 185.

69 Carsten, *Origins*, p. 177.

70 F.L. Carsten, 'The Great Elector and the foundation of Hohenzollern despotism', *English Historical Review*, 65 (1950), p. 182.

71 See Meinardus, I, pp. lvi, lxxxiii–v; L. Tümpel, *Die Entstehung des brandenburgisch-preußischen Einheitsstaates im Zeitalter des Absolutismus (1609–1806)* (Breslau/Wrocław, 1915), pp. 73f.; and in detail G. Oestreich, *Der brandenburgisch-preußische Geheime Rat vom Regierungsantritt des Großen Kurfürsten bis zu der Neuordnung im 1651* (Würzburg, 1937).

72 M. Völkel, 'The Hohenzollern court, 1535–1740', in J. Adamson, ed., *The Princely Courts of Europe: Ritual, Politics and Culture under the Ancien Régime* (London, 1999), p. 216.

73 R.A. Dorwart, *The Administrative Reforms of Frederick William I of Prussia* (Cambridge, MA, 1953), p. 20.

74 J. Schultze, 'Von der Mark Brandenburg zum Preußenstaat', in R. Dietrich, ed., *Preußen, Epochen und Probleme seiner Geschichte* (Berlin, 1964), p. 52.

75 Carsten, *Origins*, p. 255.

76 Jannen, p. 192.

77 Carsten, *Origins*, p. 257.

78 Transl. from Carsten, 'The Great Elector', p. 200, note 4.

79 Philippson, I, pp. 380f.

80 S. Isaacsohn, *Geschichte des preußischen Beamtenthums vom Anfang des 15. Jahrhundert bis auf die Gegenwart* (Berlin, 1878), II, p. 363.

81 See G. Pagès, *Le Grand Electeur et Louis XIV, 1660–88* (Paris, 1905), p. 32 for Jena's dispute with Schwerin. The Elector kept Jena on because he told him the truth, despite the Electress's hostility. She wrote to Schwerin in April 1663 that Jena was 'a little man . . . , violent' and impertinent to her.

82 Isaacsohn, II, p. 141, note 5.

83 Noble titles within the Holy Roman Empire from the level of *Freiherr* upwards could only be conferred by the emperor. Jena, who was

from Anhalt, was ennobled in 1663, Meinders in 1682 and Fuchs in 1700.

84 See Hein, p. 239, and Baumgart, 'Der Große Kurfürst', p. 53.
85 Dietrich, ed., *Die politischen Testamente*, pp. 41, 187.
86 Philippson, I, 385.
87 Waddington, *Prusse*, I, p. 266.
88 *Urk. u. Akt.*, XIV, part 2, p. 219, Goess to Leopold I, Berlin, 13 June 1665.
89 Carsten, *Origins*, p. 256.
90 Hüttl, p. 186.
91 See Opgenoorth, *Friedrich Wilhelm*, I, p. 244.
92 See Dorwart, pp. 110f., and in detail K. Breysig, *Geschichte der brandenburgischen Finanzen in der Zeit von 1640 bis 1697* (Leipzig, 1905), I, passim.
93 Spannagel, *Burgsdorff*, p. 261.
94 Hein, p. 53.
95 Erdmannsdörffer, *Waldeck*, p. 70.
96 See ibid., pp. 76f., and F. Hirsch, 'Otto von Schwerin', part 1, *Historische Zeitschrift*, 71 (1893), pp. 206f.
97 1/11 August 1680, Berlin, Southwell to Wynne, PRO, SP 105/49.
98 31 August/10 September 1681, Berlin, Poley to Conway, B[ritish] L[ibrary], Add. Ms. 37986.
99 See Opgenoorth, *Friedrich Wilhelm*, I, pp. 129ff., who is hard put to find any cultural interests of the Elector in his twenties.
100 Ribbe, I, p. 345.
101 *Der Große Kurfürst: Sammler, Bauherr, Mäzen*, exhibition catalogue published by the Generaldirektion der Staatlichen Schlößer und Gärten Potsdam-Sanssouci (Potsdam, 1988), p. 100.
102 Waddington, *Prusse*, I, p. 405.
103 Opgenoorth, *Friedrich Wilhelm*, I, p. 171.
104 L. von Orlich, *Friedrich Wilhelm der Große Kurfürst* (Berlin, 1836), p. 293.
105 See Völkel, p. 217, who calls Johann Moritz the 'prime intermediary' in a 'complex of courtly and cultural influences'.
106 J. Mirow, *Geschichte des deutschen Volkes* (Gernsbach, 1990), p. 381.
107 19/29 February 1676, Nimmeguen, Charles Davenant to Williamson, PRO, SP 84/200.

Chapter 4

A EUROPEAN PRINCE,
1648–1660

. . .

A PROTESTANT PRINCE IN THE EMPIRE,
1648–55

Although the Peace of Westphalia ended the Thirty Years War in Germany, war continued between France and Spain till 1659 and conflict was to break out once more around the Baltic in 1655. The end of hostilities in the Empire also brought no immediate relief for Brandenburg and other parts of Germany: the Swedes refused to leave till 1650 when the Empire finally paid the Swedish troops' pay arrears. Even then they would not budge from East Pomerania till the borders were settled to their satisfaction. They used their military muscle to squeeze the last drop from the surrender and to plunder the ducal manors and forests as long as possible. Before Frederick William could enter the main town of Kołobrzeg/Kolberg in 1653, he had to agree to hand over a wide stretch of the right bank of the Oder, denying him access to the river and its trade, to share half the tolls on the small East Pomeranian ports and to shoulder most of the debts of the whole duchy.

Frustration over Pomerania may have contributed to spurring Frederick William to further aggression in the Rhineland in 1651. His earlier wretched failure in Berg had not dampened his ambitions there, and he hoped the Dutch would now help him, since Duke Wolfgang William of Pfalz-Neuburg had begun to enforce the Westphalian settlement and eject Protestants in Jülich-Berg from churches they were not entitled to. Unfortunately the deaths of the two Dutch stadtholders, Frederick Henry (1647) and his son, William II (1650), had shattered the position of the house of Orange and brought supreme power in the Republic to the Regents, who were

Louise Henrietta

hostile to the Elector because of his connections with the former stadtholders. Frederick William found most of his Privy Council were still not enthusiastic, but others at court close to Louise Henrietta were: if Frederick William could defeat Pfalz-Neuburg and then tame his own Estates in Cleves, this might strengthen the Orange party in the Republic and their figurehead, the infant Prince William (later William III). There were also several pro-Orange Dutch officers in the Brandenburg army, including Waldeck.[1] Burgsdorff does not seem to have been as responsible for this war as the previous one. The main architect was Frederick William himself: convinced of his rights to Jülich-Berg and impetuous as ever, he naively disregarded his own financial, military and diplomatic weaknesses and the real risk that other states would brand him a warmonger.

In what amounted to an act of brigandage, Frederick William launched a surprise attack on Berg in June 1651, claiming (and probably believing) he was defending Protestant rights there and upholding past treaties with Wolfgang William. His 4,000-strong army was led by a Pfalz-Neuburg noble who had served in the Imperial army, Otto von Sparr. The force once again lacked the artillery needed to capture any significant towns, while the troops' behaviour recalled the excesses of the Thirty Years War. Finding no enemy to fight, they imposed contributions and seized cattle, leading contemporaries to dismiss the conflict as the 'Cow War' (*Kuhkrieg*). The adventure brought outrage and obstruction from the Cleves Estates, who ordered officials not to obey Frederick William. The Brandenburg Estates, meanwhile, called for an end to the war, and his privy councillors in Berlin were apathetic, making Waldeck complain the Elector 'was almost abandoned by all'.[2] Far worse was the international response. Schwerin reported from The Hague that 'The province of Holland [the most important one] . . . wishes everything to stay in peace and quiet'.[3] The Dutch Republic therefore pressed Frederick William strongly to leave Berg. Even more alarming was the response of Emperor Ferdinand III, who appeared ready to intervene directly to help Wolfgang William, not only because of his Catholicism: here was a chance to exert Imperial authority over one of the German princes after their collective success at Westphalia. Neighbouring Catholic rulers also threatened to invade the Elector's own lands, and the county of Mark was plundered by mercenaries under the Duke of Lorraine in August. By late summer the Elector had grown increasingly dispirited, especially as his wife suffered another miscarriage after one the previous year and the death of an infant boy in October 1649. They still lacked an heir, and Louise Henrietta seems to have felt her losses were divine retribution, and she now urged him to end the war.

In autumn 1651 Frederick William accepted the Emperor's mediation and his insistence on the restoration of the territorial and religious *status quo*. The badly prepared second Berg war had proved yet another humiliation, showing Frederick William still lacked the means to conduct his own dynastic policies. The adventure also increased his diplomatic isolation, giving him the reputation of a reckless prince willing to imperil the peace of Germany so soon after the great war. One of his ministers, Blumenthal, told him frankly in February 1652 that 'I know no one, within or outside the Empire, Your Electoral Highness can trust'.[4] While many in the Privy Council saw this isolation as further reason to conduct a passive foreign policy, the Elector came to the opposite conclusion. Encouraged by his increasingly influential and dynamic new adviser, Waldeck, he felt it essential to improve his diplomatic position and, just as important, to tame his Estates and reform his government and army.

The death of Götzen and dismissal of Burgsdorff allowed Frederick William to make a fresh start, and his instrument in coming to grips with the chaotic administration and finances left by these men was Waldeck, who soon emerged as chief minister after the Cow War. He restored the Elector's self-confidence, as well as promoting administrative reform. Although this had limited success (see pp. 66–72), the creation around the Elector of a tighter group of ministers responsible for the more important aspects of foreign and military policy, brought the discussion and conduct of these into sharper focus. Yet during the early 1650s, this focus was directed to Waldeck's own rather fanciful foreign projects, which Frederick William adopted as his own. Throughout his life Waldeck was to try to defend the interests of European Protestantism, but, as a petty German ruler himself, he was also keen to uphold his fellow princes' 'German liberties'. In the 1650s his views were still largely coloured by the Thirty Years War and he saw the Catholic Emperor and his Spanish Habsburg cousins as natural enemies.[5] These views were very similar to Frederick William's own gut reactions, and Waldeck encouraged him to believe that Brandenburg was surrounded by papist enemies: 'Danger, trouble and calamity seem in wait for us round every corner.'[6] This seemed confirmed during 1652–3, when Emperor Ferdinand III forced thousands of Protestants to leave Austria. Genuinely distressed, the Elector in July 1653 ordered his minister at the Imperial Diet, Blumenthal, to protest, adding: 'I cannot ignore the poor Protestants . . . I have written this early in the morning with a clear head, so that I cannot be accused of having had anything to drink. We must expect Catholics to behave like this, since they deny that heretics [i.e. Protestants] have any faith.'[7]

Waldeck's answer was to try to rebuild the Protestant Union of old to curb the Emperor and the Catholic party at the Imperial Diet at Regensburg and in the Empire as a whole. He described Frederick William's aims in 1654, probably correctly, as working 'to put himself in a state of defence and to live in friendship with those who claim the same liberty and the same heaven, for without their preservation he could not be Elector'.[8] During the year Brandenburg, backed by France and Sweden, was to lead the Protestant states in the Imperial Diet in rejecting Imperial taxes and the creation of an Imperial army. This culminated in the famous *Reichsabschied*, where Emperor Ferdinand was forced to agree that the princes could impose taxes to maintain garrisons and fortresses.[9] From isolation after the Cow War, Brandenburg was now at the centre of things. The French minister at Regensburg was impressed, writing home: 'Most Germans praise the Elector and consider he has restored their liberties.'[10] Some at the Diet, however, feared that the Protestant princes might plunge the Empire into another religious war.

Expanding the powers of the German princes was for Waldeck the first stage of a far more ambitious policy to limit the Habsburgs by bringing Brandenburg indirectly into the continuing Franco-Spanish war. By using French subsidies to build an army from the Protestant princes, Frederick William should prevent the Emperor from intervening on behalf of his Spanish relative, Philip IV, and ensure France conquered the Spanish Netherlands. Waldeck hoped France would then reward the Elector with Jülich-Berg. Fortunately for peace in the Empire and for Brandenburg itself, the scheme failed, partly because the German Protestants valued the hard-won German peace too much to join in a military adventure with a prince who had recently waged the farcical Cow War, and partly because it ultimately proved impossible for Frederick William to work with France. While he and Waldeck wanted an independent role for themselves as head of a Protestant league, Cardinal Mazarin hoped to turn Brandenburg and as many German states as possible,

Catholic or Protestant, into mere clients, paid to supply troops for French use. Inevitably alliance negotiations with France collapsed, as did the proposed Protestant league in 1655, when it became clear that the Rhenish states of Cologne, Münster and Jülich-Berg were forming their own Catholic league to counter this. Ironically France was soon to turn this new Catholic combination into her own satellite League of the Rhine.

. . .

THE WAR OF THE NORTH, 1655–60[11]

Waldeck and Frederick William's diplomatic manoeuvres in Germany were finally curtailed by the outbreak of war in the north in summer 1655. This was the direct result of the abdication of Queen Christina and the accession of Charles X (1654–60) the year before. The new king hankered after the military glory which had eluded him as Swedish *generalissimo* in the final stages of the Thirty Years War, and he was to find plenty of domestic support for this. Just after Charles's accession, Frederick William himself summed up the new situation perceptively: 'poverty is now great in Sweden. . . . the present King . . . is still young, is eager for war [and] will therefore hazard everything to gain something; Sweden has now had several years of peace; without war they have to fear rebellion at home.'[12] In a war to fill Sweden's treasury and her generals' and politicians' pockets, as well as to confirm her hegemony in northern Europe, the obvious victim was Poland-Lithuania under King John Casimir. But equally vulnerable was the Polish King's vassal, the Duke of Prussia, Frederick William. To complete Sweden's territorial ring round the Baltic and to extract more toll revenues, she had to make her *de facto* rule permanent in Livonia[13] (roughly modern Latvia) and annex the lands which controlled Poland's export trade – Polish Royal Prussia, with its ports of Gdańsk and Elbląg, and the East Prussian ports. The intended Polish victim was already prostrate: Cossack rebellion in the Polish Ukraine had been compounded in 1654 by the invasion of Lithuania by the Russian Tsar Alexis. The Tsar's early successes also made it wise for Sweden to seize lands from Poland before he took them and threatened Swedish supremacy in the Baltic. Charles X's Chancellor, Erik Oxenstierna (son of Axel Oxenstierna who had died in 1654), wrote at this time: 'Our chief interest is to protect the Baltic from the Russians.'[14]

A Swedish attack on Poland was bound to affect Frederick William: his lands in East Prussia lay between predator and victim, and victory for either side augured the nasty consequence of direct Polish or Swedish control of the duchy. This became clear in September 1654, soon after Charles X became king, when his minister in Berlin demanded the use of the Prussian ports as bases for a campaign against Poland. The request was rejected out of hand, for, as Schwerin remarked in January 1655: 'Do we want our throat cut? Prussia is the apple of our eye, the heart of our state.'[15] Once there the Swedes were likely to stay put and seize the revenues from the amber industry and the Polish transit trade.

Determined not to be overtaken by events and face a repeat of the disasters of his father's reign, the Elector began to prepare his defences by raising 8,000 infantry and 4,000 cavalry during the first months of 1655. Waldeck was sent to Prussia to recruit men and call out the militia. Appeals were also made to the Dutch for the protection of a Baltic fleet. Despite the Dutch Regents' dislike of Frederick William and his Orange connections, it seemed best for the Republic's commercial interests that the Prussian and Polish ports should stay in the hands of their existing weak and non-naval proprietors. By late July, therefore, an alliance was signed in The Hague, guaranteeing the Elector's lands: the Dutch appeared determined to send a fleet to back this up the next year.[16]

Frederick William had tried to warn the Poles in spring 1655 of the Swedish threat, but John Casimir was understandably more concerned with his immediate Cossack and Russian enemies. The electoral minister in Warsaw, Hoverbeck, reported as late as mid-June: 'They live in Warsaw, as though they had never heard of Sweden.'[17] Given the relentless Swedish military build-up, the weakness and indifference of the Poles and the obvious sympathy of many magnates in the Lithuanian half of Poland for Charles X, by the early summer Frederick William and Waldeck were concluding the Poles were doomed. It seemed best to throw in their lot with the Swedes and seize something themselves from Poland: what they wanted was the sovereignty of Prussia and territory lying between it and Brandenburg. The absolutist-minded Waldeck openly expressed his disgust that the Elector was a dependant of a king who 'gains the crown through the favour of senators, corruption and the rest, and he [Elector] has almost no say in this'. He also believed that, once free of Polish sovereignty, Frederick William 'could govern as he pleased like a real ruler' in Prussia.[18] But the Berlin court overestimated

Charles X's need for Brandenburg friendship – she was a minor German power in his eyes – and news of the alliance negotiations with the Dutch inevitably angered him.

In June Waldeck and Schwerin were sent to negotiate with the Swedes at Szczecin. They went with an offer of an alliance against Poland: in return they wanted the sovereignty of Prussia and a wide corridor of land to join it with Brandenburg, as well as Samogitia (most of modern Lithuania) and the bishopric of Warmia/Ermeland and Elbląg. Although these demands were hardly realistic, the Swedish negotiator Bengt Oxenstierna offered extensive concessions at this uncertain point before the war began: the sovereignty, Warmia and some of Samogitia. But in return he demanded Brandenburg join in the attack on Poland with 8,000 of her men under direct Swedish command. To Waldeck's disappointment, Frederick William rejected these proposals, the best Sweden would offer for a couple of years: he remembered all too well how his father had lost control of his own troops to the Emperor. He desperately hoped to maintain independence of action, difficult though this was.

In July 1655 the Swedish invasion of Poland began: 7,000 troops attacked from Livonia and the main force of 17,000 from Western Pomerania (crossing the Elector's lands unhindered). On the 25th Charles X himself landed at Wolgast in Pomerania, where Waldeck and Schwerin rushed to meet him, but early military successes in Poland meant Charles was in no mood to compromise. He wanted Frederick William to send 4,000 troops to join him at once. The two ministers were worried enough to advise agreement, but then on entering Poland Charles demanded what had been feared for a year: as 'insurance' for the Elector's loyalty, the Prussian ports and a share of their tolls while the war lasted, and Prussia to become a fief of the Swedish crown. Despite their alarm, these demands were too much for Frederick William and his ministers. Refusing to be reduced to a Swedish vassal, he broke off the talks.

In defying Sweden in this way, the Elector was very much on his own: neither Dutch money nor their fleet was likely to arrive before the following spring. None the less, he was far stronger than in previous disputes with the Swedes. With Waldeck's enthusiastic help, he had raised 13,000 regular troops and 6,000 inferior militia, as well as an artillery train. This army, commanded by Sparr with decent officers, was an impressive force, completely different from that of the Berg wars. In September Frederick William was able to take advantage of Charles X's campaigning in southern Poland to lead part of this army to join the rest in Prussia. He intended to defend his duchy from all sides and hoped to influence events by being closer to the war zone. Unfortunately, he was to be allowed little time to deploy his troops. By November Charles had conquered much of Poland, including Warsaw and Kráków, and now intended to winter his troops in Prussia. He then planned to annex north-west Poland, seize the Polish and Prussian ports, make Prussia a Swedish fief, and force Frederick William into vassalage.

As Charles X advanced with his victorious army into Prussia in December, the Elector and his troops retreated behind the extensive fortifications of Königsberg: confusion, and feelings of diplomatic and military weakness, led to this humiliating retreat and 'one of the weakest periods of Brandenburg history under Frederick William'.[19] Although Waldeck urged him to fight, the Elector had no experience in battle and, even though their forces were of similar size, he dared not take on the King, his seasoned generals and what was considered the best army in Europe. No outside help could be expected. The Poles were beaten and the Dutch fleet months away. The Emperor Ferdinand III was still smarting at Brandenburg's recent defiance at the Imperial Diet, and his own very poor health made him want 'peace at any price',[20] fearing the Swedes might revisit Germany itself. Eventually he answered repeated appeals from Königsberg with vague offers of help in the spring, causing Frederick William to sneer he was proposing 'to cure a man in his death throes with herbs which only sprout in May'.[21]

There was general panic in Königsberg at the prospect of a siege, and the cold that winter was so keen that soldiers suffered from frostbite and citizens kept warm by burning their furniture. The Elector himself seemed at a loss over what to do and was reported to be 'ruling in the Polish way, that is with much confusion and little good order'.[22] Eventually, in the first days of 1656, the peace party, which included Sparr and the Electress who had joined her husband in November, overcame Waldeck's calls to fight.[23] On 17 January 1656 Frederick William signed a treaty with the Swedes in Königsberg. This marked a disastrous low for him, effectively subjecting Prussia to Charles X. The duchy became a Swedish fief, her troops allowed free passage across it and her warships and merchantmen free use of its ports; the Elector had to share the Prussian toll revenues, and he was even forbidden to put his own warships on the Baltic. On the plus side, he still had control of his own army, had not been forced to join Charles in the war, and was promised the eventual cession of Polish Warmia.

Europe inevitably reacted badly. The Dutch were especially angry, believing they had been double-crossed since they had just given Frederick William a subsidy of 120,000 thalers; the leading Dutch minister, the Pensionary, De Witt, accused him of pursuing a 'foxlike policy'.[24] King John Casimir of Poland blustered that he would throw him 'into a dungeon where he will never see sun or moon again'.[25] It was generally assumed that Frederick William and Charles X were now allies, but this was far from the truth. Though they met briefly at Bartoszyce/Bartenstein, with outward signs of friendship, this was just skin deep. Almost from the start Frederick William was to struggle to free himself; and during the coming months he raised more troops, while resisting Charles's demands to enter the war. Yet he still had little idea what to do, feeling he had no control over events and desperately worried about Louise Henrietta, who stayed in Königsberg through the winter and had first miscarried and then caught smallpox.[26] Waldeck meanwhile was becoming contemptuous of the Elector and those at court who advised keeping out of the war. He wrote at the time:

> They want to be free of all risks, but have left themselves open to them; they want to stand by Poland but have deserted her; . . . they want to be free of war but also want to begin a new one; they want to have fewer troops but also want more than the enemy. In sum, they want what they didn't want and they do what they didn't think they would do.[27]

The confusion and indecision in Königsberg meant that the initiative in the war would continue to be taken by others. It was also beginning to prove a conflict which the Swedes could not win, despite their military superiority, victories in open battle and routine atrocities against the Polish population. Despite Charles X's superb infantry and artillery, the vast plains of Poland and the thousands of enemy irregular cavalry meant he could occupy only the main cities. In spring 1656 he conducted another brilliant campaign far to the south-east, only to see his conquests slip away as he returned northwards. John Casimir had meanwhile allied with his Cossack and Tartar enemies, while Tsar Alexis broke off his campaign against Poland to attack Swedish Livonia. Frederick William, however, was unable to exploit all this. The cost of his inactive troops was leading to mounting opposition from the Prussian Estates and unrest in Königsberg. When he and his ministers discussed what to do in late April, most argued against becoming involved in Swedish adventurism and some wanted to ally with the Poles. Waldeck on the other hand now urged throwing in their lot with Sweden in a Protestant alliance. He insisted that King John Casimir's recent dedication of Poland to the Virgin meant he had sworn to fight all heretics. The Elector should seize the chance to join the unbeaten Swedes and exploit the chaos in Poland to make conquests there. He also held out the prospect of future Swedish help in Germany to seize Jülich-Berg.

Waldeck's influence was growing once more and Frederick William shared his religious attitudes, but he still remained undecided for a couple of months. Ominous news was coming from Vienna that the Emperor intended to send troops to help the Poles conquer Prussia, but what finally seems to have determined Frederick William to risk joining Charles X in June was that the Poles were not offering him anything concrete. The proximity of Charles and his troops was another factor: after all, the Elector had never known Sweden defeated in battle and the new ruler was proving as great a warrior as Gustavus Adolphus. On 25 June, therefore, a new Swedo-Brandenburg alliance was signed at Charles's camp at Malbork/Marienburg. Here Frederick William at last agreed to join his troops to the Swedes, although retaining direct command over them. Charles agreed to defend Prussia and promised him Warmia and most of Great Poland (Wielkopolska) around Poznań/Posen. He refused a 'communications line' of territory between Brandenburg and Prussia, and he also retained sovereignty over Prussia and his share of the tolls. Although Frederick William was now the military ally of Sweden, this was to be another short-term measure, forced on him by circumstances rather than real design.

It seemed at first that the Elector had made a dreadful blunder: at the beginning of July a vast Polish-Tartar army, possibly 70,000 strong, seized Warsaw from its Swedish garrison. John Casimir then threatened to march on his Protestant enemies, singling out Frederick William for his special attention as a traitor. This was incentive enough for Frederick William to take 8,500 of his own men, mostly infantry, and 30 guns to join Charles's field army of 9,500 north of Warsaw. In a hard-fought three-day battle in the summer heat at the end of July, their forces decisively routed the Poles and retook Warsaw.[28] As Waldeck put it: 'All who bore the name of Pole,

Lithuanian and Tartar fled from the field.'[29] Brandenburg had essentially acted as part of a Swedish force, directed by Charles X, but the battle was the first significant one for both the Elector and his army: his troops had proved equal to the Swedes and he had fought bravely in the first ranks. The victory put him in a confident mood at last, and he refused Charles's request to follow the broken enemy, fearing a repeat of the King's fruitless pursuits of Polish cavalry over the endless plains. Just as important, complete Polish defeat would reduce him to a permanent Swedish dependant. It would suit him best for Sweden and Poland to be finely balanced: after the battle he had a medal struck with the Brandenburg eagle mediating between Polish and Swedish ones. He therefore led the bulk of his troops back to Prussia, helping to ensure that the battle of Warsaw proved no more decisive for Charles X than his previous victories.

Despite the scale of the victory of Warsaw, the Poles recovered and the Swedes were once more limited by the end of 1656 to holding various enclaves throughout Poland. The arrival of the Dutch fleet off Gdańsk in the summer had meant that Charles dared not risk offending the Republic by seizing the town or the Prussian ports. While Dutch warships offshore gave Frederick William some protection against his Swedish ally, his own duchy faced a far more immediate threat. In late summer and autumn bands of Muslim Tartar horsemen burnt towns and villages, slaughtered thousands and carried off 30,000 more to sell as slaves in such Polish towns as Lublin, which 'looked like the bazaars of Constantinople'.[30] The military danger from John Casimir and his allies was also increasing during autumn 1656. The Danes and Imperialists were preparing to enter the war against Sweden, and on 3 November the Imperialists mediated an armistice between Poland and the Tsar, who promised military help 'against the common enemies, the King of Sweden and the Duke of Prussia'. Frederick William's own forces were being depleted by sickness and desertion; Prussia had been recruited dry, and money was desperately short. Throughout the year he had been involved in bitter disputes with his Prussian, Pomeranian and Brandenburg Estates. In July the Brandenburgers complained that they had 'been forced to contribute to the limits' to illegal taxes for a foreign war.[31] Resentment was greatest in Prussia where the nobility and Königsberg appeared ready to revolt: in September some nobles approached the Imperial envoy, Lisola, offering to rise as soon as the Emperor's troops neared Prussia.[32] Frederick William's own ministers were also in disarray. At the end of August there was fierce argument over whether to stick by Sweden. Waldeck insisted on it, and this led some days later to a confrontation in a Königsberg street with two other ministers, Platen and Jena. Waldeck threatened Jena with his whip, shouting: 'You dog, you are another of those against me in the council, you clerk, you ink-shitter.'[33] He then told both men: 'Tell the Elector, if he no longer wants me, he can write and sack me.'[34] Frederick William was furious, threatening to have Waldeck's head, but he did nothing, feeling he could not afford to upset Charles X at this stage. None the less, Waldeck was becoming very isolated at court. By October Schwerin, who was gaining increasing influence, had joined those such as Platen and Jena in pushing to abandon the Swedes for a Polish alliance. The Electress had been convinced throughout the year that her husband was courting disaster because of the immorality of fighting his Polish overlord, and she was even threatening to return to Holland.

Disaster seemed to have struck on 8 October when Poles and Tartars under Gosiewski defeated a weak Brandenburg-Swedish force led by Waldeck at Prostki/Prostken on Prussia's eastern borders. The Brandenburgers, mainly raw recruits, had broken and fled. Gosiewski's army followed, plundering and seizing slaves as far as Gizycko/Lötzen, 130 kilometres from Königsberg. There was panic in the city, but Frederick William kept his head. He forbade desperate wealthy officials and citizens from shipping their families to Gdańsk and Lübeck. He told them that his wife was staying and 'you can also risk yours'.[35] Then, by threatening to change sides, he forced Charles X to send troops to help. These Swedes and Brandenburgers under Waldeck smashed Gosiewski's forces at Philipowo on 23 October. Gosiewski was so shaken that he offered a three-month armistice, which the Elector accepted despite Waldeck's opposition. Although the greatest danger for the duchy was now past, Polish and Tartar irregulars continued their raids, and burning villages could be seen from the walls of Königsberg. In the west Polish cavalry were burning and slaughtering in Pomerania and the Neumark. Even Berlin seemed vulnerable: the Elector ordered his archives and valuables removed to the safety of the fortress of Spandau. Schwerin admitted at this time to a French envoy, de Lumbres, that they had lost half their army from disease since the battle of Warsaw and were desperate for money.[36]

There is little doubt that at bottom Frederick William wanted to be rid of his Swedish alliance. He none the less stuck out against his wife and most of his ministers' wish to shift to the Polish side. This was partly because his mind was set on the sovereignty of Prussia,[37] and the Poles were still not offering him this, but there was another reason. On 28 September Schwerin had written to their envoy in The Hague, Weimann, that the Elector had replied to his advice to come to terms with the Poles: 'this is not possible, unless he [the Elector] also offers to attack Sweden, which he did not want to do ... since the common interest lay in her preservation'.[38] This 'common interest' was Protestantism and the balance of power, since Sweden's destruction would benefit the Catholic states. None the less, Schwerin continued into October to press for a treaty with Poland and her allies, arguing that even if the Swedes agreed to guarantee Hohenzollern sovereignty over Prussia, this would be worthless without Polish consent. The Elector, however, who was determined never again to have Poland as his overlord, believed she would only agree through force,[39] and he saw no alternative but to remain a largely passive ally of Charles X and to press him for further concessions. This decision was entirely his own, not that of Waldeck, whose influence had been ebbing fast and was to cease completely after his defeat at Prostki in October. By December he was even staying away from court.

Fresh talks were conducted with Charles X throughout October and November. This time Schwerin was in charge and he stuck to a demand for Prussian sovereignty. Although the King had laughed at this at first, he began to realise that his own 12,000–15,000 men, now forced once again to retreat into East Prussia, were lost if Frederick William abandoned him. For the first time he began to treat the Elector more as an equal, and on 20 November they signed their third and final alliance at Polessk/Labiau. This gave Frederick William the bishopric of Warmia and full sovereignty over Prussia. The Prussian port tolls were restored to him for 120,000 thalers (the sum he had received in subsidies from the Dutch), although Swedish ships were to be exempt. Frederick William, however, had to confirm he would not have a navy on the Baltic.[40] Charles was guaranteed vast, mostly unconquered lands in northern Poland and Lithuania. The two rulers also promised to be perpetual allies. This, of course, was mere window dressing and the alliance was very fragile. The logical next step for Frederick William, having rid himself of Swedish control, was to get the Poles to renounce their claim to Prussian sovereignty. And Charles X himself had no illusions about his ally, for during the negotiations he had remarked: 'The Elector is too powerful. His ambition, the extent of which I know better than anyone, must be set in bounds. This prince's plans must be checked: unless we watch him, he will become a threat.'[41]

Almost simultaneously with this new Brandenburg–Swedish treaty the Poles formally allied with the Emperor. The Imperial court hoped to keep the Swedes bogged down in Poland in case they revived their ambitions in Germany, and Ferdinand III promised to furnish the infantry John Casimir needed to defeat the Swedes on the battlefield. The new alliance was also clearly aimed at Frederick William and an attack on Prussia could be expected before long. Consequently, in the last weeks of 1656 the Elector pressed Charles to make peace, warning that the destruction of Poland could only benefit the Tsar, who by now had added large parts of Swedish Livonia to his earlier conquests in Polish Lithuania. But peace was far from Charles X's mind. He had recently allied with Prince George Rákóczi II of Transylvania, the Calvinist ruler of a Hungarian principality which still maintained a precarious semi-independence between Turks and Austrian Habsburgs. During the winter months Rákóczi's irregulars began to stream over the Carpathians into southern Poland, while Charles pretended to listen to Frederick William's calls for peace. It was the Poles who continued to reject these, especially ones involving territorial losses. This caused the Elector to write in early January 1657: 'We now have good hopes of peace, but these people [the Poles] must be brought to reason through force: nothing else works on them.'[42] None the less, he did not intend to do this himself. When Charles moved deep into Poland to link up with Rákóczi, Frederick William sent only a token force to follow him in March. Command of it was given to Waldeck, who had not been at court over the winter and was acting increasingly like a Swedish general. Frederick William was as apprehensive of a Swedish victory as of a defeat. At the same time he wrote to his Cleves Stadtholder, Prince Johann Moritz: 'God protect us from the tyrant [Charles X]; we will have to see how far we can depend on his promise and sworn alliance.'[43]

Charles X's new campaign was to be as inconclusive as the earlier ones and his Transylvanian allies soon returned home. By May 1657 he and Waldeck were back in northern Poland, and the King had had enough. He now decided to end the whole Polish adventure. This war, unlike Sweden's earlier ones, had not paid for itself; the Imperialists were about to enter Poland in strength; and, more importantly, King Frederick III of Denmark was invading Sweden itself. This Danish attack, which certainly posed real dangers, and produced calls for help from Stockholm, gave Charles excuse enough to abandon a war he could not win for one offering fresh pillage and recruits and more tangible conquests in the western Baltic. Announcing in Toruń/Thorn that he intended to take up Frederick III's challenge in person, Charles remarked cynically: 'The Polish and Russian wars are more difficult for me and my empire. These barbarians are so undisciplined, that you can beat them as much as you want. I have to get out of this Polish business.'[44] Before departing, he offered Frederick William the chance to join him in an alliance with France against the Danes, Habsburgs and Poles. The Elector did not respond, and Charles left Toruń in early July to march to southern Denmark, leaving enough garrisons behind to keep John Casimir occupied.

Waldeck soon followed him and entered Swedish service the next year. He complained to a correspondent in The Hague after leaving Poland: 'For almost a year now my advice had been unacceptable and now my word counts for little.'[45] Judging the Elector to have become far too cautious and pragmatic, Waldeck felt Charles was more in tune with his grandiose ideas and he also probably received money from Charles during the war.[46] His departure finally ended the period when Frederick William's policies had been identified with a leading minister, Burgsdorff in the first decade and then Waldeck. From now on the 37-year-old Elector seemed to have less need for a strong figure around him to lean on. His ministers in the future tended to be essentially functionaries, although he clearly had affection as well as regard for Otto von Schwerin. And it was now Schwerin, the practised diplomat and administrator, who in September 1657 became *Oberpräsident* of the Privy Council. Sober, patient, avoiding glib solutions, always content to see the Elector himself in real charge, Schwerin was to be the most important minister over the next twenty years.

Once Waldeck left, all Frederick William's advisers wanted to ditch the Swedes and quit the war as soon as possible, provided they could do so with the sovereignty of Prussia and a small territorial gain, such as Warmia or Elbląg. The Elector also now found himself in demand: as neither Poles nor Swedes intended peace with each other, both wanted to use his army, even though this had declined to about 10,000 men. The Swedish envoy Schlippenbach remarked: 'The Elector has many suitors, like a rich, pretty peasant girl.'[47] Even Charles X wrote warm letters from Denmark where he was campaigning with his usual success. John Casimir was at last beginning to make friendly overtures and to accept he had to make concrete offers. There was also an important catalyst for change in the person of the Imperial ambassador in Poland, Lisola. He had visited the Elector at Königsberg and was anxious to conciliate him: Emperor Ferdinand III had died in April 1657, and Vienna needed Brandenburg's vote to elect his young son, Archduke Leopold, as emperor. As the Poles still wanted Austrian military support in case the unpredictable Charles returned and the Tsar renewed his assaults, they had to listen to Lisola, who, as he boasted himself, knew how to mix 'the sweet with the sour, hope with terror'.[48] He found a vital ally in the Polish Queen, Louise Maria, who hoped Frederick William might help restore her husband's position within Poland itself.

Frederick William was prepared to play Vienna's game, and in July, during the christening of his new son Frederick, he whispered to Lisola that Leopold could depend on his vote. The ambassador at the same time was distributing large sums at the Königsberg court to the Elector's family and ministers. Whether any came Schwerin's way is not known, but during the summer he moved from urging mere neutrality to pressing for war against Sweden. For his part Lisola realised that the sovereignty of Prussia was the key, since Frederick William wanted it more than anything else. In August he convinced John Casimir that ceding this would be cheaper than handing over territory.[49] Frederick William kept his side of the tacit bargain, writing on 24 August to Johann Moritz in Cleves, in terms which would have shocked Waldeck, that he believed Leopold should be elected Emperor to prevent 'great disorder in the Empire' which 'might endanger the liberty of electors and princes'.[50]

On 1 September an armistice was announced between Poland and Brandenburg; then, on the 19th the Elector signed a secret treaty at Wehlau (now Znamensk in the Russian enclave around Kaliningrad/Königsberg) with the Polish general, Gosiewski. It was necessarily secret to keep the Swedes in the dark. This gave the duchy of Prussia to Frederick William 'with absolute power and without the previous impositions',[51] although there was a proviso 'that the treaty had to be reconfirmed by every new king of Poland and every new duke in the Duchy'.[52] The Prussian Estates were to keep their privileges and the Catholics their right to worship. The Elector also promised to help John Casimir against Sweden with 6,000 men and was to be compensated with territory to be decided when the treaty was ratified. A few weeks later, at the end of October, the Polish and Brandenburg ruling families met at Bydgoszcz/

Bromberg in Polish Royal Prussia. Here they spent a congenial week together, a particularly good rapport being established between Frederick William and Queen Louise Maria. Her French secretary, des Noyers, has left one of the few descriptions we have of the Elector:

> He is a prince of a good height, well built, with a determined appearance, a full face and large nose, fine eyes, very courteous, and he knows how to deal with people, to speak well about business and to grasp things quickly.[53]

During the week they ratified the Wehlau/Znamensk treaty and agreed on the thorny question of territorial compensation. The city of Elbląg, with control of the eastern mouth of the Vistula, was to be ceded to the Elector once the Swedish garrison was expelled, although the Poles could redeem it for 400,000 thalers. As they were unlikely ever to find this sum, Brandenburg's control seemed assured, while Polish pride was salvaged. John Casimir also ceded, as fiefs, two districts bordering East Pomerania, Lębork/Lauenburg and Bytów/Bütow, and in full sovereignty, the county of Drahim/Draheim next to the Neumark. While these territorial gains, except for Elbląg, were trivial, the real gain was ending the humiliating Prussian vassalage. The recognition of Frederick William's sovereignty by his legal overlord was far more valuable than that by Sweden, since international recognition, especially by the Emperor, was bound to follow. Above all, the Elector could now proceed to 'reduce the privileges and freedoms of its Estates'.[54]

While his alliance with Poland committed Frederick William to war with Sweden, it specified neither when nor where. On his return to Berlin in November 1657 he was in no hurry to begin, especially as he was suffering the first attack of what eventually became chronic gout. As the alliance was still secret, he feigned neutrality for many months. Although this made him appear indecisive and even devious, caution was probably still the wisest policy for a weak minor power at a time of shifting relationships among the stronger ones. Frederick William himself was also having to accept, at least temporarily, that the familiar religious divisions in Europe had been made less important because of the imperial ambitions of Charles X against Protestants and Catholics alike. And these ambitions were to produce a frightening situation: in February 1658, after the Swedes carried out a dramatic march across the frozen sea to besiege Copenhagen, the

Danes had to beg for peace and surrender vast territories on the Scandinavian peninsula at the Peace of Roskilde.

After returning to Berlin Frederick William would have liked an end to the whole conflict, but this was not possible because Charles X had almost come to see war itself as his only career. Over the winter months, therefore, the Elector had to decide whether he should invade Swedish Pomerania, which he preferred, or help the Danes directly by attacking Charles's army in the rear in Jutland. He knew neither would be feasible without Imperial help, since he considered the Poles, with their undisciplined troops, as 'dead people'.[55] He also realised that the burden of any campaign, and the brunt of Swedish anger, would fall on his own lands, especially as the Imperialists were eager for everyone but themselves to fight Charles. The eighteen-year-old Archduke Leopold was pacific by nature and, with his Imperial election in the offing, neither he nor his ministers wanted direct involvement in a war in Germany. The disastrous defeats of the later stages of the Thirty Years War were also still fresh in their minds, and they feared the French might intervene again, on the grounds that the Peace of Westphalia had been breached. Frederick William therefore had to coerce the Imperial court by hinting he might not vote for Leopold after all. As the Venetian minister in Vienna remarked: the Elector 'understands better than anyone else how to barter his friendship and his vote'.[56] The Imperialists gave way, signing an alliance against the Swedes with Brandenburg and Poland in Berlin in February 1658. Its main objective was to invade Swedish Pomerania, and a secret article promised the Elector everything the allies conquered there. The Dutch were also expected to send their fleet back to the Baltic and at least restrict Charles's movements.

Although Vienna hoped to delay action till after the Imperial election, events overtook them. The alliance was signed two weeks before Charles X imposed his humiliating peace on Denmark. Now free to move elsewhere, the King was reported to be bragging that he had 'trimmed the beard' of one brother Fritz and it was now the turn of the other Fritz, the Elector.[57] Understandably, therefore, Frederick William abandoned any idea of attacking Pomerania, and he was beginning to feel very vulnerable and even duped by Vienna. Schwerin wrote to the electoral minister at The Hague on 9 March, without much regard for the facts, that the Imperialists 'have led His Electoral Highness along this dangerous road and have now deserted him'.[58]

During spring 1658 it became all too clear that Frederick William had cause for alarm: in mid-April Charles told the Swedish Estates at Gothenburg he intended to punish the Elector, and on 1 June he wrote, 'I must fight Brandenburg' since she was a stalking horse for 'the schemes of the house of Habsburg'. He ordered a three-pronged attack on Berlin: one army was to advance from Wismar though the Uckermark, another from Holstein and Bremen through the Altmark, and another under Charles himself along the east bank of the Elbe through the Mittelmark. At the same time the Swedish garrison in Elbląg was to attack Prussia, being reinforced by 8,400 men landed on the Mierzeja Helska/Putziger Nehrung, the tongue of land on the western side of the bay of Gdańsk. As no secret was made of these schemes, Frederick William was in a state of panic: the situation was judged so dangerous that even the peasants in Brandenburg were trusted with arms. He managed to raise 20,000 men, who seem to have been in decent condition. At the same time he also personally supervised 4,000 soldiers and labourers, who worked in the sandy, water-logged soil to strengthen Berlin's defences. Desperate appeals were made to the Imperialists and Poles for troops, and they were beginning to respond slowly. Attempts were also made to negotiate with Charles himself. Schwerin was sent to Holstein, but when the King disembarked at Flensburg in late June he refused to meet him: Waldeck had denounced Schwerin as a personal enemy. At this time Charles cynically remarked to the French envoy Terlon:

> I am short of money and fear having to wage a long war; consequently I do not want this Elector as a friend, since I need his lands to quarter my troops. I can't do that if the Elector is on good terms with me. The Elector is also too powerful and I must bridle his ambition.[59]

War in Germany now seemed inevitable, and, as before, it was Charles X who had forced the pace. Once again Frederick William had had to wait on others rather than the reverse. In the event he was saved by Charles's own actions, because the plan to attack Brandenburg and Prussia was only bluff: instead in August 1658 the King sailed from Kiel to besiege Copenhagen once more, intending to raze the city, destroy the Danish monarchy and unite all Scandinavia under the Swedish crown. He boasted to Terlon: 'I will first subdue Denmark and Norway, then garrison Prussia, conquer Courland and take Danzig [Gdańsk] and Pillau [Baltiysk].' This was only the beginning: with the revenues from these, he would finance an army 100,000 strong, march to Italy and sack Rome. He saw himself as 'the Northern Alexander', and, according to the pro-Swedish Terlon, his 'first thought is always plunder'.[60] But his plans were stopped in their tracks because Frederick III refused to surrender, determined to die in his own nest. This forced the Swedes to undertake a regular siege of Copenhagen by land and sea.

The siege gave Charles's other enemies a breathing space, and his recent threats to all and sundry ensured Denmark's cries for help would be answered. Frederick William prepared to march to Jutland, hoping a Dutch fleet would ship his troops on to the Danish islands. Although several German princes warned Leopold not to interfere in case the French intervened, the new Emperor (he had been elected in July) and John Casimir were determined to do so. They gave Frederick William overall command of a substantial allied army. Most of the troops were Brandenburgers, 17,000 commanded by Sparr as fieldmarshal. The Emperor contributed 8,000 men under the Italian Montecuccoli. Although the latter still had to prove himself as an independent commander, he was later to become possibly the ablest infantry strategist of the century. Finally, Czarniecki, who had done most to free Poland from the Swedes, brought 3,000 undisciplined Polish cavalry. In mid-September the Elector led the main force rapidly across Mecklenburg into Holstein. The Polish cavalry followed, pausing to destroy many villages in the Brandenburg Neumark. They also raided East Pomerania, carrying out a pogrom against the Jewish community there for good measure. As Frederick William pushed into Jutland he met little resistance. His leisurely pace allowed most of the Swedes to escape and the peninsula was not occupied before December. Lacking strategic experience in large-scale warfare, he did not seem to have very clear military objectives, and Montecuccoli was disappointed with his leadership.[61] Meanwhile, on the main Danish island of Sjælland Charles X's siege of Copenhagen was not going well. The city was enthusiastically defended by its citizens, and in early November a Dutch fleet defeated the Swedish one, allowing supplies and Dutch troops to be landed. Then in mid-December two Danish ships took Frederick William and nearly 2,000 Brandenburgers and Imperialists from Jutland across to the island of Als, where he defeated a Swedish force. His detailed dictated account of the events afterwards showed a good grasp at least of military tactics.

Stalemate now followed. Unlike the previous winter, the frosts were not hard enough to let the allies march over the ice to the main Danish islands: they had to idle in their quarters in Jutland and on Als. Although the Dutch fleet wintered off Copenhagen, protecting it from attack by sea, the government in The Hague would not let it ship the allies to Sjælland. French diplomacy, which had supported Sweden against the Imperialists for thirty years, had been working to save Charles X. Mazarin sent him money and persuaded Richard Cromwell, the new Protector of the English Republic, to dispatch a fleet to help him in 1659. In The Hague Anglo-French diplomacy pressed the Dutch to withdraw their ships, insisting that Sweden must be saved, 'because it was such a notable part of the Protestant community and such a powerful counter-weight to Papist and Spanish hegemony'.[62] This made the Dutch leader, the Pensionary De Witt, reluctant to commit himself further against Charles in case he provoked a repeat of the recent, dis-astrous Anglo-Dutch war at sea (1652–4). The consequent Dutch refusal to provide transport ships was naturally frustrating to Frederick William, whose campaign had really collapsed. Schwerin wrote to the electoral envoy in The Hague in February 1659: 'All our hopes of achieving something here depend on the fleet; and if we do not get ships soon to reach the islands, hunger will certainly force us out . . . , to our utter disgrace and ruin.'[63]

On 20 February 1659 Charles X tried to storm Copenhagen. He was repulsed but stayed dug in outside the city. Then in April the English fleet appeared and blockaded it from the sea. Although the Dutch fleet was still there, it looked on impassively and left Frederick William's army stuck uselessly in Jutland and Holstein. His occupa-tion of the Danish peninsula was itself proving a disaster for the local population. The Swedes had already devastated the country-side, and the allies followed suit. The Poles were by far the worst, even kidnapping children to extort ransoms, but the Brandenburg and Imperial troops also behaved badly. The nobles, however, were not harmed or forced to pay contributions for the army: officers and war commissioners protected their own kind.[64] It seems the war cost the Danes 120,000 of their population of 800,000, or 15 per cent, partly through famine but above all from typhus and dysentery spread by the allied army.[65]

During the inconclusive spring and summer of 1659 French dip-lomacy was struggling to end the war, but Charles proved the most obstinate, intending to starve out Copenhagen. However, the Eng-lish fleet was withdrawn in the summer because of the disintegra-tion of the English Republic, and by August the Dutch decided to help the Danes once more. Supplies were sent into Copenhagen, and in November Dutch ships transported the allies on to the island of Fyn, where they won a clear victory over a smaller Swedish force at Nyborg on 24 November, the Swedes' worst defeat since Nördlingen over twenty years before. Charles now seemed in great danger on Sjælland, but ice made it too perilous to ship the allied troops there for a final battle.

By the time of this victory at Nyborg, Frederick William and the bulk of the allied force had left Denmark. The stalemate there had inevitably turned the allies' thoughts elsewhere. From February 1659 the Imperialists had been suggesting an attack on Swedish Pomerania as a way of forcing the Swedes out of the Danish islands to defend it. As they were worried about upsetting the Peace of Westphalia, they wanted the Brandenburgers involved, so as to share the blame. Frederick William himself was not enthusiastic, dreading the allied army would move into his electorate and repeat the kind of devastation it had visited on Denmark. In a war council on 2 May, he rejected the Imperial proposal, arguing it would be opposed by the German princes, especially the members of the French-sponsored League of the Rhine, formed the year before. It also might provoke direct intervention by France, which was close to peace with Spain. On a practical level he was concerned about the allies' infantry losses in Denmark and the Imperialists' notorious slowness in dispatching troops.

Frederick William's misgivings were eventually borne out, but in June 1659 the Imperialists and Poles pressed to transfer the war to Germany, on the reasonable grounds that their army in Jutland was not hurting the Swedes. The Imperialists also showed unusual decisiveness, hoping to end the Baltic conflict before France could act. In late June, knowing it would force the Elector's hand, Leopold sent 14,000 of his own troops into Swedish Pomerania and then urged him to send all he could spare from Brandenburg and Jutland. Although Frederick William complained bitterly about the 'labyrinth I could be put in through this action',[66] he had to follow and seize the chance to grab what he could of Swedish Pomerania. In September therefore he left Jutland with most of the troops. These behaved as badly as ever on the march south down the Danish peninsula. As usual the Poles were worst, slaughtering Lutheran pastors in a kind of holy war.

Meanwhile, the Imperial army under de Souches had seized several towns in West Pomerania. But the main ports had been reinforced by sea, and he had to raise a siege of Szczecin on 16 November after forty-six bloody days. When the Elector arrived, his troops made an early attack on Greifswald, but the garrison managed to flood the Brandenburgers' trenches. By the close of 1659, while most of the open countryside was in allied hands, the Swedes still held the ports and had free access by sea. Frederick William's troops by this stage were in such poor shape that 'on his return to Berlin early in December, a parade of the garrison troops was abandoned to hide their wretchedness from the public'.[67] Lack of money was now acute, but his short campaign in Pomerania was also conducted indecisively. This was unfortunate because time was running out.

In November 1659 France and Spain ended their war in western Europe by the Peace of the Pyrenees. Cardinal Mazarin could now assert himself in the north, where he saw the whole Westphalian settlement unravelling and with it France's recent gains in Alsace and dominance in Germany. He was determined, therefore, to save Charles X. While launching a diplomatic offensive to mediate a northern peace, France prepared to intervene militarily. Early in December Mazarin threatened to use the League of the Rhine to attack Frederick William's Rhenish lands unless he made peace with Sweden and surrendered his conquests in Pomerania. The Elector was far more exposed than his distant Imperialist and Polish allies. He knew French strength well enough and had resisted earlier invitations to join the League of the Rhine, writing to a member, the Bishop of Münster, the previous spring that France 'will enslave her friends, for she can only bear subjects or creatures'.[68] He therefore agreed to attend a peace congress at the Cistercian monastery at Oliwa/Oliva near Gdańsk in January 1660. Brandenburg, Poland, the Emperor and Sweden negotiated there under the mediation of the French minister, de Lumbres. While Frederick William pleaded for the cession of Szczecin and the mouth of the Oder, the French were resolute that Sweden should lose nothing in Germany.

Charles X himself had shown little interest in this French mediation, being determined to pursue the war. Quite unexpectedly, however, he died in February 1660 after a short illness, aged thirty-seven. The regency for his child, Charles XI, was politically weak and desperate for peace, so this strengthened Mazarin's hand. The pressures were also mounting on Frederick William to settle. His Polish allies were insisting on peace so that they could concentrate on Tsar Alexis, who had attacked them again in 1658. Vienna had lost its enthusiasm for the Pomeranian campaign now that the French were free to act. With his troops unpaid and treasury empty, Leopold dared not risk another conflict with both Sweden and France, especially as so many of the German princes favoured the French. He could no longer afford to continue the limited subsidies paid to Frederick William over the past year. Seeing the game was lost, the Elector himself eventually had to give way. France now imposed her will everywhere. On 3 May the Peace of Oliwa was signed. Here France, the Emperor, Sweden and Poland recognised Frederick William's sovereignty over East Prussia and his minor gains of Lębork, Bytów and Drahim on the East Pomeranian and Neumark borders. He did not receive Elbląg: when the Swedish garrison left, Polish troops quickly moved in and stayed put. The Poles also regained all their other lands from Sweden in return for recognising her control of Livonia. A month later at Copenhagen the Danes accepted most of their earlier losses: Sweden therefore emerged from the War of the North with huge gains, which assured her control of all the Scandinavian peninsula, except Norway, as well as the eastern side of the Sound.

Frederick William seemed to have little to show for the risks of territorial loss, the financial and material cost and the distress brought on his own subjects.[69] West Pomerania remained a distant dream and the Swedes had even refused to surrender their share of the East Pomeranian tolls. Yet, given Frederick William's perilous situation for much of the war, it was remarkable he emerged as well as he did. He had managed to raise an army to rival that of Sweden; he had proved himself a major player in the north after the humiliation of his earlier wars in the Rhineland; and he was now a sovereign European prince, if a minor one, on a political par with the leading German electors of Bavaria and Saxony. The major powers themselves had shown they considered him a suitable alliance partner in northern Europe, and they had allowed him to negotiate at Oliwa as a principal. His position was also stronger in the north after the war because of the other combatants' difficulties. Despite Sweden's conquests from Denmark, her wider Baltic imperial designs had failed and she now faced a decade of weak rule by a regency. Poland had 'emerged from the war in political and economic disarray'. The destruction and population losses mirrored those suffered by Germany the generation before.[70] The Poles also faced further war with the Tsar till 1667 and a domestic struggle to choose John Casimir's successor. The war had done much to highlight Poland's military weaknesses, but nothing was done to solve them.

The War of the North gave the Elector a reputation for crafty self-interest. The philosopher, historian and diplomat Leibniz (1648–1716) wrote later: 'When Sweden was in difficulties in Poland, Brandenburg went in for horse-trading, [saying] I will join the one who gives me the most.' But Leibniz did have some understanding of Frederick William's problem and added: 'To be neutral is rather like someone who lives in the middle of a house, and is smoked out from below and drenched with urine from above.'[71] A flexible policy was really inevitable given the Elector's own relative weakness and difficult position between the combatants. The war had also gone some way to free Frederick William from seeing international relations largely in religious terms. 'He had discovered the basis for his future policy: to keep his hands free as long as possible and then to ally with the most accommodating power.'[72] He would never pursue the naive, ill-considered actions of the Berg wars again. He now dealt more in the world of the possible and saw the need to balance the interests of the other powers.[73] This was especially important given that he was the ruler of what was still a minor power and that his separate territories involved him in the problems of both northern and western Europe. Perhaps the most important lesson he failed to learn was that the major states, particularly France, would ultimately decide the fate of the continent.

. . .

NOTES AND REFERENCES

1 For the Orange connection, see especially Erdmannsdörffer, *Waldeck*, pp. 24ff.
2 Ibid., p. 34.
3 Droysen, part 3, II 2, p. 21.
4 Ibid., p. 45.
5 Menk, pp. 38ff., and Erdmannsdörffer, *Waldeck*, p. 280.
6 Endmannsdöffer, *Waldeck*, p. 180, Waldeck to Frederick William, 31 December 1653.
7 Ibid., p. 99.
8 Waddington, *Prusse*, I, p. 303.
9 For this Diet in English see Gagliardo, p. 97.
10 Waddington, *Prusse*, I, p. 302.
11 This war has been given various names – the Swedish–Polish War, the Northern War, the Second Northern War and so on.
12 Droysen, part 3, II, p. 483.

13 Livonia and its port of Riga formally belonged to the Polish crown and consisted of present-day northern Latvia and southern Estonia.

14 Philippson, I, p. 189. A balanced discussion of Swedish policy is D. Kirby, *Northern Europe in the Early Modern Period: The Baltic World, 1492–1772* (London, 1990), pp. 184–6.

15 Philippson, I, p. 190.

16 See H.H. Rowen, *John de Witt: Grand Pensionary of Holland* (Princeton, 1978), p. 296.

17 Droysen, part 3, II, p. 145.

18 Hüttl, pp. 205, 207.

19 E. Opitz, *Österreich und Brandenburg im schwedisch-polnischen Krieg, 1655–60* (Boppard am Rhein, 1969), p. 33.

20 O. Redlich, *Weltmacht des Barock. Österreich in der Zeit Kaiser Leopolds I,* 4th edn (Vienna, 1961), p. 32.

21 Opgenoorth, *Friedrich Wilhelm*, I, p. 316.

22 Des Noyers, p. 47.

23 H. Saring, 'Zwei Missionen des danziger Syndikus Vincent Fabritius an den kurfürstlichen Hof, 1655/6', *Zeitschrift für Westpreußischen Geschichtsverein*, 72 (Danzig/Gdańsk 1935), p. 129.

24 Philippson, I, p. 222.

25 Orlich, p. 70.

26 They at least now had one healthy son and heir, Charles Emmanuel, born in February 1655.

27 Erdmannsdörffer, *Waldeck*, pp. 361f.

28 For the battle of Warsaw, see especially S. Herbst, 'Tredagarsslaget vid Warszawa 1656', in A. Stade and J. Wimmer, eds, *Polens Krig med Sverige, 1655–60* (Kristianstad, 1973). For the whole war we are fortunate to have in English Robert Frost, *After the Deluge: Poland-Lithuania and the Second Northern War, 1655–60* (Cambridge, 1993).

29 Opitz, p. 33.

30 Des Noyers, p. 237.

31 Philippson, I, pp. 247, 243.

32 Erdmannsdörffer, *Deutsche Geschichte*, I, p. 268.

33 Droysen, part 3, II, p. 494.

34 Philippson, I, p. 244.

35 Ibid., I, p. 249.

36 *Urk. u. Akt.*, II, p. 110, de Lumbres to Mazarin, Königsberg, 19 October 1656.

37 Ibid., II, p. 110, same to Brienne, Königsberg, undated, but October 1656.

38 Philippson, I, p. 246.

39 He was right, see Frost, p. 78.

40 M. Roberts, *The Swedish Imperial Experience, 1560–1718* (Cambridge, 1979), p. 17.

41 Philippson, I, p. 255.

42 Opitz, p. 41.

43 Philippson, I, pp. 260f.

44 Ibid., I, p. 264.

45 Ibid., I, p. 269.

46 *Urk. u. Akt.*, II, p. 104, de Lumbres to Mazarin, Warsaw, 6 August 1656.

47 Opitz, p. 42.

48 Waddington, *Le Grand Électeur*, I, p. 387.

49 Frost, pp. 98ff., believes the Poles were already accepting the need to compromise with Brandenburg.

50 Hüttl, p. 232.

51 Philippson, I, p. 275. The treaty is printed with a commentary in H. Duchhardt and B. Wachowiak, *Um die Souveränität des Herzogtums Preußen: der Vertrag von Wehlau, 1657* (Hanover, 1998).

52 A. Kaminska, *Brandenburg-Prussia and Poland, 1669–72* (Marburg, 1983), p. 1.

53 Des Noyers, p. 355.

54 Kaminska, p. 13.

55 Opitz, p. 48.

56 O. Klopp, *Der Fall des Hauses Stuart und die Succession des Hauses Hannover in Großbritannien, in Zusammenhange der europäischen Angelegenheiten, 1660–1714*, 14 vols (Vienna, 1875–88), II, p. 248.

57 Opgenoorth, *Friedrich Wilhelm*, I, p. 378.

58 Philippson, I, p. 290.

59 Ibid., I, pp. 295, 301f.

60 Ibid., I, p. 314.

61 Opitz, pp. 137ff.

62 Philippson, I, p. 325.

63 Opgenoorth, *Friedrich Wilhelm*, I, p. 389.

64 Opitz, p. 305.

65 A. Lassen, *Skæbneåret 1659, hungersød og pest over Sydvestdanmark* (Aarhus, 1958), review in *Historische Zeitschrift*, 191 (1960), p. 212.

66 Hüttl, p. 250.

67 Opgenoorth, *Friedrich Wilhelm*, I, p. 406.

68 Waddington, *Le Grand Électeur*, I, p. 448.

69 See the criticial assessment by Opitz, p. 282.

70 Z. Wójcik, 'From the peace of Oliva to the truce of Bakhchisarai', *Acta Poloniae Historica*, 34 (1976), pp. 257f.

71 Droysen, part 3, II, p. 15.

72 Waddington, *Le Grand Électeur*, I, p. 478. Frederick William came to enjoy his devious reputation, telling the Danish envoy (at some point in the 1660s or 1670s) that 'no one knows my mind, you know, whether I am a fox or a hare'. Beuys, p. 254.

73 Opgenoorth, *Friedrich Wilhelm*, I, pp. 410–13.

Chapter 5

BRANDENBURG-PRUSSIAN SOCIETY UNDER THE GREAT ELECTOR

. . .

THE JUNKERS[1]

The nobility of the lands east of the River Elbe sprang from a mixture of native Slav landowners and German colonists and soldiers who had settled there in the late middle ages. As many of the newcomers were the younger sons of German nobles, they were called Junkers (*Junk-herre*) or young lords. By the sixteenth century these Junkers dominated Brandenburg, Pomerania and East Prussia, at the same time as the influence of their princely overlords had declined. The Lutheran Reformation and the resulting confiscation of church property benefited the Junker nobility rather than the chronically indebted princes. Although most ecclesiastical land went to the crown – the electors owned a third of Brandenburg and the dukes two-fifths of East Prussia – the best came into Junker hands, either directly or on favourable long leases. But noble power not only profited from the decline of the princes and collapse of the Catholic church, it also benefited from a parallel downturn in urban fortunes. As the towns' political influence slipped (Königsberg was the exception till the second half of the seventeenth century), the burghers could no longer enforce their monopoly over industry and trade. Instead the Junkers bypassed the towns, exporting their own agricultural goods and importing directly what they needed. This commercial role of the Junkers coincided with burgeoning profits from an expansion of manorial farming.

From the fifteenth century a contracting population in north-east Germany and Prussia had made it difficult for the lords to live off peasant rents, unlike in the more populated regions of the German south and west. They turned instead to managing directly parts of

108

their estates, the manorial lands (the demesne), and forcing their peasant tenants into bondage, tying them to the soil and enforcing labour services of two or more days a week. These labour services and other dues were regarded as assets of an estate, having a monetary value when it was sold. This system, known as *Gutswirtschaft* (literally, manorial economy), where the manors functioned as self-contained economic units, was accompanied by the princes' abandoning judicial and taxation control of the peasantry to the Junker lords. Direct Junker authority (*Gutsherrschaft*) over the rural population allowed them to regulate who occupied peasant lands and to force the peasants to ask permission to marry or to move. Moreover, to ensure a cheap, steady supply of manorial servants, young peasants not immediately needed on the family farms had to work for their lords for a couple of years at low wages (*Gesindezwangsdienst*). This manorial economy, based on what Marxist historians called 'the second serfdom', was found in varying degrees throughout Europe east of the River Elbe and the Bohemian mountains, but also in most of Brandenburg west of the Elbe.

By enserfing their peasant tenants and directly farming their own manorial lands, the Junkers during the sixteenth century took full advantage of western Europe's growing appetite for agricultural goods, particularly grain, but also timber, wool, hemp, flax and hides. They especially benefited from the escalating price of rye in the century before the Thirty Years War, and they became 'estate-owing entrepreneurs ... orientated towards profits ... [from] external markets'.[2] Their manors were not only agricultural units: they also produced beer, textiles and other commodities, which they made their peasants buy and which they sold abroad directly as well. This contributed to the steady decline of the local towns. In 1634 Königsberg was complaining that the Prussian lords brewed beer and 'piled up corn and sold it directly to foreigners and so deprived the towns of the burghers' livelihood'. Thirty years later the city made the same charge, protesting that its own beer 'remained in the cellars and had to go bad'.[3]

In 1620 about two-thirds of all land in Brandenburg was owned by the Junkers. While most of this was farmed by peasant tenants, 10–12 per cent was reserved by the lords as manorial land. This was worked by their peasant tenants, who provided themselves, or through proxies, the usual two or three days' labour service a week. During the sixteenth century the powerful Quitzow family in Prignitz, by exploiting peasant obligations and intensive cultivation, managed a five-fold increase in the value of one estate at Stavenow in the Uckermark. But while this manor was around 2,500 acres, most were under 500 acres and yielded only 200 thalers annually, a tenth of the Quitzows' income. One result of depending on the labour services, tools and animal teams of the peasantry was to hold back agricultural improvement on noble and peasant land. Open fields, with the traditional two- or three-field rotation system, continued to be the norm. Compared with some parts of Europe, the grain yields throughout Brandenburg were remarkably low in the seventeenth and eighteenth centuries.

To maximise profits the Junkers not only bound their peasants to the soil but also seized much of their land,[4] although the crown itself was reluctant to see peasant holdings converted into manorial land, since this was exempt from taxation. While there is some dispute over the extent of these Junker acquisitions,[5] the economic success of the Junkers and the *Gutswirtschaft* system is not in doubt. Their methods were not questioned, let alone challenged, by the rulers. As landowners themselves, the electors of Brandenburg and dukes of Prussia also profiteered from their own peasant tenants. Moreover, before the military reforms of the Great Elector, the rulers had neither the means nor inclination to interfere with how the lords ran their manors. 'State authority ended at the gates of the estates.' Similarly, the Lutheran church, with pastors appointed by the Junkers, upheld the rigidly hierarchical society in the countryside, preaching 'suffering obedience' to the lords.[6]

The increasing wealth of the Brandenburg-Prussian Junkers in the century or so before the Thirty Years War coincided with their political ascendancy and the 'identification of their interests with those of the state'. By using their control of taxation in the Estates and limiting office to native Lutheran nobles by the *Indigenatsrecht*, they made the electors almost dependants. This power was shown plainly in 1620, when troops raised by George William, but paid for and recruited by the Brandenburg Estates, swore loyalty to both of them, and it was the Estates who appointed the officers. On the other hand, despite this control of the army, the Junkers as a whole were not particularly tempted by military careers: they were still not 'a military caste, and were pacific and hostile to foreign-policy adventures by their rulers'.[7] It was also inevitable, given how the Hohenzollern territories were scattered across northern Europe and had only recently come to share one ruler, that the various nobilities were not a homogeneous group: intermarriage, such as that between the Pomeranian Schwerin and his Prussian wife, was the exception. The Brandenburg and Magdeburg nobles had more in common with their Saxon and Brunswick neighbours, and the Prussians with the Poles.

What the Hohenzollern nobility did have in common was that they were all predominantly minor nobles. Historians, however, have paid most attention to those in Brandenburg, where at the beginning of the seventeenth century the nobility was made up of around 260 families, all told about 3,600 men and women. This was under 1 per cent of the total population of probably 400,000, and the ratio was similar in Pomerania and Prussia. In each local circle (*Kreis*) in Brandenburg an elite of three or four families held most land, dominated political and social life, and acted as 'patron of the numerous petty nobles'. In 1620, although there were thirty-eight noble families in the Prignitz, half the land there was owned by the Quitzows, Winterfelds, Putlitzes and Rohrs. Yet these leading families were insignificant, compared with aristocrats elsewhere. While a Bohemian and Polish noble often owned thousands of villages, a 'wealthy Junker in Brandenburg might have fifty'.[8] None the less, in Brandenburg terms, there was a 'power elite' of around fifteen intermarried families, who made the running in local and central politics. Their power was obvious in the local Estates (*Kreistage*), in the diet (*Landtag*) on the rare occasions it met, and in the permanent committees or deputation/representative diets (*Ausschüße* and *Deputationstage*) when it did not. The elite's position had been formalised in 1540 when eighteen members of the leading families, including eleven who held electoral office, set up the *Kreditwerk* to manage loans given by the Estates to pay off Elector Joachim's debts. Successive electors became heavily dependent on, and indebted to, this institution. It was to be monopolised by the same families for a century, and the electoral loans it repaid were largely to them.[9] This meant the elite families, such as Schulenburgs and Knesebecks in the Altmark and Arnims in the Uckermark, were the prince's creditors as well as his leading councillors. At the start of the Thirty Years War thirteen families owned nearly half the manorial lands in Brandenburg and the same families had filled almost half the electoral offices for more than a century. They also administered or held the leases of much electoral land as security for the loans.[10]

The dominance of the elite families and general prosperity of the Junkers was to be undermined by the devastation of the Thirty

Years War and the agricultural depression following. (In Prussia much the same happened after the War of the North, 1655–60.) Their political and economic influence was to decline, as that of the crown increased. Abandoned peasant holdings meant lower rent incomes and a shortage of labour. For example the Arnim estate at Boitzenburg in the Uckermark had only 20 peasant families in 1653 compared with 225 thirty years before.[11] This, together with a parallel collapse in agricultural prices and land values, meant there was little recovery after 1650. The 1660s and 1670s saw manorial incomes and grain prices at their lowest point for the whole century. At the same time Frederick William's competing taxation and military exactions on the peasants left these even less to spare for their lords. The peasants' payment of their dues in kind, when prices were falling, also contributed to the Junkers' falling incomes – these may have fallen by two-thirds.[12] In addition the nobility found that building material, such as iron, held its price, while population loss made labour more expensive to hire. In 1667 the Brandenburg nobility declared: 'What we receive from the peasants goes mostly on repairing houses and essential restocking of animals . . . We can hardly support ourselves or raise our children in the proper noble virtues . . .'.[13] Of course the same difficulties were also besetting peasant tenants on their own farms, since these often employed paid labour, and, unlike the lords with their tax and billeting exemptions, peasants faced the state's growing financial and material demands. Relief for all those depending on labour was a long time coming, but agricultural prices slowly recovered and wages began to fall during the last quarter of the seventeenth century.

After the Thirty Years War the Brandenburg and Pomeranian nobles, like those in Prussia after the War of the North, tried to solve their economic difficulties by squeezing their peasant tenants harder. They seized the best empty plots, usually to graze cattle and sheep, and demanded more labour services and dues. This, however, does not seem to have been as successful as was once thought, at least during Frederick William's reign.[14] William Hagen has argued that the Junkers' authority actually collapsed under the Great Elector: the catastrophe and dislocation caused by the war, together with the resulting chronic labour shortage, meant that the Brandenburg peasants 'ceased to obey their noble overlords'. It became very difficult to get them to perform labour services, as is shown by Junker complaints in the diet of 1652. The Junkers were having to hire costly labour and animal teams to farm their manors instead. Consequently the 'first half century of absolutism did not witness the binding of the rural population's neck under a yoke of seigneurial domination heavier and more irresistible than before the Thirty Years' War'. The Junkers' problem only began to be resolved in the early eighteenth century when a recovery in population allowed dues and rents to be enforced.[15]

Although more detailed studies are needed on the power of the Junkers in the countryside, it is clear the elite's political grip on the Brandenburg state had weakened some time before Frederick William died. This did not stem from his agreement with the Estates of 1653, which merely confirmed existing Junker privileges; nor did it come from the final demise of the general diet, the *Landtag*. Elite power had been exercised for more than a century through the provincial diets, the deputation/representative diets, the permanent committees, and a monopoly of office. The role of the general diet had been far less significant because it met so rarely, whereas the provincial diets met once or twice a year, deputation/representative diets sometimes annually, and the permanent committees, of course, much more often. The real pointer to how relations between the Elector and the Brandenburg elite had tipped decisively towards the crown was how Frederick William from the 1660s began to treat the committees and deputation diets as rubber stamps.

There was more than one reason for the contraction of the elite's political power. An important factor was that they lost the financial whip hand as their own wealth began to slip away during the seventeenth century. They no longer had the spare cash to lend to the crown and to insist on conditions for the loans. The rulers therefore had to look elsewhere, especially to meet the demands of war. One German historian has remarked trenchantly: 'the economic conditions for a strong *Ständetum* [rule by Estates] were over. And this led the way to absolutism.'[16] Just as significant, however, were the effects of Elector John Sigismund's conversion to Calvinism in 1613. He almost immediately began to ignore the *Indigenatsrecht* and to choose his closest advisers from his own faith. Then Brandenburg's entanglement in the Thirty Years War and Schwarzenberg's absolute rule led to a complete, if temporary, eclipse of the Estates and the elite. The accession of Frederick William restored their influence and one of the elite, Knesebeck, drew up the agreement of 1653, while the leading councillors of the early years, Götzen and Burgsdorff, belonged to families allied by marriage to them. From the beginning, however, Frederick William preferred his councillors to be Calvinists, as Götzen and Burgsdorff were. In his *Political Testament*, he advised his successor to choose advisers 'of the reformed [Calvinist] religion, . . . [from] inside and *outside* the country'.[17] By this time, in the late 1660s, most of the original councillors from the elite families were dead and had been replaced from elsewhere.

Soon after his first marriage Frederick William had reinforced his preference for Calvinist advisers by deliberately recruiting prominent co-religionists from outside his own lands to serve as stadtholders or important officials for his various lands. The most important was Prince Johann Moritz; others were members of princely families in the Empire, such as Waldeck and Anhalt, but there was also the Polish-Lithuanian Prince Radziwiłł. Amounting almost to a dynastic nobility, they were not associated with the particularist interests of any of his territories. They also brought distinction and a touch of cosmopolitan glamour to his north-German backwater of a court. At the same time Frederick William was also recruiting his privy councillors from outside and these had usually travelled widely and shared his political assumptions.

By the second half of Frederick William's reign, his court and the Lutheran noble estate in Brandenburg had grown increasingly apart. Now none of his leading noble ministers, Schwerin, Canstein, Gladebeck, Grumbkow or Knyphausen, was even from the elector-ate. Although as nobles they inevitably felt some empathy with the Junkers and the Estates, there were always the commoners, Jena, Meinders and Fuchs (all also from outside Brandenburg), to check this. Of the seventy-four privy councillors of the reign, twenty came from the Empire or abroad, twenty-four from Prussia, twenty from Brandenburg (less than a third), nine from Pomerania and one from other Hohenzollern lands.[18] Between 1640 and 1740 under 'ten per cent of the leadership at court, the diplomatic corps, and the high bureaucracy' were Brandenburg Junkers. And even in the army there was competition from Pomeranians, Prussians and then French Huguenots. By 1689 Huguenots made up at least a third of the 1,000 officers.[19] While Frederick William certainly tried to per-suade Brandenburgers to join his colours and to discourage ser-vice elsewhere, it was only during the reign of his grandson and namesake that it became the norm to serve in the (by then) royal Prussian army.[20]

In contrast to Frederick William's court and ministers, the native Brandenburg nobility appeared boorish, ill-educated provincials.[21]

Some of these began instead to enter the service of the neighbouring Saxon and Brunswick courts, where their Lutheranism was an asset, not a liability. Consequently, by the end of the century the old close relationship of elector and native nobility had dissolved.[22] The latter's alienation must have been compounded in Frederick William's final years by the influx of the Calvinist Huguenots. It is not true, therefore, as Francis Carsten wrote, that the 'political power of the nobility . . . survived in a new form . . . re-born as a working alliance between the absolute ruler and his higher officials and army officers. The squirearchy was transformed into a service nobility.'[23] This change did not occur till the next century. For much of the Great Elector's reign the Junkers sulked, unwanted, in the provinces. Most of course had never had any political influence and had been 'passive' supporters of the elite families.[24]

The collapse of elite influence at the centre also went together with the undermining of their other power base in the deputation/representative diets and permanent committees of the Estates through administrative and tax changes. Their influence was increasingly restricted to the localities, although even here there was growing electoral interference. On the other hand, Frederick William had no intention of abolishing the increasingly symbolic Estates committees, representative and provincial diets or of challenging the Junkers' economic and social privileges. In this way the Brandenburg nobility could believe that their interests were represented and their privileges guaranteed.

While Frederick William used his increasingly elaborate and lavish court to stress his own separateness and elevation above the nobility, he was not hostile to nobles as such, considering them his natural servants and ensuring commoners he employed were ennobled. The membership of the Privy Council shows this: between 1641 and 1651 he appointed sixteen councillors, all but three nobles. Of the thirty-four named between 1653 and 1687, only seven were commoners. The same aristocratic bias was found in other bodies, and there was no equivalent of the French lawyer-cum-administrative class, the *noblesse de robe*. The issue of a decree in 1682,[25] forbidding nobles to pursue commercial careers, reflected his own, and contemporary, belief that social hierarchy and discreteness should be maintained. Like most of early modern Europe, the Hohenzollern lands were 'a society of orders' (*Ständegesellschaft*), groups socially and legally separate from one another, and an essential function of government was 'to police the barriers' between them.[26] The leading role of Paul Fuchs (1640–1704) as Frederick William's secretary in his last years does not mean commoners were replacing nobles at the centre. Fuchs began life as the son of a Pomeranian Lutheran pastor, studied at Leiden, converted to Calvinism and married a Huguenot. In 1683 Frederick William ennobled him (he also became a baron of the Empire in the next reign), and he eventually had the same wealth and properties as a noble minister. Much the same went for Fieldmarshal Derfflinger (1606–95), whose entry into the electoral army eventually led to an Imperial baronacy and the stadtholdership of Pomerania, with an annual salary of 18,000 thalers besides the revenues from six Brandenburg and fourteen Prussian estates.[27]

Frederick William's patronage of the nobility comes out strongly in his relations with Cleves-Mark. Here the nobles were far fewer and had not exercised the power of those in Brandenburg and Prussia, and even in the countryside their influence was limited. Very few farmed directly; instead they practised what was called *Grundherrschaft*, living off the rents of peasants on hereditary leases. In the diets they played second fiddle to the urban estate. From the beginning of his reign Frederick William tried to favour them, especially in their claims to be free of taxation. He was soon able to count on the support of the Protestant nobles in the diets, although many Catholic ones were among his fiercest critics (see pp. 54–5).

Far less research has been carried out on the Lutheran nobles of Prussia than those of Brandenburg, but we know from a tax census at the beginning of the eighteenth century that there were around 2,000 male nobles.[28] During the Great Elector's reign these included members of a dozen substantial families, including the Dohnas, Wallenrodts and Finckensteins, who owned thousands of acres and were recognised as a separate group, the *Herren*. While these families were far wealthier than the Brandenburg elite, they were not in the same league as the Polish magnates. Their political influence moreover had always been tempered by the mass of Junkers and the city of Königsberg.[29] The Junkers themselves were small fry, like those in Brandenburg, owning a thousand acres or less. Since the sixteenth century they had similarly farmed their manorial lands and controlled their peasants under *Gutsherrschaft*. Although escaping the devastation of the Thirty Years War, they did suffer badly from the War of the North and were affected by the general collapse in grain prices. While Junker power in the diet, like the influence of Königsberg, lasted well into the 1670s, the whole logic of Frederick William's policies was to prise political control from the Junkers at the centre and to restrict it to the provinces. Although usually an absentee ruler, he gradually had his own officials usurp the functions of the traditional Prussian government and extend the military-financial administration of the General War Commissariat, especially in the last ten years of his life. The great families, in particular the Calvinist Dohnas, who were the wealthiest and most cosmopolitan, tended to accommodate themselves to the new order. The real resistance came from Junkers such as Kalckstein (see pp. 142–3), although this opposition never developed on the scale of that of Königsberg.[30] Yet the Great Elector's influence certainly had its limits, especially away from the centre. A year after his death, a Prussian noble, possibly a Dohna, complained to Fuchs that the Junkers were monopolising the office of *Landrat* and excluding the great families, so that 'all good has come to an end in the land, and the sovereign must at all times negotiate with these district councillors [i.e. the *Landräte*] about his rights, even his very bread; so long as this goes on, the Elector will be ruler more *nomine* than *omine*'.[31]

. . .

THE PEASANTRY[32]

The peasant population of the Hohenzollerns' almost completely rural lands was as diverse as elsewhere in seventeenth-century Europe. The Rhenish territories of course were completely different from the rest, with mixed farming, prosperous peasants, few serfs and no large estates. But in the eastern lands the peasantry came in many guises as well. There was a whole hierarchy from so-called 'full peasants' (*Vollbauern*), with substantial holdings of up to 140 acres and often employing their own labourers, down to near-landless cottagers (*Kossäten* in Brandenburg/Pomerania and *Gärtner* in Prussia). The 'full peasants' had secure, and often hereditary, tenancies on lands owned by the lords or the crown, and they usually farmed these with their own families and paid labourers. 'Half peasants', and others with various names, occupied smaller tenancies, often on a precarious legal basis. The far more numerous cottagers rented a small plot at best, working for larger peasants or lords. At the bottom of rural society were the landless labourers and domestic servants, who depended totally on wages or on their keep.

In seventeenth-century Brandenburg and Prussia nearly all the population of the countryside was servile in some way, subject to the manorial economy and the landlords' law courts. Strict personal serfdom (*Leibeigenschaft*), where the actual bodies of the peasant and his family belonged to the feudal lord, was mainly confined to Pomerania and parts of the Uckermark and Neumark in Brandenburg. Elsewhere in the electorate (and in Prussia) there was hereditary bondage (*Erbuntertänigkeit*), which was attached to the land itself rather than to the person: it therefore only applied to the peasant while he was a tenant there. In theory, he could leave his farm, if he found someone to replace him and if the lord approved. In reality, however, these *Erbuntertanen* were little different from serfs and just as bound to the soil, performing labour services, needing the lord's permission to marry and forced to send their children to work for a time as manorial servants. Contemporaries drew little distinction between *Leibeigenschaft* and *Erbuntertänigkeit*, and 'in practice it meant the same thing'.[33] While some *Erbuntertanen*, especially in the Altmark west of the Elbe, had what amounted to hereditary tenure and fixed rents, dues and labour services, far more peasants to the east of the river and in northern Neumark, Pomerania and most of Prussia only had tenancies for life. It was easy to evict them and to raise their rents and obligations, and their successors were usually chosen from their sons by the landlord's bailiff, who charged a fee. The one exception to this general pattern of servility was a group of free peasants in Prussia called *Kölmer*, who held 8 per cent of the land as late as 1701. None the less, even they, while personally free and owning their holdings, had to render some feudal dues to lords or crown.[34]

For the Junkers to pursue the successful, intensive cultivation of their manors, that is to practise *Gutswirtschaft*, they needed to squeeze as much labour as possible from their dependent peasants and to do so at a time of year most inconvenient for the latter. Services, which also included the use of peasants' horses and oxen for ploughing and carting, seem to have increased throughout Brandenburg from a few days a year in the mid-sixteenth century to a couple of days a week, and every day during the rye harvest, by the Thirty Years War.[35] Peasants also had to wash and shear the lord's sheep, catch his fish, collect firewood and perform other tasks. These heavier services, which the wealthier peasants fulfilled by sending labourers or younger sons but which the other peasants had to perform themselves, were upheld by decrees from the rulers, who stood to gain from similar labour on their own estates. For example, in 1572 and 1593 the crown ordered the peasants in the Neumark to perform unlimited services at harvest time.[36] Although the Prussian dukes were just as indifferent to burdens on the peasantry, there was some resistance. This came from the city of Königsberg, which tried occasionally to limit Junker demands until its own political influence collapsed in the late seventeenth century. In 1634 it proclaimed that peasants were 'free people', whose children 'can move where they want'. The city also refused to hand back peasants who had fled there, and a pamphlet published in 1640 compared peasant bondage with that of the children of Israel in the land of Egypt.[37]

Modern research is beginning to suggest that before the Thirty Years War the increasing peasant burdens of dues and rents to the lords and taxes to the ruler were not intolerable, at least in Brandenburg. On the contrary, the peasants there seem to have been rather prosperous, benefiting from high grain prices and fairly light taxes, especially given the disproportionate payments by the towns. However, the catastrophe of the Thirty Years War in the electorate and Pomerania (and of the War of the North in Prussia) changed the situation and led, as we have seen, to ruined and deserted farms and to population collapse. Agricultural recovery was slow: in 1687 'nearly two thirds of the Uckermark's pre-war peasant and cottager holdings stood abandoned',[38] and by 1700 a third of the arable land in the electorate was still lying fallow.[39] Demographic recovery was also delayed, and it is likely that Brandenburg's 'rural population did not return to its 1618 level until the 1720s'.[40] Yet this reduced peasant base was to be called on to fulfil its traditional obligations to the landlords *and* to meet the new fiscal demands of the Great Elector. This was made more difficult because of the severe agricultural depression and low prices after the Thirty Years War, a slump which lasted till 1690. Falling agricultural profits affected peasants as well as Junkers.

The Junkers seem to have had difficulties in getting their peasant tenants to perform services or to render dues after the Thirty Years War. The American historian William Hagen has pointed out that the war left the peasants themselves desperate for labour to cultivate their own farms. Those with large holdings needed to hire cottagers and the landless, so there was competition for the reduced and costly pool of labour between peasants and Junkers, as well as among the Junkers themselves. Peasant tenants also resisted providing labour services for the manor. This was the reason for electoral edicts issued in the Altmark in 1635 and then in the Mittelmark and Neumark in 1644–6, forbidding peasants from abandoning their farms and ordering the performance of existing services. Even in the Uckermark, where personal serfdom was more widespread, a similar edict had to be issued in 1643. This was evidently ineffective, because in 1644 and 1649 the Junkers in the Uckermark were complaining that their 'absconded subjects refused all compliance and would not return to their cabins'. In the Prignitz, where there was little personal serfdom, the peasants were even more recalcitrant. In 1643 they protested to Frederick William about exorbitant rents, heavier labour services and the contribution taxes. He was unsympathetic, answering: 'We cannot in any way approve the peasants' independent undertaking, especially since they do not constitute a corporate body (*Universität*).[41] It looks more like a sedition that, if not stopped in time, might burst out in action.'[42] The next year, he tried to help the Prignitz landowners with an ordinance to restrict wages paid to labourers, shepherds, herdsmen and others. In 1648 armed peasants there defied the local noble circle commissioner (*Kreiskommissar*), seized the baggage of Swedish troops and tried to refuse them quarters. In February 1650 the commissioner complained to the Elector that the peasants were still in arms and now would not feed and quarter his own troops. The unrest persisted: in 1656 peasants were still banding together against contributions and manorial services, and in May the Junkers got the Elector to decree that peasants in arms or refusing services would be imprisoned. Four ringleaders were then seized and taken to Berlin, and more were gaoled two years later.[43] There were also disturbances against heavier labour services during the 1650s in the Wendish (Slav-speaking) districts of Bärwalde and Cottbus on the Silesian border, and 800 electoral troops were needed to restore order.[44] While this peasant resistance made it difficult for the lords to cultivate their manors, its scale hardly posed a serious threat to the government or to the social order itself.

Given the difficulties in finding cultivators (whether by labour services or by hire) for their manors, it is not surprising that the Junkers used the meeting of the full Brandenburg diet (*Landtag*) in 1652 to appeal as an estate to the Elector. In his response, in the *Rezess* of 1653, the Elector tried hard to maintain the *status quo* in the countryside. He confirmed the jurisdiction of the Junkers' manorial courts over tenants and effectively discouraged the peasants from any legal contact with the ruler by a clause laying down that:

'When a peasant brings an action [in the electoral courts] against his lord and his complaint proves not to be well founded, he shall be punished with imprisonment . . . that others may refrain from similar mischievous complaints.' The same applied to townsmen who accused their magistrates 'rashly, frivolously, and maliciously'. Peasants and townsmen did, however, have the right to appeal. The Elector also warned the Junkers against ejecting tenants except on very serious grounds. While he decreed that rents should be paid at the same rate as before the Thirty Years War, he pressed the lords to cancel arrears, as he had done on his own domains. On the other hand the Elector was determined to maintain strict personal serfdom 'where it has been introduced and is the custom', and he ordered those who had 'absconded' to new masters to return. Peasants were also not to claim freedom from personal serfdom without a proper legal title or their lord's consent.[45] Although, strictly speaking, hereditary serfdom was limited to the Uckermark and Neumark, the clause was meant to apply, and did, to the less rigorous form of subjection, *Erbuntertänigkeit* (hereditary subjection), found throughout the electorate.[46] It is unlikely, however, that this clause had much effect on the existing situation, and it does not seem that the lords used it 'on any large scale' to extend personal serfdom.[47]

Long after the agreement of 1653 the crown was to continue to insist the peasants should fulfil their labour obligations: in the 1680s decrees previously issued in various parts of the electorate in the 1640s and 1650s were repeated.[48] The Elector also tried to satisfy the lords' complaints by edicts to limit the cost of hiring labour, declaring in 1681 that:

We . . . have received many complaints about the pride and insolence of the domestic servants, the peasant farmers and the farm workers . . . And that they refuse to conform to Our previous ordinances and edicts, instead they do as they please, and through their contrariness, stuborness and all manner of aggravations make themselves almost intolerable to their masters.

The crown would have preferred the landlords not to hire labourers at all: it naturally wanted as many peasants as possible settled on vacant farms in Brandenburg, since they paid the contribution tax, whereas day labourers did not. Edicts urging the settling of the latter were issued in 1651 and 1670, and then again in 1683, the Junkers being pressed to get all peasants' sons to take over vacant plots and to force all peasants and servants to marry by twenty-one.[49]

More research needs to be done on the peasantry under the Great Elector to be clear about its overall condition, but a picture seems to be emerging now of a rural population affected less by the exactions of the Junkers than by the increasing tax and military demands of the crown.[50]

THE TOWNS

While the towns in Cleves and Mark were to retain their predominance throughout the seventeenth century, elsewhere in the Hohenzollern lands their influence and prosperity continued to decline, and the devastation of the Thirty Years War had accelerated this. In Brandenburg and Pomerania the urban deputies had long played an inferior role within the Estates. This was reflected in towns' shouldering a completely unequal share of the contribution taxes, which put them heavily in debt. The introduction of the excise (the rate after 1667 was 2 per cent), which shifted the tax burden from property to consumption and services, meant the towns no longer attended what was left of the diet and it also led to the rapid disappearance of urban self-government. This political collapse was accompanied by economic decline. Like most contemporary rulers, Frederick William did little to protect or foster the towns' commercial interests or even to help them recover from the wars.[51] The Junkers were also allowed to continue enterprises on their own estates. But even more damaging were the Elector's actions in Prussian Königsberg. In the 1640s this was still a rich, major Baltic port, politically almost on a par with the nobility; by the end of his reign the city had been battered into submission, its influence within the diet destroyed and its autonomy undermined. The Elector not only made repeated assaults on Königsberg's political power after the War of the North, he also seems to have resented its economic independence, since this facilitated the city's political resistance. From the very beginning of his reign, he was uninterested in helping individual merchants and industrialists there. In 1643 two citizens wanted to build a causeway between Königsberg and neighbouring Baltiysk/Pillau to provide better shipping facilities than at Gdańsk. But Frederick William refused: instead, he had it built himself fourteen years later and pocketed the profits. He was also more interested from the 1660s in trying to attract foreign Calvinist traders to the Prussian ports with offers of a period of exemption from taxes and billeting. Although the native Lutherans opposed this on competitive and religious grounds, by 1668 the Königsberg magistrates had to agree.

Under Frederick William, Königsberg's trade declined sharply, in his last decade by more than a third. His reign recorded the lowest number of ships using the port between the sixteenth and nineteenth centuries. Partly this was a reflection of the decline of Dutch trade to the Baltic, but it has been argued convincingly that by allowing the entry of foreigners, creating monopolies systematically in the 1670s and 1680s, and interfering in the freedoms of his native bourgeoisie, Frederick William destroyed the latter 'economically and . . . also politically', not only in Königsberg but throughout Prussia and Brandenburg as well.[52]

The one town to benefit to any extent from Frederick William's reign and show significant growth was Berlin.[53] By his death the twin towns of Berlin-Cölln had become the permanent seat of court and government, as well as *de facto* capital of the Hohenzollern lands. Yet Berlin only grew slowly till after the War of the North, when it was helped by a burgeoning garrison and its position on the improved waterway of the Havel and Spree. When the Elector returned there in the early 1640s, Berlin was dilapidated and dirty, with many buildings having been burnt down. The bridge connecting Cölln, on its island in the River Spree, to Berlin on the northern right bank was in ruins. The Cölln *Schloß*, which doubled as fortress and electoral palace, was barely habitable because of gaping holes in the roof. Frederick William's frequent absences and the heavy contributions on the city all inhibited recovery, even to the level of the early years of the century.[54] However, when Frederick William brought Louise Henrietta to Berlin in the early 1650s, not only was the *Schloß* repaired but swampy land to the south-west of Cölln was drained and a few buildings erected. This was the later suburb of Friedrichswerder, planned and begun by Frederick William's Piedmontese architect-cum-engineer, Philippe de Chièze. By 1666 there were ninety-two houses here (half belonging to courtiers). The introduction of the excise helped it expand and in 1672 it had a church, magistrates and town hall. Friedrichswerder was also enclosed in the fortified walls of Berlin-Cölln, when Frederick William undertook extensive and costly rebuilding of these during and after the War of the North. It had been obvious that the crumbling medieval walls were useless to defend the city; in 1658, therefore, new fortifications were begun, worked on extensively in the 1660s but not completed till 1683, the burghers paying much of the construction cost. These were a huge defensive structure in the Dutch manner, with thirteen bastions, towers, 8-metre high walls and a 55-metre wide moat. They were planned first by the Dutch Memhardt, then Chièze and finally Johann Nehring. Frederick the Great later was very critical of the works, describing them as 'poorly constructed'.[55] Despite their size, they lagged behind the simultaneous urban expansion. In the 1670s a fourth quarter, Dorotheenstadt, was begun on the left bank of the Spree. This was on further marshy ground to the west of Friedrichswerder, given by the Elector to his second wife, Dorothea. She divided it up into lots which were quickly sold and houses built on them. She was also responsible for its most imposing feature, the famous avenue of lime trees, the Unter den Linden. By the end of the reign there were 150 houses in this suburb, many occupied by French Huguenots.

In 1660 Berlin's population had still not recovered from the losses of the Thirty Years War, and the city had a civilian population of only 5,000, with a garrison of 1,500 and their 900 dependants. This meant that the military and their families were a third of the population; as there were no barracks, it also meant they lived beside or billeted on the rest.[56] Population growth over the next twenty years remained slow, not quite reaching 10,000 by 1680. But there was rapid expansion in the 1680s – to 17,000 in 1685 and almost 20,000 at Frederick William's death.[57] Although many of the new citizens were Huguenots (6,000 settled there between 1685 and 1700), the rest were natives.

Within its walls the city seems to have been improving as well as growing. A visitor in the mid-1660s had not been impressed by Berlin as an economic centre. He wrote that 'Trade is limited; the goods manufactured here are used on the spot. The court has most of its needs supplied from Holland and Hamburg.'[58] But by 1687 the Italian traveller Gregorio Leti enthused about the wide streets, churches and statues. He admitted it was 'not one of the greatest towns in Germany but is certainly one of the most beautiful and pleasant, although it is too sandy and surrounded by forests'.[59] Considerable effort had been made to improve the city in the 1680s, as it became more obviously the centre of the Hohenzollern lands and the permanent home for the court. The governor of Berlin was made responsible for overseeing street cleaning, paving and lighting. A decree of 1674 had already ordered all peasants entering the city with carts to take loads of rubbish out with them. In 1684 householders were told to make sure the frontages of their properties were kept clear and the paving in repair. Citizens were also forbidden to fatten their pigs by letting them wander and scavenge. In 1680 street lighting, oil lamps on poles outside every third house, was introduced, to be lit on dark nights throughout the year. Efforts were also made to keep the water supplies clean and the wells open, and numerous regulations were issued to prevent fire in the still largely wooden city. While some attempt was clearly made to make Berlin more tolerable for the court and its citizens, the other electoral towns were ignored. And in the regulations for Berlin itself, there was very little of the rigid ordering of urban life so typical of the Prussian state of the Elector's successors.

· · ·

NOTES AND REFERENCES

1 Edgar Melton, 'The Prussian Junkers, 1600–1786', in H.M. Scott, ed., *The European Nobilities in the Seventeenth and Eighteenth Centuries* (London, 1995), II, pp. 71ff. provides the most useful analysis. For the background see R.L. Gawthrop, *Pietism and the Making of Eighteenth-Century Prussia* (Cambridge, 1993), pp. 14ff.; F.L. Carsten, *Origins*, passim, *A History of the Prussian Junkers* (Aldershot, 1989), passim, 'The Origins of the Junkers' in *Essays*; and H. Rosenberg, 'The rise of The Junkers in Brandenburg-Prussia, 1410–1653', *American Historical Review*, 49 (1943–4). A detailed account of the pre-Thirty Years War Brandenburg nobility is P.-M. Hahn, *Struktur und Funktion*, and for after the war see his 'Landesstaat und Ständetum im Kurfürstentum Brandenburg während des 16. und 17. Jahrhundert', in Baumgart, ed., *Ständetum*. See also G. Heinrich, 'Der Adel in Brandenburg-Preußen', in H. Rössler, ed., *Der Deutscher Adel, 1555–1740* (Darmstadt, 1965) and R. Endres, *Adel in der frühen Neuzeit* (Munich, 1993). Useful are R.M. Berdahl, *The Politics of the Prussian Nobility: The Development of a Conservative Ideology* (Princeton, 1988), pp. 14ff.; H. Schissler, 'The Junkers: notes on the social and historical significance of the agrarian elite in Prussia', in R.G. Moeller, ed., *Peasants and Lords in Modern Germany* (Boston, 1986), pp. 24ff., and 'The social and political power of the Prussian Junkers', in R. Gibson and M. Blinkhorn, eds, *Landownership and Power in Modern Europe* (London, 1991). H. Kaak, *Die Gutsherrschaft: Theoriegeschichtliche Untersuchungen zum Agrarwesen im ostelbischen Raum* (Berlin, 1991), provides a massive

historiography of the manor. And there is the theoretical and rather abstruse J. Peters, ed., *Gutsherrschaft als soziales Modell: Vergleichende Betrachtungen zur Funktionsweise frühneuzeitlicher Agrargesellschaften*, Historische Zeitschrift Beihefte 18 (Munich, 1985). The essential works by W. Hagen are listed in note 32 below.

2 Schissler, 'The Junkers', p. 26.

3 Carsten, *History of the Prussian Junkers*, pp. 16, 26.

4 Schissler, 'The social and political', p. 102.

5 According to W. Hagen very little land was seized before the Thirty Years War. Using a census of 1624, he disputes Carsten's claim, based on the same source, that manorial land in the Mittelmark grew by 50 per cent over the previous half century. He puts the figure at 7.3 per cent. See Hagen, 'Seventeenth-century crisis', p. 311, and Carsten, *History of the Prussian Junkers*, p. 11. Melton, 'Population structure, the market economy, and the transformation of *Gutsherrschaft* in East Central Europe, 1650–1800: the cases of Brandenburg and Bohemia', *German History*, 6 (1998), p. 299, says noble holdings of arable land in the Uckermark increased between 1500 and 1620 from one-eighth to one-third. Junkers in the same Mittelmark also seem to have acquired a further 18.2 per cent from seizing holdings deserted during the Thirty Years War. E.E. Rich and C.H. Wilson, eds, *Cambridge Economic History of Europe* (Cambridge, 1977), V, p. 111.

6 Schissler, 'The social and political power', pp. 102f.

7 Carsten, 'Origins of the Junkers', pp. 17, 40.

8 Melton, 'The Prussian Junkers', pp. 75f., 80.

9 Hahn, 'Landestaat und Ständetum', pp. 62f. and his *Strucktur und Funktion*, p. 191.

10 Melton, 'The Prussian Junkers', pp. 78f.

11 Ibid., p. 82.

12 Hagen, 'Seventeenth-century crisis', pp. 322, 335; Hahn, *Struktur und Funktion*, pp. 252–6.

13 W. Abel, *Geschichte der deutschen Landwirtschaft vom frühen Mittelalter bis zum 19. Jahrhundert*, 2nd edn (Stuttgart, 1967), p. 266.

14 See Rosenberg, 'The rise of the Junkers', pp. 239f., and Carsten, 'The Great Elector', p. 187, who believed subjection increased.

15 Hagen, 'Seventeenth-century crisis', pp. 315, 329.

16 V. Press, 'Formen des Ständewesens und den deutschen Territorialstaaten des 16. und 17. Jahrhunderts', in Baumgart, ed., *Ständetum*, p. 301.

17 Nachama, p. 35. My italics.

18 Heinrich, 'Der Adel in Brandenburg-Preußen', p. 299.

19 Melton, 'The Prussian Junkers', p. 85; Hagen, 'Seventeenth-century crisis', p. 333.

20 R. Wohlfeil, 'Adel und Heerwesen', in Rössler, ed., *Deutsche Adel*, pp. 331ff.

21 In the first years of the eighteenth century only 3.7 per cent of Brandenburg nobles had been to university. Heinrich, 'Der Adel in Brandenburg-Preußen', p. 308.

22 Hahn, *Struktur und Funktion*, pp. 386–8.

23 Carsten, 'The Great Elector', pp. 182, 200f., and see his *Origins*, p. 273. Similarly, the Marxist argument that the nobility supported Frederick William's absolutism and military expansion in return for control over the peasantry hardly holds water. The nobility did not welcome any increase in the ruler's power or need his military protection from the peasantry. See K. Deppermann, 'Der preußische Absolutismus und der Adel', *Geschichte und Gesellschaft*, 8 (1982), pp. 544ff., and Asch, 'Estates and princes', pp. 120ff.

24 Between 1470 and 1620 around '60 per cent of Junker families in Brandenburg never held office at any level', Melton, 'The Prussian Junkers', p. 81.

25 For several from 1550 to 1720, see W.G. Benecke, 'Stand und Stände in Preußen vor den Reformen', dissertation, Friedrich-Wilhelms Universität, Berlin, 1935, p. 19.

26 Gagliardo, p. 152.

27 Abel, *Geschichte der deutschen Landwirtschaft*, p. 267.

28 Carsten, *History of the Prussian Junkers*, p. 30.

29 See G. Schramm, 'Adel und Staat: ein Vergleich zwischen Brandenburg und Polen-Litauen im 17 Jahrundert', in M. Biskup and K. Zernack, eds, *Schichtung und Entwicklung der Gesellschaft in Polen und Deutschland im 17. Jahrhundert* (Wiesbaden, 1983), pp. 70f.

30 W. Görlitz, *Die Junker* (Limburg an der Lahn, 1964), p. 50.

31 O. Hintze, 'The Hohenzollern [sic] and the nobility', in F. Gilbert, ed., *The Historical Essays of Otto Hintze* (New York, 1975), pp. 44f.

32 Most research on the peasantry has concentrated on the Brandenburg heartlands. For the various levels of peasant society, see H.-U. Wehler, *Deutsche Gesellschaftsgeschichte* (Munich, 1987), I, pp. 170f.; and in English there is the useful R.M. Berdahl, *The Politics of the Prussian Nobility* (Princeton, 1988), pp. 28ff. There is now a good deal of analytical work on the peasantry in English, and guidance on the extensive German material can be found there. See especially the important articles by W.W. Hagen, 'Seventeenth-century crisis', pp. 302ff., 'Working for the Junker: the standard of living of manorial laborers in Brandenburg, 1584–1810', *Journal of Modern History*, 58 (1986), pp. 143ff., 'How mighty the Junkers? Peasant rents and seigniorial profits in sixteenth-century Brandenburg', *Past & Present*, 108 (1985), pp. 80ff., 'Village life in East-Elbian Germany and Poland, 1400–1800: subjection, self-defence, survival', in Tom Scott, ed., *The Peasantries of Europe* (London, 1998), pp. 145ff., 'Subject farmers in Brandenburg-Prussia and Poland: village life and fortunes under manorialism in early modern Central Europe',

in M.L. Bush, ed., *Serfdom and Slavery: Studies in Legal Bondage* (London, 1996), pp. 296ff., and 'The Junkers' faithless servants: peasant insubordination and the breakdown of serfdom in Brandenburg-Prussia, 1763–1811', in R.J. Evans and W.R. Lee, eds, *The German Peasantry: Conflict and Community in Rural Society from the Eighteenth to the Twentieth Centuries* (London, 1986). In the same collection is H. Harnisch, 'Peasants and markets'. See also E. Melton, 'Population structure', pp. 297ff. Two impressive modern studies of the whole Uckermark and of an estate there are L. Enders, *Die Uckermark: Geschichte einer kurmärkischen Gesellschaft vom 12. bis zum 18. Jahrhundert* (Weimar, 1992) and H. Harnisch, *Die Herrschaft Boitzenburg. Untersuchungen zur Entwicklung der sozialökonomischen Struktur ländlicher Gebiete in der Mark Brandenburg vom 14. bis zum 19. Jahrhundert* (Weimar, 1968).

33 Kellenbenz, p. 67. Otto Hintze commented in his *Die Hohenzollern und ihre Werk*, 7th edn (Berlin, 1916), p. 206, that what was later officially called *Erbuntertänigkeit*, was actually generally known at this time as *Leibeigenschaft*. This meant that the clause in the agreement with the Estates of 1653 over *Leibeigenschaft* had a much wider application.

34 For the *Kölmer* see H. Aubin and W. Zorn, eds, *Handbuch der deutschen Wirtschafts-und Sozialgeschichte* (Stuttgart, 1971), I, p. 502.

35 G. Vogler, 'Die Entwicklung der feudalen Arbeitsrente in Brandenburg vom 15. bis 18. Jahrhundert', *Jahrbuch für Wirtschaftsgeschichte*, 1 (1966), p. 152.

36 Carsten, *Origins*, p. 12.

37 Carsten, 'Gutsherrschaft und Adelsmacht', in Schlenke, ed., *Preußen*, pp. 36ff.

38 Hagen, 'Seventeenth-century crisis', pp. 311, 313, 317, note 29.

39 Gagliardo, p. 129.

40 Melton, 'The Prussian Junkers', p. 106.

41 The implication was that the peasants were not an estate in their own right like the nobles and towns.

42 Hagen, 'Seventeenth-century crisis', p. 317.

43 Ibid., p. 318, J. Schultze, *Die Prignitz, aus der Geschichte einer märkischen Landschaft* (Cologne, 1956), pp. 202f., 297 and *Mark Brandenburg*, IV, p. 41.

44 See J. Brankačk and F. Mětsk, *Geschichte der Sorben* (Bautzen, 1975), I, pp. 235f.

45 All quotes from Macartney, pp. 232–7. The crown intended to retain *Leibeigenschaft* where it existed on its own estates. In 1673 the administration in Ravensberg was ordered to enforce it and warned against freeing peasants without very good cause. See Spannagel, *Minden*, pp. 174ff.

46 See reference to Hintze in note 33 above.

47 Hagen, 'Seventeenth-century crisis', pp. 318f.

48 Schultze, *Mark Brandenburg*, IV, p. 39.

49 Hagen, 'Seventeenth-century crisis', pp. 302, 325–7.
50 Melton, 'The Prussian Junkers', pp. 105ff., and 'Population structure', pp. 302ff.
51 See especially Nachama, pp. 66ff.
52 Ibid., pp. 124–7, 184.
53 See Waddington, *Prusse*, I, pp. 409ff., Philippson, III, pp. 117ff., and Ribbe, I, pp. 343ff.
54 M. Arendt et al., *Geschichte der Stadt Berlin* (Berlin, 1937), p. 175, and Philippson, I, p. 427.
55 J. Luvaas, ed., *Frederick the Great on the Art of War* (New York, 1966), p. 63.
56 Schultze, *Mark Brandenburg*, V, p. 44, and Ribbe, I, p. 349.
57 Aubin and Zorn, I, p. 580.
58 Arendt, p. 206.
59 Beuys, p. 399.

Chapter 6

THE MATURE RULER,
1660–1679

After War of North FW began to
see the "absolutist" role of troops

. . .

DEALING WITH THE ESTATES

After the War of the North not all Frederick William's troops were disbanded, since he was determined to keep at least some as a standing army. The war had shown how soldiers could be used to impose taxes whether the Estates agreed or not. Consequently, when the Brandenburg Estates' permanent committee and successive representative diets refused to continue the contributions in the early 1660s and pressed instead for the remaining troops to be dismissed, Frederick William showed his tougher and increasingly arbitrary side. In January 1662 he insisted to the Estates that 'the preservation of his lands depended next to God on arms',[1] and he followed his wartime practice of simply informing them what money he required and then seeing this was collected, sometimes by force. His promise of 1653 to consult the Estates was forgotten, as he became more convinced that he could only keep a permanent force by freeing himself from their financial shackles. Frederick William's impatience comes out clearly in tart comments written on a document presented by the Estates' deputies in July 1666:

Deputies. We are sorely grieved that in matters touching the weal [welfare] of the land and entailing the loss of our property and our total ruin, you no longer call us together in the diet to ask our advice.

Frederick William. Tie the secret and weighty matters to a bell-rope by giving them to the Estates to deliberate over, indeed!

Deputies. It is with the greatest pain that we have seen how you continue to levy 22,000 th[alers] a month . . . as if it were a permanent tax.

Frederick William. I could wish that we lived with such neighbours that we could get along with less.

Deputies. The military taxes [contributions] ... cause the decay of the towns and the villages.

Frederick William. For the decay in the towns the town magistrates themselves are responsible. It is due to the inefficiency of their administration, which smells to high heaven.

A few days later he told the deputies bluntly: 'The burden of taxation in the present circumstances is unavoidable . . . for our safety and welfare.'[2]

During the 1660s Frederick William brought all meaningful opposition from the Brandenburg Estates to an end. From then till his death their permanent committees and representative diets had to accept what he demanded, although there was still some grumbling over the level of taxation. The situation seemed satisfactory enough for him to say little about these Estates in his *Political Testament* of 1667, where he described the Brandenburgers, unlike those elsewhere, as 'true subjects'.[3] None the less, the system was to be far from ideal, while tax collection still depended on using the Estates' officials and while only peasant holdings and urban properties were taxed. The solution was to develop institutions separate from the Estates (see pp. 165–9 for General War Commissariat) and to use different kinds of taxation (see pp. 162–5 for urban excise).

The War of the North led to a similar reordering of Frederick William's relations with his Estates outside Brandenburg, although resistance here was to be more overt and tenacious. The war considerably strengthened his position, even in the Rhenish lands, by allowing him to use the threat of force to get his way, and he was to employ the same tactics in peacetime. One new advantage he enjoyed was the relative isolation of the Cleves-Mark Estates. Although Dutch garrisons remained and the urban elite in control of the Republic was particularly hostile to Frederick William as uncle of the young William of Orange, over the next decade the Dutch regime faced too many domestic and foreign problems of its own to interfere directly as in the past.

In August 1660, just a few months after the Peace of Oliwa, the Elector sent his Stadtholder, Johann Moritz, a new agreement (*Rezess*) for the Estates to accept in full. The inevitable fierce opposition, led by the Cleves towns, brought the angry response from Frederick William in October that 'we are not minded to allow any more delay, and if the Estates will not agree . . . , then we know how to do what we want'. Johann Moritz, therefore, insisted to the diet that the previous agreements of 1649 and 1653 had to be abandoned, because these undermined 'His Electoral Highness's princely sovereignty and . . . lead to . . . a condominium'. Warnings that the Elector would be driven to bring an army and deal 'harshly' with them had the desired effect, and he believed 'the Estates were well frightened'. Within a month the *Rezess* was accepted, since the Estates wanted, as the Stadtholder put it, 'to be good children'. In this struggle Johann Moritz had the advantage of his own experience and prestige, but he also had a stronger hand because most Calvinist nobles and smaller towns wished to compromise and the native officials within the Cleves government were becoming increasingly loyal to him and the Elector. Especially supportive was the forceful and competent Chancellor, Daniel Weimann, who in March 1657 had even told the diet that 'subjects must not grumble but pray when their prince was fighting . . . and must remember that kings and princes encountered danger and war for the sins of the people'.[4]

Frederick William himself came to Cleves in December 1660 and the new *Rezess* was formally completed the following March. It was essentially a compromise, showing he did not intend to abolish the Estates and rule as an absolute prince here. However, the Estates' more offensive privileges were removed – their right to negotiate with foreign powers, to oppose the stationing of troops, to oversee the appointment of officials and to have these swear to uphold their privileges. Yet, very significant privileges remained – restricting office to natives, the Estates' right to assemble unsummoned, *and* their right to vote taxation. But at the same time the Estates effectively 'recognised their duty' to provide taxation,[5] since they agreed to pay 110,000 thalers in 1662.

The dynasty's grip over its Rhenish territories and their dependence on Berlin were to be increased five years later. In 1666 a definitive settlement over the whole Cleves-Jülich succession was signed with Duke Philip William of Pfalz-Neuburg (see pp. 202–3), finally removing any possible doubts that the Hohenzollerns were there to stay. This settlement, together with the *Rezess* of 1661, set the parameters of relations between ruler and Estates for a century. There was no further serious constitutional conflict, unlike in Jülich-Berg where the traditional strife continued. The Cleves-Mark Estates had managed to hold on to a significant political role in return for effectively accepting they had to pay for their ruler's army in their midst.[6] The diet continued to meet almost annually, and it dutifully voted Frederick William revenues of 110,000–180,000 thalers a year with little complaint till the end of the reign, and even double that on occasions after 1675, although this was still considerably less than that paid by the much poorer population of Brandenburg. While mainly native officials continued to be appointed, they proved ever more dependable, especially as Frederick William and Johann Moritz deliberately appointed nobles. The crown also forced the Cleves diet in the mid-1660s to free the nobility from taxation and to increase the towns' share from a sixth to a fifth. This meant that most tax continued to fall on the peasantry, who the Elector himself had admitted in 1664 were 'notoriously overburdened'.[7] Excise taxes, like those in the neighbouring Dutch Republic, would have been the best way to tap urban wealth, and Frederick William tried nine times to introduce one between 1667 and 1687. As the towns continually refused and he would not force their agreement, Cleves and Mark remained the only Hohenzollern lands without the excise.

It has to be asked why Frederick William did not reduce the power of the Cleves-Mark Estates further, especially as the Dutch garrisons did not return after the Dutch War of the 1670s. The most likely explanation is that regular payment of tax and the acceptance of Hohenzollern troops gave him no further reason to interfere. He clearly did not set out to impose absolutism for its own sake there. While the rulers of Jülich-Berg had continually stressed their divine right in negotiating with the Estates, Frederick William had argued 'more pragmatically'. Attacks on their privileges were justified by employing the formula 'necessity knows no law'.[8] Although he undoubtedly believed in divine right, he never laboured the point and also accepted that he could override the Estates' privileges only to safeguard his dynasty and his territories. He 'saw his role as ruler as part of the traditional system of political and social hierarchy, which had a religious basis, and he accepted the right of traditional institutions to exist'.[9]

The War of the North was to transform Frederick William's political position even more significantly in Prussia. During the first years of his reign he had not dared to risk a trial of strength with the diet and his 'own' government there, and he had kept only a few garrison troops in the duchy. This all changed with the threat posed by Charles X of Sweden's accession. In April 1655 Frederick William summoned the diet in Königsberg, appointing Waldeck and Hoverbeck, the experienced envoy to Poland and Calvinist convert, as his commissioners. The deputies, however, dismissed their warnings about an imminent Swedo-Polish war and proposed relying on the traditional, ineffective militia for defence. It was not till August, when the danger from Sweden was obvious to all, that the diet agreed to an excise on agricultural and other goods for a year to raise 70,000 thalers. Even then goods for the nobles' own use were exempted and the Estates were to collect the money and control how it was spent.

This sum was hardly enough to defend the duchy, and as soon as Frederick William arrived in Prussia with his large army at the end of 1655, he used the threat of this to raise far more money. In August 1656 he went further by setting up his own war chest and appointing one of the few great Prussian nobles, Johann von Wallenrodt, as war commissioner. Wallenrodt's war commissariat soon began to side-step the Estates' officials, assign and collect taxes and seize food, animals and billets. But Frederick William's demands were only part of the burden on a population facing incursions by Swedes, Poles and Tartars. Plague appeared and killed off even more. There was widespread famine and crowds of refugees flocked to Königsberg. The duchy seemed to be suffering as much distress as Brandenburg in the 1630s. With Königsberg's trade collapsing under the strains of the war and the excise, there were inevitably bitter protests and real anger in the diet every year of the war. Open revolt appeared only a matter of time.

His subjects' misery mattered less to Frederick William than wresting the sovereignty of Prussia from Poland. Although interference from Warsaw had been only spasmodic since his accession, ending the feudal overlordship was fundamental to the development of his dynasty there and the creation of the monarchy in Prussia by his son in 1701. The triangular relationship of Polish king, Prussian duke and Prussian Estates would be finished, and with it a main prop of Estates power dislodged. The future was made immediately clear to the diet in October 1657, as Frederick William prepared to return to Berlin. Determined not to restore authority to the independent *Oberräte*, he created the position of stadtholder to represent him, giving it to a relative, the Lithuanian Calvinist Prince Bogusław Radziwiłł.[10] The Elector intended the Prince to rule together with the *Oberräte*, and future orders were sent to them jointly. In addition the Prince had total charge of the troops, and the *Oberräte* were instructed to consult him over supplying and paying these.

Radziwiłł's appointment inevitably evoked protests and a string of complaints from the diet about breaches of the *Indigenatsrecht*, as well as about the military occupation and illegal taxes. The deputies eulogised: 'When we think back and consider the happy situation of our forefathers, who lived in true peace and secure freedom . . . we [now] have only a mere shadow of that old happiness.'[11] However, enough troops remained in the duchy during the last years of the war for Radziwiłł and the military commissariat below him to be able to ignore the diet. It was not even consulted about the transfer of sovereignty, which was probably illegal, and it was only informed formally a year after the 1657 treaties settling this with Poland.[12]

Once peace was made in 1660, Frederick William had two priorities in Prussia: to have the diet acknowledge his full sovereignty and to keep enough troops there to deter Swedish or Polish invasion. Concern about the latter, rather than to frighten or destroy the Estates, was the main reason for maintaining the troops. But the recent war had clearly shown their value in enforcing taxation, and by this stage in his life (he was now forty) Frederick William had had enough of the continual interference by his overbearing subjects here as in his other lands. In this more arbitrary temper he was not alone: in 1660 the Danish monarchy became absolute, the Stuarts were restored in Britain, and the next year Louis XIV embarked on his personal rule.[13] While the Danish, British and French crowns enjoyed substantial domestic support, Frederick William had few friends in Prussia and usually tried to rule from a distance in Berlin. Probably because of his weakness he shied away from an immediate showdown over the diet's privileges and was willing to try to work as far as possible within the existing system. Instead he asked the diet early in 1660 to continue the unauthorised taxes, still running at 20,000 thalers a month, to maintain his troops. Even if the diet had agreed, which it did not, these would have been a heavy burden on the population, given the destruction of the war and then poor harvests in the early 1660s. In 1661 the diet claimed that 7 million thalers, or 1 million a year, had been levied since 1655 – 4.5 million in contributions, 1 million in the excise and 1.5 million in kind.[14]

Inevitably opposition began to well up, and most members of Frederick William's government in Königsberg sympathised with it, especially the *Landräte*, who made up the upper house of the diet. For his part Radziwiłł believed the *Landräte* were 'indifferent to the defence of the country; they are true neighbours of the Poles',[15] who were of course notorious for their rebelliousness. The

Stadtholder was finding both the *Oberräte* and *Landräte* hostile, obstructive and incompetent, especially in the management of the ducal domains. Frederick William himself was to complain that 'when there is a diet in Prussia, I am unlucky that my own servants cause me the most opposition'.[16] This opposition in the central government, however, was largely passive; that outside was far more dangerous. The ending of Polish sovereignty, heavy taxation and the suspicion that Prussian liberties were under threat were leading to demands to restore the old system. By the end of 1660 Radziwiłł was reporting that malcontents were accusing Frederick William of being 'the greatest tyrant and enemy of the people'.[17] In January 1661 six members of the diet appealed to the Polish Grand Marshal, Lubomirski, to invade and free them from 'the present tyranny'.[18] When the Elector heard about this, he wrote angrily in April to his envoy in Warsaw, Hoverbeck:

> It distresses me that evil people are denouncing me as a tyrant, who abuses his subjects. You know how I have humoured these Estates, and you are well aware how I treat my subjects in Brandenburg, Pomerania, Halberstadt and Minden.[19]

Although the Poles failed to respond, a crisis in the duchy was inevitable because Frederick William needed the diet to agree formally to his sovereignty. The task was given to Schwerin, who was sent to Königsberg in 1661 to work with Radziwiłł in holding a new diet. Schwerin was not only the leading electoral minister, but since the reorganisation of the Privy Council ten years before, he had handled Prussian affairs (largely from Berlin) and his second wife was a Prussian with lands there. His instructions, however, were not going to make his mission easy: besides getting the sovereignty accepted, he was to confirm only privileges which did not encroach on this, to have taxes voted for the troops, and to reform the domain revenues.

Both Schwerin and Radziwiłł were moderate-minded men who did not want to rile the Prussians. But when they opened the so-called 'Great Diet' in Königsberg in 1661, this began a year-long tussle.[20] Even before the diet met, during preliminary discussions with leading deputies, the ever-sanguine Schwerin was given a nasty foretaste of what was in store. He was told bluntly by Hieronymus Roth, a rich merchant and president of the court of aldermen of Kneiphof, one of Königsberg's three towns, that 'every duke carried a tyrant in his breast' and this one intended to make them paupers and then 'slaves'.[21] The diet itself seemed determined to reject the sovereignty: the deputies insisted that signing the treaties with Poland without their consent was illegal. They set out their own contract theory of the constitution, claiming Prussia had voluntarily associated with Poland two centuries before. This made the two countries one body which could be dissolved only with the consent of king, duke and Estates.[22] They then insisted all three parties draw up a new agreement, containing a right of appeal to Warsaw. In July they presented a long memorial, which demanded the end of illegal taxes and the suppression of the posts of stadtholder and war commissioner, both of which were dependent on the duke rather than on them. They also insisted all troops should leave except for garrisons at Baltiysk/Pillau and Klaipeda/Memel, on the restoration of the militia under their control, strict observance of the *Indigenatsrecht*, and a diet to be called every two years. They further demanded that Polish commissioners should mediate disputes between Estates and ruler. Outside the diet the Lutheran pastors were also vociferously attacking the new sovereignty. Schwerin, who was no enemy of diets, was aghast and told the deputies that 'such liberties' were 'not found among any Christian people'.[23] He wrote miserably to Berlin that some deputies were accusing the Elector of trying to destroy Prussian freedom and prosperity, so 'that not even cats and dogs can stay there'.[24] He was also alarmed at the growing attraction of all things Polish: 'Your Electoral Highness would never believe . . . how fond they have grown of Poland and seek all their prosperity therein.'[25]

Schwerin now decided to change tack and in August 1661 used an outbreak of plague in Königsberg as an excuse to prorogue the diet, hoping tempers would cool. The city in any case was also becoming politically unhealthy, with frequent, large and excited meetings against the excise taxes and their 'tyrannical' ruler. Hieronymus Roth was emerging as an impressive and fiery spokesman, determined to safeguard Prussia's ancient constitution and rule by the traditional elite. He was defending existing feudal liberties rather than proclaiming new democratic ones. His weakness was that few of his fellow burghers were as convinced and as resolute, and he had limited influence in the diet among the Junkers, even the rebellious ones.[26] Schwerin, with his inherent restraint, found Roth impossible to understand or to deal with, declaring he could not fathom 'whether the fellow was *sanae mentis* or full of brandy'.[27]

In October 1661 Schwerin reconvened the diet 50 kilometres to the south in Bartoszyce/Bartenstein, well away from the noxious plagues and citizens of Königsberg. But he was now faced by opposition from the equally intractable, if less volatile, Junkers. At the opening service the Lutheran pastor repeated the traditional formula of asking the delegates to pray for their overlord, the King of Poland. When the diet reopened, Junkers and towns discussed appealing to Warsaw, and the usual protests were made about illegal taxes. Weeks passed without the deputies' softening, and in mid-November they denied Frederick William had any right 'to go to war or make an alliance on behalf of this duchy of Prussia without the humble advice of the Estates'.[28] When Schwerin, despite his own reservations but on direct orders from his master, pressed for religious freedom and access to some offices for Calvinists, the diet angrily rejected this assault on the Lutheran monopoly. It subsequently declared toleration 'a most injurious liberty' and demanded: 'The preservation of the Lutheran religion alone, pure and simple, to the exclusion of all others, till the end of the world.'[29]

This session in the provinces was proving no more successful for the Elector than the previous one. Meanwhile Königsberg had continued to seethe: Radziwiłł described it at the beginning of 1662 as 'breathing war'.[30] In March Roth went in person to Warsaw to appeal for military help. Although he received only sympathy there, when he returned home Schwerin and Radziwiłł dared not arrest him in case it inflamed Königsberg further. Frederick William in Berlin would have preferred tough action and had already written in late February: 'I have never considered taking away the Prussians' liberties, but . . . they have claimed and usurped things . . . not part of their liberties . . . The Estates must [take] the oath of homage . . . and if this is not done, they must be forced to it.'[31] And a week later he wrote that 'the reason why I wish to have all things clearly defined, is that I may leave to my children no difficulties after my death'.[32]

By spring 1662 the Junker deputies, realising the Poles would not help, began to move towards accepting Frederick William's full sovereignty and agreed to an excise on the towns in return for concessions over rural taxation. Inevitably this upset Königsberg, where by late May Radziwiłł reported that 'every day 400–500 burghers . . . protest against the introduction of the excise'.[33] The city refused to pay this and remained in ferment throughout the summer. In July the citizens, with Roth's encouragement and the blessing of their Lutheran pastors, formed a confederation to safeguard their relationship with the Polish crown. They also began to arm and to strengthen the city's walls, leading Radziwiłł to conclude 'open rebellion has begun'.[34] Although he was desperately short of money to pay his troops, he reinforced the castle garrison and blockaded Königsberg to prevent help arriving from Poland. Conciliation had clearly failed and the situation was getting out of hand. In July, therefore, Frederick William decided to recall Schwerin and to follow Radziwiłł's urging to come in person. Consequently, in October 1662 Frederick William entered Königsberg at the head of 2,000 troops. He had heeded Radziwiłł's advice not to bring any more, so as not to antagonise the population further by having to support more troops. When he arrived, he found Königsberg's increasing radicalism had alienated the bulk of the nobles and news of his coming had cowed most of the city. There was still unrest, however, in Kneiphof, led by Roth, whom Radziwiłł still considered as dangerous 'as an enemy army'.[35] But all resistance soon collapsed here, when cannon were trained on it from the castle and troops appeared on the streets. Roth was seized and accused of treason. Frederick William intended to hang him, writing to Schwerin: 'Roth will be interrogated tomorrow, condemned the next and executed on Monday or Tuesday.'[36] In the event he was never brought to trial, presumably because he might have been acquitted. Instead he was carted off to Brandenburg, where he stayed imprisoned, refusing to ask for pardon, till he died sixteen years later.

With Königsberg's resistance broken, Frederick William next had to deal with the diet. Inevitably agreement over the sovereignty and taxation proved slow. Delays over the winter of 1662–3, and a crippling attack of gout, which Frederick William blamed on the diet, made him increasingly angry. He called the Prussians 'evil people . . . , who make those of Cleves saints'.[37] By early February 1663 he was so frustrated that he was warning those around him he would 'use the power given me by God, and, if anyone opposes me, he will find his head at his feet'.[38] But as the weather and his gout improved with the spring, he reached a favourable settlement with the diet, which was dissolved in May. The Estates were allowed to keep all those privileges which did not limit ducal sovereignty, a diet was to be called every three years, and its approval was necessary for taxation or war. The clause about war, however, was effectively nullified by the addition of 'except in case of necessity, when we and our successors do not need to ask our true Estates' advice and approval'.[39] Whether troops could be kept in the duchy was passed over in silence, clearly to Frederick William's advantage. Although he also agreed to suspend the excise, the diet voted to pay 70,000 thalers a year till 1666, enough for a small permanent army. Almost half the sum was to be paid by Königsberg, but the city, the other towns and the nobility were to raise and collect the money how they wished – this seemed to end the role of the war commissioners. The Lutheran monopoly was slightly breached, with Calvinists' being admitted to a few minor offices and allowed to have churches in the ports.[40] The post of stadtholder, and Radziwiłł's own position, were confirmed, and the difficult process of converting the four *Oberräte* into loyal ducal officials was begun when the diet agreed these should be bound by the Duke's instructions.[41] Finally the diet was recalled and swore homage to Frederick William as its sovereign ruler. He could then return to Berlin after a year away.

Very much a pragmatist, Frederick William had not set out to exercise unlimited power in Prussia, and he was, for the moment at least, satisfied with the agreement. He wrote to Schwerin on its conclusion: 'the constitution of the government is quite altered here'.[42] However, the opposition was far from over: calling a new diet was always to be the signal for further conflict, as Frederick William himself recognised well enough. In his *Political Testament* of 1667, he advised his successor to control his spending, so that 'you do not have to look to the Estates for money . . . then you will not have to hold many expensive diets, since the more you hold, the more of your authority will be taken away'. He also warned about the influence of the *Oberräte* and concluded: 'Caress the Prussians, but watch them . . . I have come to know them during my rule and God preserve you from knowing them still more . . . beware of them.'[43] He knew well enough, of course, that almost the whole administration in Prussia remained in the hands of potentially hostile Lutheran members of the Estates. Moreover, he still did not have real control of his own domain lands and revenues there. During his recent stay in Königsberg he had begun to overhaul these, discovering no accounts had been kept for six years (i.e. from when he had left during the last war) and that firewood for the castle was even being bought from outside his own huge domains. Yet little was to change. Though Canstein in Berlin was given ultimate control of the Prussian domains, the *Oberräte* and *Landräte* continued underhand to prevent significant reform. Over the next decade, despite Frederick William's new sovereignty, 'his' government in Königsberg continued to manage the domains, tolls, mines and amber trade for the benefit of fellow nobles.[44]

As the 1660s were free of major warfare and heavier expenditure, there was little open conflict with the Prussian Estates. In 1666 the *Oberräte* and *Landräte* agreed to continue the existing taxes for a further two years but insisted a new diet would then have to be called. They also rejected Frederick William's pleas to raise a thousand troops to use in his conflict with the Bishop of Münster (see pp. 200–2), claiming it did not concern Prussia. While he had to swallow this, it hardly endeared them to him. And when he returned to Königsberg in autumn 1668 to be on hand for a new Polish royal election, he was frustrated to find lax administration had put the tax revenues 90,000 thalers in arrears. In May 1669, therefore, he called a new diet and asked for open-ended taxation. Inevitably, all three houses complained about existing taxes, and the Junkers were particularly vexed over new domain leases. They also seem to have been caught up in the excitement of the election in Warsaw, where a native noble was to be elected king in June. Frederick William himself returned to Berlin after this, and the diet would only renew current taxes for a further year. It was unfortunate, therefore, that the experienced Stadtholder, Radziwiłł, died at the end of 1669. He was replaced the next year by another Calvinist, the Pomeranian Duke Ernst Bogislav von Croy, who met his first diet in July 1670. Despite the distribution of presents and pensions to the deputies, as had been done in 1661 and 1666, this diet predictably refused to renew the taxes. During the autumn some of the nobles began to play the Polish card once more, appealing for support to the new king, Michael, who had not yet confirmed the 1658 treaties (he eventually did so in January 1672). Although Croy wanted to be conciliatory, he was becoming increasingly worried, reporting the 'evil humour' of the country in February 1671.[45]

Renewed opposition in Prussia was the last thing Frederick William needed because of his growing concern about a Franco-Dutch conflict, one likely to involve him in the Rhineland and even spread to the north (see pp. 206–12). He was being offered conflicting advice from those around him in Berlin. Schwerin as usual was for compromise, explaining in January 1671: 'During my long service in your various lands, especially in Cleves, I have found you gain most by trying to satisfy the Estates.'[46] The Elector himself, however, now in his fifties, and used to getting his way in Brandenburg and even in Cleves, was more attracted by advice from Jena to stand firm. Frederick William did not believe that he had any contractual relationship with the Prussian Estates, insisting to Schwerin in February he was answerable only to 'God and posterity'.[47] He had also insisted to the Prussian *Oberräte* the previous month that they were just 'advisers and servants, who simply and solely depend on their master and are not empowered . . . to decide their lord's affairs contrary to their instructions . . . , and it is for His Electoral Highness to resolve and judge what is most valuable and best'.[48] Croy was, therefore, ordered to ignore the diet and collect the taxes, and more troops were sent to Prussia to ensure this. These sufficiently intimidated the deputies, who became more compliant over the spring and summer. By September 1671 they finally agreed to taxes for another two years, although insisting their own officials should collect these. The diet was then dissolved, having lasted for fourteen months, and Frederick William was to call no more, despite annual requests from the nobility. Until he died he merely called together the upper house, made up of the *Landräte*, to approve the extension of the taxes. Prussia was now, in effect, following the Brandenburg pattern of a permanent committee of the Estates.

The diet of 1670–1 coincided with the related Kalckstein affair. This occurred because of the death in 1667 of Count Albrecht von Kalckstein, a leading critic of Frederick William's sovereignty. His death produced a bitter quarrel over the inheritance between his son Christian Ludwig (1630–72) and his other children. Christian Ludwig was accused by his siblings of plotting to murder Frederick William and invite Polish troops into the duchy. This seemed plausible, as he had served in the Polish army and was as opposed to ducal authority and sovereignty as his father. Frederick William therefore had him banished to his estates in 1668.[49] Then in March 1670 Kalckstein fled by sledge across the snow to Warsaw, where he urged all and sundry to invade Prussia. Brutal and corrupt, and quick to consider rebellion, he seemed a dangerous model for those Junkers determined to challenge Frederick William's sovereignty once more in the diet, meeting in July 1670.

King Michael would not surrender the fugitive, so at the end of the year the Brandenburg envoy, Brandt, had him seized, bundled in a carpet and carried by covered waggon back to Prussia. Despite Polish protests, Frederick William refused to release him, convinced that Michael, as the German metaphor has it, would not 'make an elephant out of a gnat'.[50] He was proved right and was now determined to be rid of Kalckstein and to make an example of him. During 1671 he had him tried, probably illegally, before a special court, made up mostly of non-Prussians. This condemned Kalckstein to death in January 1672 and he was beheaded. Encouraged by Jena, Frederick William also had him tortured in a vain search for accomplices. It says much for Frederick William's character and the mildness of his rule, however, that despite his fiery temper, this was the only political execution during his reign.

The last diet had agreed to new taxes for two years in 1671. These produced, through the usual mixture of land tax and excise, about 100,000 thalers a year. This was hardly adequate for Frederick William's needs when he became involved in Louis XIV's Dutch War, 1672–9. As he had no intention of calling a further diet, he had the *Landräte* informed in July 1673 that 'the highest law must be . . . the security of the country'.[51] These were unimpressed, and war commissioners had to use force to collect further heavy, unauthorised taxes. Another meeting of the *Landräte* was told in March 1674, after complaining that the war did not concern Prussia: 'It would hardly make sense for the head to trouble its limbs without any need; the head, however, recognises a need not always obvious to all the limbs.'[52] This was all very well but the new onerous taxes were being imposed at a time of real distress in the duchy: in spring 1674 Croy sent samples of bread made of chaff and bark peasants were having to eat. General discontent at all levels of society soon produced yet another political crisis. In the first two months of 1674 an unsummoned assembly of nobles met in Königsberg and joined local burghers in demanding a full diet be called. Although Junker protest soon evaporated (possibly Kalckstein's execution was too fresh a memory), Croy feared a repeat of the previous disturbances in Königsberg and even actual revolt. And over the coming months the city refused to pay taxes unless a new diet approved them. Having faced such a crisis before, Frederick William believed force was the answer. Therefore, in May 1674 he ordered Croy and the hawkish commander of his troops in Prussia, General Görtzke, to occupy Königsberg. The troops surprised the citizens and smashed down the gates, disarming the civic militia and damaging many properties. Although Görtzke wanted punitive action, Croy persuaded the Elector to accept the city's submission and to fine it instead. This armed assault marked both the end of Königsberg's resistance and of burgher autonomy. From 1676 Frederick William began to reduce the city's

power to manage all its own affairs, while burgher unity was undermined by encouraging non-Prussian merchants to settle there.

Open opposition to taxation was now over, but noble protests
against paying for a non-Prussian war continued at meetings of the
Landräte.[53] In 1678 a *Landrat* complained they had lost their 'still
unforgotten blissfulness, liberty and peaceful tranquility', and he
wanted to know why they 'let themselves be exploited to death since
the [Holy] Roman Empire is . . . not of the slightest concern to
them'.[54] And exploited they were, for between October 1677 and
the end of 1679 Prussia was paying 150,000 thalers a month, 4
million altogether, money which was going directly into the war
treasury, controlled by the War Commissariat. This heavy taxation
continued into the 1680s, when Frederick William was at peace. He
still had 30,000 a month collected, three times what had been paid
in the 1660s. While these sums were heavy, they were still lighter
than those imposed on the smaller population of Brandenburg. In
1676 Schwerin had remarked, 'It is well known that no territory
contributes so little as Prussia', which he compared unfavourably
with 'tiny Pomerania'.[55] The burden of annual taxation for the main
provinces is shown in Table 1.[56]

Frederick William found it easier to impose heavier taxation both
in Prussia and Brandenburg because he gradually freed himself
from the Estates' own officials. During the War of the North, and
even more in the Dutch War, these traditional functionaries were
elbowed aside, as the Elector depended on war commissioners directed by a General War Commissariat in Berlin (see pp. 165–9) to
collect taxes and supplies for the army. The military commanders
much preferred these commissioners to the old officials with their
scruples and their ties to the Estates, and in the 1670s the 'military
command formed a kind of independent government' in Prussia,
hostile to the Estates.'[57] With the return of peace in 1679, the war
commissioners stayed put and continued to collect the taxes.

Table 1   Annual taxation in the main provinces (in thousands of thalers)

	1654	1659	1661–3	1674	1679	1680–8
Brandenburg	75	600	240–260	288	549	341–452
Cleves-Mark	50	250	100–108	150	200	150–200
Prussia	6	600		93	140	380	300–336
Pomerania	108	406 [1658]	?	?	?	?

Throughout the 1680s they and the Stadtholder tended to decide the levels and allotment of taxes, merely informing meetings of the *Landräte*. Frederick William also used the commissioners in Prussia to impose the Brandenburg taxation model, where towns and countryside were taxed separately. Königsberg and the other towns paid through an excise, while the rural population paid various land taxes. Protests from the *Oberräte* about the separate forms of taxation were ignored, and instructions to the commissioners in 1683 and 1685 told them specifically to insist on this. In this new atmosphere even the Stadtholder, Croy, was beginning to be edged aside together with *Oberräte* and *Landräte*. In 1680 one of the war commissioners wrote: 'the Stadtholder no more than the *Oberräte* . . . can command the commissioner what to do, since he [commissioner] depends entirely on His Electoral Highness'.[58] When Croy died in 1684 Frederick William evidently felt the situation in Prussia was satisfactory enough not to replace him before his own death.

The taxation imposed on the duchy, particularly in the 1680s, when threats of invasion had diminished, seemed to bring Prussia itself no tangible advantage. It weighed particularly heavily on the unfree peasants, who paid twice the rate on the nobles. The burden probably held back, and may have reversed, the economic development of the duchy, with around 10 per cent of peasant farms vacant in 1685. Königsberg continued its downward spiral as the excise and high tolls made foreign merchants prefer Polish Gdańsk and Swedish Riga. By the last two decades of Frederick William's reign the Prussian port was being used by half as many ships as earlier in the century.[59]

When the Great Elector died, the rule of the Prussian Estates was over for good. His government here, as in Brandenburg, can be described as absolute. The English envoy, Southwell, in 1680 believed 'he is little less absolute here than is the King of France at Paris' and 'obey'd as much by his subjects'.[60] Under Frederick William the new sovereignty and his firmness against Königsberg and the leading dissidents had finally cut the potentially dangerous ties with Poland. The Estates' autonomy had been undermined in various ways. Their militia had been replaced by a standing army controlled by the crown through its War Commissariat, which assigned and collected taxation. The *Oberräte* and *Landräte* were being marginalised, and ducal officials were beginning to regulate the trade and lives of the citizens of Königsberg and the other towns. Yet the ruler's absolute power should not be exaggerated: there were definite limits to it. Frederick William's bureaucracy was tiny and not fully under his own control. Moreover, he had no desire to override vested interests except over taxation and in defence of his territories. In February 1687 he repeated to the *Oberräte* what he had told the Cleves Estates decades before, that 'necessity knows no law'.[61] He did not press his victory over the Estates to extremes. Meetings of the *Landräte* were still allowed and they usually formally approved the limited taxation, giving a semblance of consultation. In the religious sphere he was satisfied with the minor gains made for his fellow Calvinists in the 1660s, and his policy was essentially defensive, to prevent persecution by the Lutheran majority. While the Prussians had accepted Frederick William's new system sullenly and resentfully, they were to find it far less centralised and disciplined than the one his grandson, King Frederick William I (1713–40), was to impose.[62]

In his struggle with the Estates in Prussia and elsewhere, Frederick William was fortunate that the opposition never responded with an overtly political programme as in contemporary England or sixteenth-century Holland. The Estates in his various territories also made no attempt to cooperate with each other and were usually divided among themselves.[63] In Prussia, as well as in Brandenburg, while the Junkers lost most of their political power, their social, economic and judicial predominance was unaffected. It was they who continued to rule most of Frederick William's subjects. He accepted this hierarchical system and wanted to work with it. Although the Prussian nobles did pay some tax, it was much less than anyone else, and troops were not billeted on them. While the crown tried to reform its own domain leases, it was still the nobles who continued to hold these. Almost all the central and local offices below stadtholder and commissariat were in the hands of native Lutheran nobles at the end of the Great Elector's rule, and the evidence from Cleves, where he did have the opportunity to employ commoners, shows that he preferred nobles.

· · ·

A 'CHAMPION OF RELIGIOUS FREEDOM AND TOLERANCE'[64]

In the eighteenth century Prussia under Frederick the Great enjoyed a European reputation for religious tolerance, matched only by the Dutch Republic and Britain. The foundations for this were already established during the previous century and stemmed from the rulers' peculiar religious position. When Elector John Sigismund converted to Calvinism in 1613, he had expected his subjects would follow. Unfortunately for him, the Lutheran church in Brandenburg was very traditionalist in belief and practice and firmly rooted throughout society: there was no enthusiasm among the clergy or laity for further religious reform.[65] Instead there were riots in the towns and open hostility from pastors and Junkers. After a year the Privy Council concluded that 'Among the nobility not more than five have actually embraced our religion'. As John Sigismund was too weak to impose the Reformed faith on his Brandenburg subjects, let alone those he acquired in Prussia, he tried to argue that Calvinists and Lutherans shared the same basic Protestant beliefs and should unite against Rome. A policy of toleration more accidental than planned was forced on him. In 1615 he assured the angry Brandenburg Estates he did not claim 'dominion over consciences and therefore does not wish to impose any suspect or unwelcome preachers on anyone'.[66] The following year he promised there would be no forced conversions 'since belief is no one's property but an act and gift of God'.[67]

The limits to religious change were shown by John Sigismund's difficulties over appointments. Calvinists became his close advisers and court preachers, and they were also admitted to Brandenburg's sole university at Frankfurt an der Oder and to the gymnasium, or grammar school, at Joachimsthal in the Uckermark, but the Estates insisted only Lutherans could be presented to clerical livings. John Sigismund, and his successors, however, remained head (*supremus episcopus*) of the Lutheran church, while not members of it, and filled senior appointments. This allowed them to pick men for the church hierarchy less hostile to their own faith.[68] Overall, nevertheless, the very incomplete conversion meant Calvinists were a minority in Brandenburg (and a phantom presence in Prussia), limited to the court.[69] The political and personal weaknesses of John Sigismund's successor, George William, weaknesses compounded by the Thirty Years War, ensured Lutheran dominance remained unchallenged.

The traditional view that Lutheran communities were passive ones, because of Luther's own direction to obey secular rulers, falls down when applied to Brandenburg or Prussia. 'Instead of encouraging political submissiveness and governmental authoritarianism, . . .

Lutheranism in Brandenburg-Prussia actually promoted the very opposite: constitutionalism and political engagement.' Consequently John Sigismund's action 'weakened rather than strengthened the ruler's hand'.[70] On the other hand the Lutheran Estates' combativeness at home went together with passivity towards the outside. As we have seen, when Frederick William succeeded to the electorate he immediately accepted their demands to withdraw from the Thirty Years War and to restore their domestic power. This meant the new ruler's Calvinism appeared less relevant at first. As he came, however, to develop a more adventurist foreign policy in the late 1640s and 1650s and to strengthen his position within Brandenburg, the difference in religion between Elector and subjects became more important. Although Frederick William eventually won the upper hand over the Lutheran Estates in Brandenburg and Prussia, his political victory was not accompanied by a religious one but by the compromise of toleration.

Much has been made of the contribution of Calvinism to the Great Elector's political success. For instance Otto Hintze even claimed Calvinism 'formed the bridge by which western European raison d'état made its entry into Brandenburg', allowing her to become 'in the seventeenth century a progressive European state, comparable to France or Holland, in which regional political and confessional interests were subordinated to the general welfare of the state'. Gerhard Oestreich developed this further by stressing the simultaneous influence on the Hohenzollern dynasty of neo-stoic ideas fashionable in the late sixteenth and early seventeenth centuries in the Dutch Republic.[71] While all this can be exaggerated and Calvinism and neo-stoicism did little for the weak John Sigismund and George William, such ideas may have had a more positive effect with the more dynamic Frederick William, especially when events moved in the crown's favour. The influence of Calvinism, with its hold on the ruler and court, was inevitably out of all proportion to the size of its communion. Calvinism and neo-stoicism probably did encourage elitist and absolutist attitudes in Frederick William and those closest to him, as well as a more open approach to ideas from outside, especially from western Europe. An important direct influence was the Calvinist cleric Johann Bergius, court preacher in Berlin for over forty years till his death in 1658. Bergius continually emphasised the rights of the ruler before those of his subjects, and he argued, like Luther, that the latter had no other recourse but passive obedience, since 'The worst tyranny is always better than a state without any sovereign at all'.[72] Whereas Calvinism was often associated elsewhere with rebellious Estates and parliaments, in seventeenth-century Germany it identified more with ruling princes. Like Pietism later, Calvinism here did not question absolutism or lead to dissent.[73] Moreover, the Calvinist church in Brandenburg was tied closely to the ruler. There was no independent system of synods as in Scotland or the Dutch Republic, and even the Huguenot refugees were not allowed them. Instead the ruler appointed the few Calvinist ministers and court preachers, at the same time circumventing the traditional Lutheran patronage system.

It was not till Frederick William's reign that the sovereign's own faith ceased to be a serious political handicap, at least in Brandenburg. The Peace of Westphalia made his position much stronger than his predecessors': it legitimised his Calvinism in the eyes of Emperor and Empire and of most of his own Lutheran subjects. None the less, the Elector did not capitalise on this to undermine the predominance of the Lutherans or convert them. He continued the pragmatic toleration of his predecessors. In the agreement of 1653 with the Brandenburg Estates he pledged never to use 'compulsion or force' against his Lutheran subjects, 'since we have never thought to claim for Ourselves dominion over consciences'. He pointed out that they enjoyed far more freedom than Lutheran rulers allowed his co-religionists. While confirming Lutheran patronage rights over livings and schools, he did insist that control of the university at Frankfurt an der Oder should be shared with the Calvinists.[74] He also assured the Estates that toleration in Brandenburg of public or private worship would be limited to the two mainstream Protestant faiths. Although he repeated in this agreement his own, and his predecessors', promises to prefer native Lutheran nobles for ecclesiastical and secular offices (the *Indigenatsrecht*), in practice he was to appoint Calvinist nobles, commoners and foreigners as his chief servants. In this way he confirmed Calvinist control at the centre; the eclipse of the Estates of course was to make this easier.

To flout the *Indigenatsrecht* would have been impossible in Prussia, where Calvinism effectively existed only in the person of the Hohenzollern duke, disappearing when he left the country. As the duchy was outside the Empire, the religious provisions of Westphalia were immaterial, and even Frederick William's assumption of sovereignty in 1657, while strengthening him politically, produced no fundamental religious change. His hope to extend the existing toleration of Catholics there to his fellow Calvinists was whistling in the wind. While a few offices were opened to Calvinists and three churches allowed in the ports in the 1660s (see p. 140), this scarcely affected the Lutheran monopoly and little changed before his death. He did, however, discourage the Estates from persecuting Protestant sectaries who had fled from Poland in the 1660s and 1670s. He wrote to Schwerin in May 1673, granting the petition of one group, the Arians, to stay in Prussia: 'It is wrong to deny people this, if they remain peaceable'.[75]

The eclipse of the Estates in Brandenburg from the time of the War of the North might have been expected to have led to an assault on the Lutheran position there. This did not happen: Frederick William was not a zealot in the mould of Ferdinand II or James II. He shared the views of theologians, including Bergius, who believed Calvinists and Lutherans should tolerate each other and reconcile doctrinal differences. Unfortunately, many Lutherans considered syncretism worse than conversion to Islam, and in 1662 some pastors even followed divines at the Saxon University of Wittenberg, the cradle of Lutheranism, in protesting against the toleration of Calvinists by the Peace of Westphalia. Determined to maintain religious peace within his own lands, Frederick William responded in June 1662 with an edict confirming this clause of the peace and ordering all pastors to do the same in writing. They were also warned not to censure fellow Protestants but to live peaceably together. At the same time he forbade his subjects from studying in Wittenberg and instructed his Privy Council to deny livings to dogmatic Lutherans. The following year Lutheran and Calvinist clerics were invited to the Berlin *Schloß* to resolve their differences under Schwerin's chairmanship. Inevitably this generated more dissension than harmony. The most distinguished Lutheran there, the hymn writer Paul Gerhardt, accepted that an individual Calvinist might be a Christian but denied Calvinism in itself could make a man one. Frederick William, therefore, issued two more edicts in 1664 and 1665, calling on both sides not to condemn each other. As Gerhardt and two other pastors refused, they were stripped of their livings. After being given a further chance to conform in 1667, they were again dismissed, and Gerhardt left for Saxony.[76] This was the end of attempts at reconciliation, although Frederick William continued to hope for Protestant union for the rest of his life. This was well known enough for William III in 1685 to speak of 'This reunion [of Protestants] which he wishes to bring about in his own lands and by his example'.[77]

Although Frederick William's decrees of the early 1660s are often called toleration edicts, they were merely further attempts to reassure the two main Protestant faiths and to persuade them to live harmoniously together. They certainly did not extend formal toleration to Catholics and Protestant sectaries in Brandenburg (unlike in Cleves and to some extent in Prussia), both being forbidden to hold private or public services. It was not till the reign of the Elector's grandson, King Frederick William I, that Catholics were allowed a church in Berlin. However, the few Catholics in the electorate were not disturbed, and as early as 1647, in pressing his claims to Minden in the Westphalian peace negotiations, the Elector had assured the French that Catholics there would be left in peace, as 'in our other hereditary lands'.[78] Jesuits, however, were different: the French minister, Rébenac, noted in 1687 that in the few years he had been in Berlin, 'Frederick William has expelled more than twenty people accused of Jesuitry'.[79]

The peculiar religious position of his dynasty in Brandenburg-Prussia meant Frederick William, like his two predecessors, had to reject the contemporary belief, one also held by his Lutheran subjects, in religious conformity and unity of church and state. This was to push him inevitably towards ruling as a more secular prince. Hohenzollern absolutism could not be a confessional one like that of Catholic France, Spain, the Austrian Habsburg Monarchy or even Lutheran Denmark or Sweden. While this was essentially practical politics on his part, his attitude towards the sectaries in Prussia and the Jews in Brandenburg (see pp. 186–7) does show he was unusually tolerant. As early as 1649 he told his Privy Council: 'In religious matters we have never approved the public exercise of a forbidden religion, but that one or two should hold a service in their own home in private, no one hopefully will take offence.' In 1670 Prince Johann Moritz of Nassau and Frederick William's second son, the later King Frederick I, attended a Jewish wedding. Frederick William also pressed his government in Halberstadt to pay to restore a synagogue destroyed there by a mob in 1669.[80] And in 1686 he had his secretary, Paul Fuchs, draw up a letter for the Duke of Savoy, explaining why he was allowing the Waldensian refugees from Savoy into his lands:

> Differences between religious communities certainly produce violent hatreds, yet older and holier is the law of nature, which obliges men to support, tolerate and help one another . . . since without these bonds

151

of human society, which tie civilised and uncivilised people together throughout the world, they can never communicate with each other.[81]

There can be no doubt about the Elector's own religious convictions. We find him telling the English minister, Southwell, in 1680: 'I am very grateful for the blessings I have received from God. I will never forget God: he has never deserted me.'[82] His mixture of piety and tolerance comes out in his *Political Testament* for his successor in 1667, at the time of his spat with dogmatic Lutheranism. This was full of Protestant concepts of the paternalistic godly ruler, whose authority like that of Old Testament kings came from God, and who had to set his subjects an example by a God-fearing, 'sober and sensible life'. He urged his heir to 'love the subjects God has given you, regardless of their religion, as a proper father of the country [*Landesvater*], always willingly to further their profit and well-being in right things, above all to develop commerce, and to keep in mind increasing the population, especially of the electorate of Brandenburg'. In this convoluted way he was clearly trying to justify some form of toleration on economic and demographic grounds. But at the same time he warned against being completely disinterested: he urged his heir to appoint Calvinist advisers and ensure 'the Reformed religion . . . is firmly planted in all your lands, although without using force and dispossessing the Lutheran church'. He should do this out of his 'own pocket' by inviting Calvinists into the country and giving them positions. While insisting past promises not to impose Calvinism should be kept, and describing the Lutherans as allies against Catholicism, he advised expelling bigoted and intolerant Lutheran pastors. Clearly hostile to the Catholics, he said he was relieved Brandenburg and Pomerania 'are quite free of the papists' gross abominations and idolatry except what the Lutherans have kept of papist ceremonial in their churches'. He therefore urged they never be allowed to celebrate the mass openly or privately there, although the treaty commitments to allow this in Prussia and the Rhineland should be honoured.[83] In practice, however, the non-Jesuit Catholics in Brandenburg and Pomerania were to be left in peace.

Despite the advice in his *Political Testament*, Frederick William did not attempt vigorously or methodically to spread his own religion. He merely encouraged Calvinist communities in the chief towns by appointing court preachers there from the 1650s and filling a few livings in the Neumark with sympathetic pastors. A far more effective way of expanding the Reformed faith of course was his policy of attracting foreign immigrants and refugees. Yet in 1680, before the main influx of Huguenots, there were only around sixteen Reformed churches in the whole of Brandenburg.[84] On the other hand systematic efforts were made to ensure that the central government remained almost completely in Calvinist hands. While a few advisers, such as Canstein, remained Lutheran, the rest, such as Burgsdorff, Waldeck, Schwerin, Somnitz, Meinders and Fuchs, were all Calvinists or converts.

Official toleration for Lutherans in Brandenburg and Prussia, for Catholics in Cleves-Mark, Minden and Prussia, and tacit toleration of sundry sectaries and Jews, where the Estates would allow it, probably made the Hohenzollern lands under the Great Elector, even if more by chance than design, more tolerant than contemporary Britain or Holland.[85] The Hohenzollerns' conversion also produced lasting effects internationally. Dynastic alliances were now mainly contracted with Reformed families, such as those of the Palatinate and Hesse and, more importantly, with the Dutch house of Orange. This allowed the crown to break free from the narrow policies of its Lutheran Estates, whose horizons were restricted to Brandenburg, her immediate German neighbours and the emperor. The dynasty began to mix with another more cosmopolitan and commercially minded world, that of the Dutch, English and French.[86] These family connections, and the diverse problems thrown up by ruling such far-flung territories, allowed, as well as forced, the Hohenzollerns to lift Brandenburg above the other German principalities and to play a significant, if secondary, role in the European arena.

In Frederick William's case, this European role cannot be seen in purely political terms. He also saw himself very much as an evangelical ruler. Like the Calvinist Oliver Cromwell and Frederick William's own nephew William III, but also like his uncle, the Lutheran Gustavus Adolphus, he believed Protestantism in Europe had to be protected from resurgent Catholicism. A constant thread through his foreign policy was its *Protestantism*. In the 1650s and 1660s his actions in the Imperial Diet showed that he certainly thought of himself as part of the Protestant community in the Empire,[87] and he often conducted his diplomacy in terms of religious leagues. He was always uneasy about his cooperation with the Catholic Emperor during the War of the North, and in his *Political Testament* he urged his son to try to cooperate with fellow-Protestant states, especially in Germany, against the Emperor, who threatened both Protestant and princely liberties. Above all he should work with the Dutch, the dynasty's oldest and closest ally, chiefly because of their Calvinism. In the 1670s Frederick William's great work was to help the survival of Dutch political independence, the bastion of Protestantism. His political alliance with Louis XIV in the 1680s, a sound one on financial and even strategic grounds, finally collapsed when it became all too obvious that French hegemony was endangering European Protestantism. It distorts Frederick William's foreign policy, however, to call him 'the champion of religious freedom and tolerance in Europe'. The religious freedom and tolerance he was seeking was for European Protestantism. It is true that he saw no particular merit in persecuting individual Catholics. But his appeals to universal principles of toleration should be read as intended to guarantee this above all for endangered Protestants.[88]

If Frederick William had little effect on his subjects' religious beliefs and practices, he had even less on their intellectual life and institutions. Because of the success and influence of the nineteenth-century Prussian educational system, historians have inevitably tried to trace his hand in this. It has been a futile task. Although Frederick William has sometimes been credited with founding the Calvinist university of Duisburg in 1655, it was mainly the work of the Cleves Estates. He merely gave the project his blessing, and its development was stymied by lack of money. The two existing universities at Königsberg and Frankfurt an der Oder had the same problem, and their faculties remained unimpressive, despite Frederick William's occasional attempts to attract foreign scholars there. The odd gift of a scientific instrument was no substitute for cash.[89] At a lower level, the Elector did issue several edicts, urging towns and villages to set up schools. But these were little more than pious gestures and were never followed up. Those schools in church hands before the Thirty Years War had disappeared during it, and there was no rebuilding before the end of the century.[90] More was done in Berlin, however, where there were two grammar schools. The small Calvinist gymnasium at Joachimsthal had been destroyed during the Thirty Years War. Frederick William allowed it to be housed in the Berlin *Schloß* and in 1667 he bought it a new building. He showed less interest in the much larger Lutheran Graues Kloster gymnasium, which eventually had around 400 pupils, but in 1682 the Electress Dorothea seems to have persuaded him to give it some financial help. The year before he had also set up a new gymnasium in the suburb of Friedrichswerder. This school took boys from both Protestant faiths, and it received some funds from him. In Prussia there were three gymnasia, established in 1588, but none appears to have been supported by Frederick William himself.[91]

. . .

NOTES AND REFERENCES

1 F. Hirsch, 'Die Armee des Großen Kurfürsten und ihre Unterhaltung während der Jahre 1660–1666', *Historische Zeitschrift*, 53 (1885), pp. 231ff.
2 Fay, 'The beginnings', pp. 774f.
3 Dietrich, *Die politischen Testamente*, p. 51.
4 Carsten, *Origins*, pp. 244–6, and Droysen, part 3, II, pp. 377, 515. For increasing support for the Elector see Kloosterhuis, p. 107.
5 E. Opgenoorth, 'Stände im Spannungsfeld zwischen Brandenburg-Preußen, Pfalz-Neuburg und den niederländischen Generalstaaten: Cleve-Mark und Jülich-Berg im Vergleich', in Baumgart, ed., *Ständetum*, p. 247.
6 See R. Vierhaus, 'Die Landstände in Nordwestdeutschland im späteren 18. Jahrhundert', in Gerhard, ed., *Ständische Vertretungen*, p. 83, and D. Stievermann, 'Absolutischer Zentralismus oder Ständischer Regionalismus? Preußen und seine westlichen Provinzen im 17. und 18. Jahrhundert', *Westfälischer Zeitschrift*, 138 (1988).
7 Carsten, *Origins*, p. 247.
8 Opgenoorth, 'Stände im Spannungsfeld', pp. 258f.
9 Opgenoorth, 'Johan Maurits as the stadtholder', pp. 41f.
10 For him see Jacoby.
11 Philippson, I, p. 395.
12 J. Małłek, 'Eine andersartige Lösung. Absolutischer Staatsreich in Preußen im Jahre 1663', *Parliaments, Estates and Representation*, 10 (1990), p. 181. This article can also be found in Małłek's, *Preußen und Polen: Politik, Stände und Kultur vom 16. bis zum 18. Jahrhundert* (Stuttgart, 1992).
13 For the whole question of seventeenth-century absolutism, especially in Germany, see the intelligent and wide-ranging *Absolutism in Central Europe* by P.H. Wilson (London, 2000), passim.
14 Carsten, *Origins*, pp. 209f.
15 Droysen, part 3, II, p. 383.
16 *Urk. u. Akt.*, IX, p. 830, Frederick William to Schwerin, Cleves, 2 June 1661.
17 Pagès, p. 54.
18 Philippson, II, p. 165.
19 Meinardus, 'Kurfürst Friedrich Wilhelms', p. 63.
20 For this see especially Małłek, 'Eine andersartige Lösung', passim, and Carsten, *Origins*, pp. 210ff.

21 Małłek, 'Eine andersartige Lösung', p. 182.
22 B. Schumacher, *Geschichte Ost- und Westpreußens*, 2nd edn (Würzburg, 1957), p. 174.
23 Waddington, *Prusse*, I, p. 351.
24 Rachel, *Große Kurfürst*, pp. 28f.
25 Małłek, 'Eine andersartige Lösung', p. 181.
26 For him see ibid., p. 179; Rachel, *Große Kurfürst*, pp. 60f.; and Carsten, *Origins*, p. 214.
27 Fay, *The Rise*, p. 61.
28 Tümpel, p. 40.
29 Lackner, p. 96.
30 Waddington, *Prusse*, I, p. 351.
31 Hüttl, p. 278.
32 L. von Ranke, *Memoirs of the House of Brandenburg and History of Prussia during the Seventeenth and Eighteenth Centuries* (London, 1849), I, pp. 50f. He was particularly worried in case of a minority, see *Urk. u. Akt.*, IX, p. 836.
33 Małłek, 'Eine andersartige Lösung', p. 185.
34 Droysen, part 3, II, p. 453.
35 Jacoby, pp. 141, 143.
36 Waddington, *Prusse*, I, pp. 352f.
37 *Urk. u. Akten*, IX, pp. 846f.
38 Pagès, p. 79.
39 Tümpel, p. 53.
40 See K. Deppermann, 'Die Kirchenpolitik des Großen Kurfürsten', *Pietismus und Neuzeit*, 6 (1980), p. 109, and Lackner, pp. 167ff. In 1668 Frederick William also forced Königsberg to accept Calvinists as citizens.
41 Hartmann, 'Gefährdetes Erbe etc', in Heinrich, ed., *Ein sonderbares Licht*, p. 121.
42 Philippson, II, p. 183.
43 Dietrich, *Die politischen Testamente*, pp. 52f., 198–200.
44 Rachel, *Große Kurfürst*, p. 57.
45 Ibid., p. 39.
46 Hein, p. 264.
47 Rachel, *Große Kurfürst*, p. 13.
48 Tümpel, p. 67, and Waddington, *Prusse*, I, p. 356.
49 For the episode see Nachama, p. 100, and Opgenoorth, ' "Nervus rerum" ', p. 105.
50 Philippson, II, p. 196.
51 Ibid.
52 Tümpel, p. 48.
53 See Hartmann, 'Gefährdetes Erbe', p. 126.
54 H. Rosenberg, *Bureaucracy, Aristocracy and Autocracy: The Prussian Experience, 1660–1815* (Cambridge, MA, 1958), p. 34.

55 Rachel, *Große Kurfürst*, p. 237.
56 Figures from Fay, 'The beginnings', p. 771, note 18, and Rachel, *Große Kurfürst*, p. 237. The figures for Pomerania are sic. In 1697–8 Prussia, with 38.4 per cent of the whole population, was still paying 16.4 per cent of taxation, while Brandenburg, with 24.3 per cent of the population, paid 32 per cent.
57 Rachel, *Große Kurfürst*, pp. 300f.
58 Tümpel, p. 101.
59 Carsten, *Origins*, p. 226.
60 1/11 June, 7/17 July, Berlin, Southwell to Jenkins, PRO, SP 105/49.
61 Rachel, *Große Kurfürst*, p. 199.
62 Hartmann, 'Gefährdetes Erbe', p. 130.
63 Opgenoorth, '"Nervus rerum"', pp. 107ff.
64 Lackner, p. 304.
65 He had been a secret Calvinist since 1606 and probably converted through personal belief, rather than to win Dutch and Palatine support over the Cleves-Jülich dispute: it would have made more political sense to have stayed Lutheran because of his claims to Prussia, since his action alienated Catholic Poland and Emperor as well as Lutheran Saxony. See Nischan, *Prince, People*, pp. 81ff.
66 Ibid., pp. 196, 209.
67 Deppermann, 'Die Kirchenpolitk', pp. 100f.
68 See G. Heinrich, 'Religionstoleranz in Brandenburg-Preußen: Idee und Wirklichkeit', in M. Schlenke, ed., *Preußen: Beiträge zu einer politischen Kultur* (Reinbeck bei Hamburg, 1981), pp. 36, 63, and Lackner, p. 56.
69 B. Nischan, 'The second Reformation in Brandenburg: aims and goals', *Sixteenth Century Journal*, 14 (1983), pp. 37f.
70 Nischan, *Prince, People*, pp. 247f.
71 For a useful summary see ibid., p. 246.
72 B. Nischan, 'Calvinism, the Thirty Years' War, and the beginning of absolutism in Brandenburg: the political thought of John Bergius', *Central European History*, 15 (1982), pp. 219–22. The most important neo-stoic thinker, Lipsius, had similarly emphasised princely authority, see E.P. Bos and H.A. Krop, eds, *Franco Burgersdijk, 1590–1635, Neo-Aristotelianism in Leiden* (Amsterdam, 1993), p. 146, and Oestreich *Neostoicism*, pp. 39ff.
73 See P.S. Fichtner, *Protestantism and Primogeniture in Early Modern Germany* (New Haven, CT, 1989), p. 153. For the alliance of Calvinism and one German court, see Clasen.
74 Lackner, p. 112. He repeated much the same formula to the Prussian Estates in 1661: 'We wish to have no conscience constrained', Philippson, III, p. 127.
75 Philippson, III, p. 155.
76 See Deppermann, 'Die Kirchenpolitik', pp. 110ff.

77 Droysen, part 3, III, p. 277.
78 Spannagel, *Minden*, p. 12.
79 R. Fester, 'Zur Kritik der Berliner Berichte Rebenacs', *Historische Zeitschrift*, 92 (1904), p. 5.
80 Beuys, pp. 134, 298, 303f.
81 Lackner, p. 300.
82 Philippson, III, p. 126.
83 Dietrich, ed., *Die politischen Testamente*, pp. 179ff.
84 Philippson, III, p. 137.
85 This is the conclusion of Lackner, p. 307, and G. Birtsch, 'Pflichthandeln und Staatsräson. Die Gründer des preußischen Staats Kurfürst Friedrich Wilhelm im Spiegel der Geschichtschreibung', in Heinrich, ed., *Ein sonderbares Licht*, p. 148.
86 See C. Hinrichs, *Der Große Kurfürst* (Berlin, 1956), p. 56.
87 See A. Schindling, 'Der Große Kurfürst und das Reich', in Heinrich, ed., *Ein sonderbares Licht*, p. 63.
88 See footnote 81 above about Savoy. In July 1677, in urging Leopold I to stop mistreating his Hungarian Protestants, he wrote 'past and present experience shows that forcing men's consciences inevitably leads them to desperate actions and decisions'. Philippson, III, p. 145.
89 See Opgenoorth, *Friedrich Wilhelm*, I, p. 296, II, p. 60.
90 Schultze, *Prignitz*, p. 317.
91 Philippson, III, pp. 171–3.

Chapter 7

FISCAL AND MILITARY POWER

· · ·
FINANCES AND THE TAX SYSTEM

Frederick William's ambitions were continually hampered by his territories' poor resources. Although various attempts were made to bring some order to the financial system, success was inevitably limited: first, because of his disparate possessions, and second, because his revenues came from two main sources, those more or less under his direct control and those dependent on the cooperation of the Estates. He had most freedom of manoeuvre over his personal revenues, those produced by his domain lands (he owned around a third of Brandenburg and more than half of Prussia) and what were usually known as the *regalia* – tolls, mines and monopolies. Initial attempts to manage these personal revenues in Brandenburg through committees in the early 1650s had been disappointing (see pp. 166–72) and from 1655 they were largely entrusted to a single minister, the head of the treasury for the domains (*Amtskammer*, known after 1689 as the *Hofkammer*). This minister had various titles, *Kammerdirektor*, *Kammerpräsident* or *Hofkammerpräsident*, and most holders of the office were non-native. Each tried to extend his control over the ruler's personal revenues in Brandenburg to the other Hohenzollern lands as well, usually meeting resistance from the local administrations there. In August 1655 the Westphalian Raban von Canstein was appointed Brandenburg *Kammerpräsident*, and after four years he was also put in charge of the personal revenues elsewhere.[1] He proved diligent and competent and had the advantage of not being distracted by other duties. When he retired in 1674 he had achieved a fivefold increase in the Brandenburg domains and *regalia* revenues on the 1652–3 figure of 100,000 thalers.

This was managed by tighter accounting, insistence on revenues being paid in cash not kind, and sustained efforts to claw back alienated and mortgaged domain lands. Attempts were also made to do the same in the other Hohenzollern territories, since Frederick William himself, by now, had grasped that he needed some overall supervision of all his personal revenues, and he was determined to support Canstein's systematic approach, promising in 1663 'to hold his hand'.[2] With able subordinates in Prussia and the Rhenish lands, Canstein provided Frederick William for the first time with 'an orderly and centralised financial administration' and a much clearer idea of income and expenditure.[3] He lacked imagination, however, and avoided innovations, often feeling the job itself was beyond him. In 1669 he offered to resign, writing:

> Prussia sends nothing, Lauenburg and Bütow nothing; only 2,000 thalers have come from Pomerania; the Neumark revenues are spent on officials' salaries and fortifications; the Electorate's domain lands only provide grain, which goes to the court . . . ; Halberstadt largely consumes its own revenues; Minden has paid more than it should; Ravensberg is in debt; Cleves pays nothing and invents complaints.[4]

After Canstein's retirement in the middle of the Dutch War, Jena, Gladebeck and then Meinders tried to cope inadequately, while filling other posts. At last in 1683 the East Friesland noble Dodo von Knyphausen was put in charge, although he was not given the actual title *Hofkammerpräsident* till 1687. He had experience in the Estates administration of East Friesland, and Frederick William recruited him specifically to bring real order into the personal revenues of all his territories. He stayed in office till 1697 but never had a staff of more than six or even his own room for meetings.[5] From the start, however, he was determined to get the finances right, and his appointment was the turning point in their management under both Frederick William and his successors.[6] Knyphausen was probably 'as significant in his influence upon the financial administration of Brandenburg-Prussia as Colbert was in France', and has even been credited with establishing 'the principles of the administration of [King] Frederick William I'.[7] Although Knyphausen's most important work lay in the next reign, of Elector Frederick III (King Frederick I), much was done beforehand. In 1689, in a move planned before Frederick William's death, he established the *Hofkammer*, 'a central financial college', which was independent of the Privy Council and supervised not only the Brandenburg treasuries (there were still three) but also those of the other lands.[8] It was institutionalised so that it could survive from one head to the next. Previously, in 1685–6, he had drawn up a proper budget for all the Hohenzollern lands, giving the Elector for the first time in his reign an accurate idea of the state of his revenues and expenses. He also established a far more profitable supervision of the leases of the domain lands. Between 1681 and 1695 the revenues from these throughout the territories more than doubled.[9] His policies seem to have had an almost immediate effect, although the recovery in agriculture in the 1680s and 1690s certainly helped. In the Privy Council in October 1685, he felt confident enough to promise that increased domain revenues would make good the French subsidy of 200,000 thalers a year if Louis XIV withdrew it.[10]

The Hohenzollerns' domains and *regalia* had always provided their most dependable income. Far less sure were those revenues voted by the Estates and imposed on town and countryside as the contributions: these were irregular at best, and both the collecting and spending of the money had been largely controlled by the Estates' own officials. But from 1651 the Brandenburg contributions were paid into a War Chest (*Kriegskasse*), and over the next two decades this gradually began to receive similar contributions from the other Hohenzollern lands. By 1674 it had become the General War Chest (*Generalfeldkriegskasse*) and had long since been taken from the Estates' control. As these were revenues approved, if increasingly notionally, by the Estates' representatives specifically for military ends, they were kept separate throughout the reign from the Elector's personal domains and *regalia* revenues. By the 1660s Frederick William had managed throughout his territories to turn the contribution from what had been considered an emergency tax during the Thirty Years War into a permanent one to pay for a standing army and future conflicts. Until the 1680s the level of these taxes fluctuated, depending on whether the Elector was at war or not. The signature of peace with the French and Swedes in 1679, however, was not followed by the usual reduction. Instead, during the 1680s taxes remained almost at a wartime level (see table on p. 144).

While Frederick William's main difficulty was persuading all his Estates to vote what he considered adequate contributions, a further one was that taxes were allotted according to the balance of elite power within the various Estates rather than the actual wealth of his different lands. For example, in Cleves-Mark, where the rich towns were in the ascendant, the peasantry bore the greatest burden, while in Brandenburg the weak and impoverished towns paid most, since the dominant Junkers wanted to limit the taxes paid by their dependent peasants, especially as the latter were also usually burdened by the military's demands for animals, victuals and fodder. The ideal solution would have been to increase taxation on the towns in the Rhineland and to end the Junkers' exemptions in the electorate, but it was hardly realistic to tax the most powerful the heaviest. Moreover, while Frederick William would have welcomed taxing the urban elite of Cleves-Mark, he shared the contemporary assumption that nobles did not pay direct taxation. In Cleves-Mark he worked to exempt them and he had no intention of challenging their tax privileges elsewhere. Yet Frederick William and his ministers did see the need to widen the tax base and also felt some unease at the burden on the Brandenburg towns, especially because tax there was paid on land and property, which discouraged rebuilding houses and workshops. In 1661, therefore, he suggested to a Brandenburg representative diet that the contribution taxes on urban and peasant land should be replaced by an excise tax on the sale of goods in town and countryside. Such a tax was already a success in the Dutch Republic and neighbouring Saxony. The noble deputies, however, rejected the proposal in horror: it would bring the Junkers within the tax net, end their exemption and reduce them to the same tax level as the peasantry. They were doubly concerned because they also enjoyed the traditional right to import and export goods to and from their manors free of tolls. Their vehement opposition, and doubts among his own noble councillors, caused Frederick William temporarily to shelve the proposal. But the idea had aroused great interest in the towns as a way to reduce their unequal tax load. Consequently in 1663 burghers from some of the Brandenburg towns wrote to Frederick William in support of it.

While the Elector was encouraged by this, it was not till January 1667 that he again proposed a general excise to another representative diet. As the noble deputies would still not give way and he was reluctant to override them, a compromise was worked out over the following months. He issued a decree promising to save the towns 'from final ruin and complete destruction' by ensuring 'the public burdens were somewhat more evenly distributed, not all laid only on the poor, nor levied exclusively on land and houses'. The towns were allowed, if they wished, to introduce an 'excise, towards which all inhabitants without distinction shall contribute, . . . according to whether his consumption is large or small'. It was to be imposed at various rates on sales of food and drink, the movement of goods, and on slaughterhouses, mills and breweries. The magistrates were warned to ensure that tradesmen did not use it as an excuse 'to raise their prices excessively'.[11] Pressure from urban taxpayers soon led to many towns' adopting the new excise, and the Elector himself remained in favour, declaring in February 1671 that it was 'the most Christian and fairest' tax of all.[12] The excise certainly had an immediate benefit, encouraging the first serious urban rebuilding since the Thirty Years War. In Berlin, for example, 150 houses were rebuilt in the two years after 1667, and the city council in 1671 claimed that because of the excise, 'almost all waste plots have been built on, old houses repaired; and there is a rush to buy houses'.[13] On the other hand the new tax undoubtedly increased the cost of living for the urban poor because it was chiefly on staple goods. However, as the poor's interests were never considered, more and more towns adopted the tax during the 1670s. Eventually between 1680 and 1682 Frederick William imposed it on all Brandenburg towns. As in many other spheres, he also extended the Brandenburg pattern of the excise to Prussia, Pomerania, Magdeburg and Halberstadt during the 1670s and 1680s. In Minden, where the excise was adopted in 1674, it was imposed on countryside as well as towns, although three years later nobles and officials were exempted from paying on some articles after the Estates protested.[14] Cleves and Mark, nevertheless, escaped completely, since the urban-dominated Estates there were still too strong to challenge.

Except in Minden, the contribution taxes remained in force elsewhere in the countryside. This dual pattern of rural and urban taxation continued till the nineteenth century, and it meant an administrative as well as socio-economic divergence between country and town. While taxes were now imposed, ostensibly, more fairly on the towns, the excise ultimately retarded urban recovery and growth;[15] trade and industry conducted in the countryside, especially on the Junkers' manors, could develop free from the excise. The excise system suited Frederick William because of his reluctance to attack the economic interests of the Junkers, but it was hardly an ideal way to extract most revenues from his eastern territories. It worked best in countries with more developed commercial economies and urban centres, such as Holland, England and even Saxony. In the predominantly agricultural economies of Brandenburg and Prussia what was needed was a land tax to tap noble as well as peasant wealth.

One attraction of the excise for Frederick William was that the Estates had no hand in administering it. Moreover, because of disputes over its collection by the urban magistrates, he imposed an 'excise director' on Berlin in 1667 and commissioners in the other towns afterwards. These new officials soon began to interfere in other areas and thereby undermine urban autonomy. Variously called *Steuerrat* or *Commissarius loci*, these tax commissioners soon took over the duties of the war commissioners and received orders from the General War Commissariat (for this body see pp. 165–9). This led to much tighter central control over the towns.[16]

As the excise was imposed directly, with no discussion with the town magistrates or the representative diets, the Brandenburg urban deputies ceased to be invited to the latter or the permanent committee. These now came to represent the Junker nobility exclusively. Although after the War of the North these bodies were too weak to refuse the crown's contribution demands, they were still an irritant because they often raised grievances. The Elector therefore came to prefer dealing directly with the nobility at a local level, through assemblies in the provincial circles, the *Kreistage*.[17] Here consultation proved even more of a formality, and the contributions were effectively imposed on the countryside. This was made easier because of the gradual replacement over the coming years of the Estates' officials by the Elector's own administration to collect taxation here as well as in the towns.[18]

While the tax burden was shared unfairly among different social groups, there was territorial disparity as well. Prussia and Cleves-Mark, richer and more populated than Brandenburg but where political opposition was strongest, paid less. The newest and weakest territories, Halberstadt, Magdeburg, Minden and Pomerania, contributed most of all. For example, Halberstadt, a sixteenth the size of Brandenburg and with a tenth of its population, paid nearly a quarter of what the electorate paid. Overall Frederick William's reign probably saw a trebling of total revenues from all sources.[19] At his accession they were about 1 million thalers on paper, 40 per cent from the contributions and 60 per cent from his domains and *regalia*, although very little was in fact received by the crown. When he died, the revenues of nearly 3.5 million thalers were coming half and half from both sources; while prices for most goods doubled during the reign,[20] this was probably more than compensated for by most revenues actually reaching him. In addition to his domestic income, Frederick William often benefited from foreign subsidies.

These of course varied from 250,000 thalers in 1685 to 64,000 three years later.[21]

• • •
THE GENERAL WAR COMMISSARIAT

Frederick William received far more of his tax revenue in his last years because he acquired direct control of the collection and use of the contribution taxes through the development of a new institution, the General War Commissariat (*Generalkriegskommissariat*). This body was eventually to elbow aside the Estates, their local officials, and even the Privy Council. Its combination of tax collecting with its original function, military administration, owed much to the example of Louis XIV's France. But in Brandenburg-Prussia it went far beyond this French model to become the basis for the whole government into the next century. The General War Commissariat grew out of the system of war commissioners, existing in Brandenburg and throughout Germany in the early seventeenth century.[22] During the Thirty Years War the Brandenburg Estates had followed the conventional practice of appointing the leading official of the local circle (*Kreis*) to raise the contributions and to cooperate with the regimental colonels in recruiting, paying, supplying and quartering troops. Whether called war commissioner (*Kriegskommissar*), provincial commissioner (*Landkommissar*) or circle commissioner (*Kreiskommissar*), they were the same official.

As with much else in Brandenburg, the impetus for setting up the General War Commissariat and closer crown control came from Count Waldeck after he ousted Burgsdorff. From 1651 Waldeck gradually began to detach supervision of military affairs from the Privy Council, and as war between Sweden and Poland became inevitable early in 1655, he drew up a memorandum for Frederick William, suggesting 'a permanent War Council [*Kriegsrat*] ... responsible for organizing and maintaining the army and its logistic support, including responsibility for raising and distributing money for the army'. This resulted in April in the appointment of a General War Commissioner (*Generalkriegskommissar*).[23] While Otto von Sparr, as *de facto* commander-in-chief (the Elector himself was nominally this), was responsible for deploying the army, the new General War Commissioner and his rudimentary commissariat (*Generalkriegskommissariat*) ensured that it could actually function. The man appointed was

Klaus Ernst von Platen, a Prignitz noble, member of the Privy Council and former *Kriegskommissar*, who had studied at Leiden. Although he was assigned to Brandenburg, from the start there was also an *Oberkommissar* in both Cleves and Prussia, Ludwig and Wallenrodt, who acted as his deputies. With Frederick William's approval, Platen quickly freed his *Generalkriegskommissariat* from control by both Privy Council and commander-in-chief, although it was formally subordinate to both. There was inevitably some friction, especially with Sparr. Areas of responsibility were not sharply defined, and this was inescapable in the seventeenth century. Real separation of function in offices could not develop easily in any case under such an energetic ruler as Frederick William, who believed everything was done in his name and expected to decide most things himself.[24] None the less, Platen began to develop an office and role, unifying the state's military and financial administration, in the same way as the two French secretaries of state for war, Le Tellier and Louvois. Like the French ministers, if on a smaller scale, Platen drew up contracts with regimental commanders and oversaw recruiting, paying, supplying and billeting the troops. But allotting and collecting the contribution taxes was still left to the Estates, despite their open hostility to paying for the war. The money itself was paid into a War Chest (*Kriegskasse*) in Berlin, with separate ones in Cleves and Prussia, under Platen's direct control. Overall, it seems likely that the surprising effectiveness of the Brandenburg army in the War of the North, after its disasters earlier in the reign, owed much to the new body.[25]

Platen kept his post in a slimmed-down form at the end of the War of the North, when a small permanent army was maintained. But when he retired in 1667 his replacement, Meinders, was simply given the title of War Councillor (*Kriegsrat*), not becoming a member of the Privy Council till August 1672, when the Dutch War (1672–9) had already begun. This is a clear indication that Frederick William had not yet realised the value in peacetime of the new system. Meinders' position 'radically changed' in importance once the Dutch War broke out,[26] and it was much to his credit that the Brandenburg army did not fall apart in the two Rhine campaigns. But he had none of Platen's independence and was essentially an agent of the Privy Council. Then in June 1675, just after the battle of Fehrbellin, the post of General War Commissioner was revived and given to Bodo von Gladebeck, who had held a similar one in Brunswick service. He was able to carry on Meinders' work with

more independence and to develop the General War Chest
(*Generalfeldkriegskasse*), set up in 1674 to centralise the collection
from all Frederick William's possessions of those revenues intended
for the army, i.e. the contributions, excise and foreign subsidies.
At the end of the war in 1679, Gladebeck was replaced by the
Pomeranian noble and officer Joachim von Grumbkow, who had
already worked with him and was to hold the post till 1690.
Grumbkow's appointment was a watershed on two counts: first, it
showed that the post of *Generalkriegskommissar*, with its subordinate
war commissioners (*Kriegskommissare*), had become as permanent
as the standing army, and second, the man himself was an able
and energetic administrator. Initially, the commander-in-chief,
Derfflinger, was shown Grumbkow's instructions, but this soon
became a mere ritual: '... in practice the *Generalkriegskommissar*
combined the functions of chief of the general staff with those
of the ministers for war and for finance and thus held a key position
in the whole state'.[27] He soon shook off any constraints from the
Privy Council and installed his commissioners throughout the
Hohenzollern territories. He worked side by side, sometimes overlapping, with the *Hofkammerpräsident*, who still managed the revenues intended for non-military purposes. Grumbkow also took
the decisive step to free the Elector almost completely from any
dependence on the Estates. Although the war commissioners had
often acted heavy-handedly in the provinces during wartime, the
circle officials (*Kreiskommissare*), nobles responsible to the Estates,
had always been involved. In peacetime, these *Kreiskommissare* had
collected the contributions on their own and with an eye to protecting their own localities and limiting the effects of the passage and
quartering of troops.[28] Grumbkow now brought them directly under
his control, often combining their functions with the more military ones of his war commissioners. As in the past, the names given
to these officials varied, but now all were essentially servants of the
General War Commissariat, a sign that the rudimentary electoral
bureaucracy was being militarised. Although most were nobles, still
chosen by their fellow Junkers, they were increasingly employed
outside their native circle or province. As Grumbkow's dependants,
these officials, besides deciding what each circle should pay in contributions, began to develop a judicial and police function. They
dealt directly with local grievances rather than passing them on to
the Privy Council as in the past. While their social origins and
continuing family relationships meant their loyalty to the crown

Grumkow

could never be total, the Junkers as a whole strongly resented their interference and their undermining the traditional territorial system of government. In 1683 at a meeting of a representative diet, the Altmark deputies protested that their institutions and privileges were being destroyed; deputies from the Uckermark complained of the Commisariat's 'insufferable usurpations'; and the deputies altogether concluded that their privileges were being 'annulled and emaciated so that no *umbra libertatis* [shadow of liberty] seemed to be left'.[29]

While these complaints from the Brandenburg Estates were just ignored, a more cautious approach was adopted in the Rhineland. In 1684 the General War Commissariat appointed a local noble, Johann von Wilich Bötzlar, as *Oberkommissar* in Cleves. Besides his military duties, he was charged with assessing and collecting taxes, and he soon quarrelled with the Estates. These complained that the traditional government was being usurped. Surprisingly, Frederick William sided with them, and in March 1687 Bötzlar was ordered not to interfere in the taxation voted by the Estates or to meddle with the administration of the towns.[30] It would also be wrong to exaggerate the omnipresence of the General War Commissariat under the Elector. Its staff in Berlin was only 21 in 1691, whereas the total in the other government departments there was 206. None the less, expenditure on the military, for most of Frederick William's reign, amounted to about two-thirds of all his revenues. And the population as a whole has been described as entering a stage of 'proto-militarisation', with the presence of troops and their demands a permanent factor in all their lives.[31]

In the Great Elector's last years his *Generalkriegskommissariat*'s competence was even extended into the general economic sphere. Grumbkow and his commissioners aimed to make Brandenburg self-sufficient in woollen textiles for military uniforms, and they had some success in the 1680s in encouraging the production of coarser weaves. Then in 1685 a French section was added to the Commissariat, to settle the Huguenots. As this also meant helping them start their businesses, the town guilds had to be persuaded to accept the refugees; a by-product of this was to bring the guilds under the Commissariat's control. This acquiring of an economic as well as financial and military dimension was of course very much in line with the ideas of contemporary mercantilist thinkers and practitioners, especially Colbert in France, who linked a state's economic health with its military strength.

By making the *Generalkriegskommisariat*, as well as the *Antskammer*, independent of the Privy Council and by concentrating decision-making in a small cabinet under him, Frederick William had really ensured that these bodies, rather than the Council, would develop over the next half century as the centralising instruments for all the Hohenzollern lands.

. . .

THE ARMY

The hallmark of the early-modern European absolute state was the control exercised by the ruler through the twin pillars of a standing army and an administration.[32] By the eighteenth century in Prussia these institutions were also interdependent. While this synergy began under the Great Elector, above all through the role played by the General War Commissariat, its completeness, or inevitability, should not be overstated before the time of his grandson, King Frederick William I. Until then development was both slow and hesitant, and the late-seventeenth-century army itself was very different from the famous Prussian regiments of Frederick the Great.

At his accession as elector, Frederick William had done his best to rid himself and Brandenburg of his father's useless undisciplined army. By doing this, however, he made even more certain that the Imperialists and Swedes could treat the electorate as they wished. Their continuing depredations, and his own difficulty in garrisoning the few fortresses in his hands, led him to adopt Norprath's schemes to create a small army in Cleves from 1643. But, as the two wretched invasions of Berg showed, lack of funds and the barrage of complaints and active obstruction by the pacific Estates rendered the small force almost worthless.

The situation began to change with the Brandenburg diet of 1652–3, not because this increased Frederick William's army – it actually reduced his mainly garrison troops to 1,800 men – but because the Estates tacitly accepted a force should exist in peacetime, paid for out of taxation. Far more significant than this diet were the steps the Elector took, mainly under Waldeck's influence and justified by the Imperial decree of 1654, to raise huge sums throughout his territories to support his burgeoning army during the War of the North. Despite all the Estates' hostility, by November 1655 systematic recruiting and imposed taxes produced the remarkable number of 19,000 men (including 6,000 militiamen), and by 1658 there were 25,000 in Brandenburg and Pomerania, with a further 5,000 in Prussia.[33] This army's success in the war came in part from greater tax resources, but also from the experienced generals employed, veterans from both sides in the Thirty Years War. Although Frederick William always accompanied his army on campaign, command was exercised by Otto Christoph von Sparr (1599–1668). He had fought in the Imperial army, entered Brandenburg service in 1649, was put in charge of the artillery in 1654 and then of the whole army a year later. Sparr was a thoroughly competent soldier, although not of the top flight. The French ambassador to Poland, de Lumbres, remarked tartly that he was 'better at carrying out the plans of others than at formulating his own, better with a small army than a large one, and better at defensive war than in a battle'.[34] None the less, he enabled the Elector to enter this war with an artillery train of seventy-two pieces, with standardised calibres, reflecting Frederick William's own determination to copy the Swedes' successful use of field guns. Sparr was also important for creating a rudimentary general staff under his unified command, although in the first years of the war there were some problems because Waldeck also played a major role, trying in effect to be war minister and general. As his experience had been in the Dutch army, he was quick to mock 'the ways of officers [i.e. Sparr] who have been in Imperial service'.[35] Tensions eased in 1657 when Waldeck left the Elector's employ.

The effectiveness of the new army owed much to its tactical training under Georg Derfflinger, later Frederick William's most successful general. A Lutheran from a prosperous Austrian peasant family, he had joined the Swedish army in 1630, becoming an outstanding cavalry officer. War made him rich, with an estate and a noble wife in Brandenburg, where he settled after the Peace of Westphalia. Knowing his reputation, the Elector appointed him general of cavalry in 1655. Most of the officers below Derfflinger and Sparr were Brandenburg nobles, many having served in the Swedish and Imperial armies. Their ability immediately impressed de Lumbres, who described the army in November 1655 as 'very good', although he felt that because the officers 'came from such diverse schools [of war], they often had very different ideas which they stuck to obstinately'.[36] Generally, however, Dutch and Swedish practices were adopted. The drill-book of 1654 was based on that of

Prince Maurice of Orange and the 1656 articles of war on those of Gustavus Adolphus.[37]

Although the Elector, like the Poles, had proportionally more cavalry (over half his men) than the Dutch and Swedish armies, the infantry regiments were soon increased. The infantry was the conventional two-thirds musketeers and one-third pikemen. Musketeers, as in other European armies, were armed with heavy matchlock guns, which had to be rested on stands and fired by smouldering wicks. Like the Swedes they lined up in three rows, one kneeling, one stooping and one standing. Blocks of pikemen stood beside them to fend off enemy cavalry. Unusually the Elector's infantrymen were beginning to wear uniforms: in the Danish campaign in 1659 they were 'all dressed in blue woollen cloth', the colour of Frederick the Great's army. But there was no hard-and-fast rule, and the cavalry continued to sport assorted colours, the troopers themselves having to provide most of their horses and weapons.[38]

At the beginning of the War of the North Frederick William probably did not intend his new army to be anything more than temporary, with most troops disbanded at the peace. The men were raised like those of the Thirty Years War: some were militiamen called out by Waldeck in Prussia and persuaded to stay on, but most were the usual mercenary soldiers. Colonels had provided regiments in the traditional way, signing contracts, or 'capitulations', with the Elector and receiving lump sums to raise these. Since peasants with their own farms were not encouraged to enlist and the Junkers wanted to hold on to scarce labour, the recruiting captains were forced to look outside the Hohenzollern lands, especially to the more populated areas of Westphalia. Although a basic military administration was created by Frederick William during the war (see pp. 165–6), the regiments still showed many of the faults of earlier ones. Wives and children accompanied soldiers on campaign, giving the army a 'tail' of non-combatants: in 1660 245 men in two companies had 53 wives and 29 children with them. While efforts were made to pay the troops and provide bread, the old practice continued of living off the countryside, especially in enemy territory. Frederick William, however, laid great emphasis on building up magazines to store food and arms and tried to protect his own subjects from his troops to prevent another collapse of Brandenburg society and economy. For, as he told his successor in his *Political Testament* of 1667, 'When you need to wage war, maintain good order in your own lands and do not let your subjects be oppressed or terrorised'.[39] In 1657, therefore, when his army of 14,000 moved into Brandenburg and Pomerania from Prussia, he warned his officers to respect the Brandenburg civil magistrates, to enforce contributions only on his orders, and to keep their troops from plundering and demanding free quarters.[40] Similarly when his Polish and Imperial allies passed through the electorate in 1658, adequate magazines were set up to feed them. The Imperial ambassador was astonished that, despite the exhaustion of the country, 'so many troops have left hardly a trace in the countryside, . . . [since] they have been checked so strictly'.[41] When the Brandenburg army returned from Denmark in 1659, it followed – remarkably for the period – a designated route home, with prepared magazines. This was to prevent its disintegrating on the march, rather than to protect Frederick William's neighbours, and there was still much looting. Real improvement in discipline would have to wait till the embryonic military administration developed and troops were paid and supplied properly.

The Prussian and other traditional militias were absorbed into Frederick William's army during the War of the North, but militiamen were useless on their own. Although the Brandenburg militia, a feudal levy of cavalry and infantry, had signally failed to protect the electorate during the Thirty Years War, the Estates liked it because it was cheap, and Frederick William still called it out in his early years, making a special effort in November 1654. The results were invariably poor; success in any case would have spelt economic disaster for labour-scarce Brandenburg, if the one in twenty summoned had responded. During the War of the North the Elector finally accepted the militia was worthless, and further summonses, in the 1660s and again in 1678, were issued only to make those liable buy exemption. In Prussia the militia, a cherished institution, controlled by the Estates, had formed the basis for Waldeck's makeshift force of 5,000 there in 1655. Yet Frederick William was never satisfied with this militia, and after the war he wanted to be rid of it, especially because of the Estates' involvement. In his *Political Testament* he advised substituting an annual cash levy, because the 'Prussian militia is no good for any kind of war, as I have found out myself'.[42] None the less, the Estates insisted on keeping it. During the Swedish invasion in 1678–9, it collapsed and Frederick William had to bring in regular troops from Brandenburg. This gave him the final excuse to force the Estates to pay for a permanent force.

The success of the Brandenburg army from the time of the War of the North depended heavily on Frederick William's insistence on imposing what taxes he wished. During this war, when he rode roughshod over the Estates' objections, to collect increasingly heavier contributions, they tacitly accepted his demands and there was no resistance. In the event they were prepared to pay, especially those in Brandenburg, because they 'realised . . . a well-armed ruler' had saved them from the horrors of another Thirty Years War. When the new conflict was over they wanted most of the troops dismissed but they did accept 'that a complete reduction of the army was unwise'.[43] During this conflict the total taxation from contributions on all Frederick William's lands rose sixfold. Beforehand Brandenburg and Pomerania had borne the brunt of the contributions, but now they were imposed heavily in Cleves and Prussia as well. Inevitably the soldiers also made their own demands on the population.

The Elector's growing financial independence from the Estates allowed him to field forces which did not disintegrate at the close of each annual campaign and actually improved during the war. Even after three years of conflict, in 1658 an Imperial envoy commented that Frederick William's army was 'well-clad' and 'very disciplined'.[44] In the War of the North the troops enjoyed, in Platen's General War Commissariat, the beginnings of a military administration to feed and pay them. The new body also established at least some of the kind of bureaucratic control over the troops that Louis XIV exercised, including limiting the colonels' power over their regiments. The General War Commissariat's survival in skeletal form after 1660 moreover helped Frederick William take one of the most important decisions of his reign. Instead of reducing his army to a few garrison troops and personal guards, he discharged half and kept the other 12,000 men – 5,200 of them in garrisons and the rest 'as a permanent field army'. 'This is the true origin of the Prussian standing army.'[45] It had become possible through his ruthless imposition of contributions and creation of an elementary general staff and military bureaucracy.

The conflict itself convinced Frederick William that his dynasty's survival depended on such a permanent army. He wrote in his *Political Testament*: 'alliances are certainly good, but a force of your own that you can depend on confidently, is better. A ruler is not treated with respect unless he has his own troops and resources. It is these, thank God, that have made me important since I have had them.'[46] Although financial constraints meant that the army had to be reduced during the 1660s, it never fell below 7,000 men and rose temporarily to 12,000 in 1666 during the dispute with Münster.[47] Numbers often fluctuated monthly, depending on the cash available, and troops were put to civil tasks, on the Frederick-William Canal and the reconstruction and expansion of Berlin.[48] Many discharged soldiers were also settled on the electoral domains on favourable conditions. While the ranks could be made up fairly easily in wartime, a cadre of officers could not. Consequently, proportionally more officers were kept on and others put on reserve with half pay. The higher officers were employed as commanders of fortresses, and of his sixteen generals at the outbreak of the Dutch War in 1672, all but two had already served in the War of the North.

At the beginning of the Dutch War Frederick William's field army, not counting garrison troops, was 20,000 strong – 12,000 foot and, a high proportion, 8,000 horse – with 50 artillery pieces. By 1678 the army was a remarkable 45,000 (now two-thirds infantry), and the Elector brought 180 cannon to the siege of Stralsund that year. In addition he had many lighter cannon, taking thirteen of them on the lightning Fehrbellin campaign. The condition of the army in September 1672, however, had not impressed the French envoy, Vauguion. He reported that only the 6,000 or so guards were any good, several regiments were under strength, the cavalry was poorly equipped and the whole could only march very slowly.[49] But Derfflinger's work during the war led to a great improvement, and the quality seems to have been maintained right to the end, despite the huge rise in numbers. The re-establishment of the General War Commissariat at the same time (see pp. 166–7) undoubtedly contributed to this. In 1678 the French diplomat and soldier Rébenac commented on the force which took Stralsund: 'I was surprised how fine his troops were . . . , and I can only compare them with the *regiment du roi* and five or six of the finest regiments I have seen in France . . . The dragoons are very fine, the cavalry well turned out, although with poor mounts.'[50] Discipline, however, could still break down on occasions. In 1674 another French diplomat, Verjus, had reported that troops being assembled in the electorate were ransacking it, reducing the population to 'beggary and despair'. 'It was as if a fire had passed through.'[51] They none the less proved far more disciplined than the Emperor's troops during the Rhine campaign of that year.

With the return of peace in the 1680s the standing army remained. Its numbers were usually around 25,000, increasing to 31,000 in the critical months before Frederick William's death in 1688

(about two-thirds were available as a field force, the rest for garrisons).[52] The infantry continued to eclipse the rest, although they
were undergoing significant change. Since the battle of Warsaw, a
generation before, they had been made up of two musketeers for
every pikeman. But the pike's long history on European battlefields
was almost over, and during the 1680s Frederick William's musketeers followed the Imperial armies in using the forerunner of the
bayonet, the short boar spear. This was stuck in the ground in front
of them to repel cavalry, providing similar protection to that from
pikemen. At the same time matchlock guns were being gradually
replaced by lighter, faster-firing flintlocks. Further progress was also
being made in standardising the calibres of artillery pieces, using a
gun foundry in Berlin; and a string of artillery parks was built from
the Rhine to the Niemen/Nemunas. Following the French example,
in 1679 Frederick William established two veteran companies for
old and crippled soldiers. The men were used for garrison duties
and no longer had to beg to survive, the fate of most ex-soldiers.

The quality of Frederick William's troops continued to impress
in the 1680s. In November 1684 Rébenac reported that the 11,000
men assembled to welcome the bride of Crown Prince Frederick to
Berlin were 'the finest I have seen in Germany'.[53] More telling was
the action of the Brandenburg contingent at the bloody storming of
Buda, in the 1686 Imperial campaign against the Turks. The officers
kept tight control and their disciplined troops did not join other
contingents in sacking the city.[54] This reflected Frederick William's
continual attention to matters of discipline. An ordinance of 1679
had threatened to cashier officers who allowed troops to pillage, and
one of January 1688 ordered soldiers guilty of serious indiscipline in
peacetime to be beaten. Although electoral troops, like all others,
did desert,[55] it was probably not a serious problem: only one edict
was issued against it, in 1683.

It was perhaps fortunate that the army was not tested by a full-
scale war in the 1680s because there was confusion over who would
lead it. The Elector himself always fought with his troops, but he
largely left their handling to his commanders-in-chief, unlike his
great grandson, Frederick the Great. Unfortunately, in his last years,
as Frederick William became increasingly infirm, his commander
Derfflinger was also really too old to take the field. Always insuffer-
ably rude, Derfflinger had never been an easy servant. Now in his
late seventies, he had made it clear that if his master's tortuous
diplomacy led to war against the Emperor, he would resign: 'I would

hack myself to death rather than command the electoral army contrary to Your Electoral Highness's honour and conscience and to Your well-being and the Empire's.'[56] Consequently, in 1683 Frederick William tried to get Louis XIV to allow Schomberg, a French general and Palatinate Protestant, to enter Brandenburg service. Although the King refused, Schomberg left France in 1684 because of the persecution of the Huguenots, and three years later he was made Frederick William's commander-in-chief. He was the most important of the refugees from France, but there were enough of them to form two whole regiments.

By Frederick William's death his army was second in size in Germany to the Emperor's and was possibly as well-trained and armed as that of Louis XIV, perhaps even better because the French were slower in phasing out the pike and matchlock. The army's dramatic growth in the 1680s owed most to the crisis engendered by Louis's policies on the Rhine and the repercussions of the Turkish assault on Vienna. Although its numbers were exceptional, other German states were also trying, if with less success and determination, to establish standing armies. In 1683 the Brunswick dukes raised a combined force of 28,000, but these troops were raised to face the immediate danger of a French-inspired attack; the numbers soon declined and the dukes did not unite militarily again. The Bavarian army on occasions reached 15,000 men, although no sizeable permanent force was maintained, despite the absolute rule of the Bavarian electors, and in 1682 it was down to 12,800. In Saxony, where the Estates remained powerful, the army was next in size to Brandenburg's in the Empire. In 1675 it was 8,260, about 10,000 in the 1680s and 20,000 in the 1690s, when it bore much of the brunt of the war against the Turks.[57] The Emperor himself had only 38,400 men to face the Turkish invasion in 1683, but numbers probably doubled during the year. These German armies of course paled beside that of Louis XIV: the King had 290,000 men at the end of the Dutch War and kept at least 130,000 under arms in the early 1680s.[58]

The officer corps of Frederick William's army was drawn from the domestic nobility, but the latter as an estate had still not merged its interests with the Hohenzollern state and army (p. 114). It was not yet the eighteenth-century service nobility, where 'the relationship between Junker and serf was reproduced in the army in the relationship between officers and men'.[59] The soldiers in the army were as mixed as any contemporary German one: a muster roll for one regiment from 1681 shows that half the 1,100 men came from the Hohenzollern lands and two-thirds of the rest were Germans. The remaining 200 or so included Danes, Swedes, Poles and Czechs.[60] While his own recruiters went outside his borders for men, Frederick William forbade those of foreign states within his own territories, issuing fourteen edicts against this between 1665 and 1687. Unlike the mercenary troops of Frederick William's early years, with their shifting loyalties from one colonel and ruler to another, now soldiers usually spent their whole careers in the Hohenzollern army. In this way they were more like the regular professional troops of the eighteenth- and nineteenth-century armies.

Frederick William had the same problem as other European rulers in establishing direct control over his army. Subordinating the officers to the crown proved a slow process, as even Louis XIV found. In the early years the colonels were independent contractors: they had invested their energies and their own cash, as well as the Elector's, in raising regiments, and they expected a financial return. However, the General War Commissariat under Platen and his successors began to erode their power by taking over many of their administrative functions, such as paying wages, providing bread and fodder, and clamping down on false muster numbers. The soldiers' regimental pay was now less misused and paid more regularly. Just as important, the Elector decreed in August 1673 that he could veto the colonels' choice of regimental officers. This was to encourage the junior ones to give their ultimate loyalty to the crown, although the colonels continued to appoint most of their officers till the end of the reign. However, the role of the colonels themselves was changing significantly. Until the 1670s they could disobey orders by sticking to the letter of their contracts, but from the time of the Dutch War fewer were drawn up and colonels were often directly appointed to command new regiments.[61] They could no longer remove themselves and their regiments to another employer: the private conduct of war was effectively over.

At the Great Elector's death the eighteenth-century pattern had been established of funding the army through the contribution tax on the countryside and the excise on the towns. The sums collected had been increasing throughout his reign. In the electorate the contributions, 270,000 thalers a year in the 1660s, were 430,000 in 1688.[62] But by this date 60 per cent of the cost of the army was being borne by the excise tax, which in that year produced 850,000 thalers. The total direct cost of the army in 1680 was 1.5 million thalers.[63] In addition, of course, during peacetime and wartime the population had to billet and feed the bulk of the troops – infantry in the towns and dragoons and cavalry in the villages. Although the Elector was supposed to reimburse his subjects for this, usually by reducing their taxes, this was often ignored. It is true that the money to feed and clothe the expanding army was being spent in the Hohenzollern lands, but it is doubtful if it boosted the domestic economy, since resources were being diverted from more productive use.[64]

Despite the burden of the army on Frederick William's subjects, they did not even bear the full cost. Like other German princes, the Elector also depended on foreign subsidies, increasingly so as the army grew. This led him to shift his policies for 'short-term gain', and some alliances, especially with Louis XIV, were made less for political and territorial advantage than for money. Similarly other rulers saw his main value as an ally in the number of troops he could offer. His army, therefore, had to be kept up, in part, to maintain their interest. This dilemma was to continue through his son's reign and was only solved by his grandson, King Frederick William I, who made himself financially independent.[65]

. . .

THE DEVELOPMENT OF INDUSTRY
AND TRADE

While Frederick William's reign had a rather negative effect on his native bourgeoisie and did not arrest the general decline of the towns (see pp. 108, 122–3), this is somewhat surprising because he undoubtedly tried to develop industry and trade.[66] His four years as a youth in the Netherlands led to his life-long interest in these matters, as well as in a navy and overseas expansion. Dutch economic success was too obvious for him not to be impressed. Yet he never contemplated turning his territories into an eastern Holland, since he did not want to rule in a commercial state with urban elites: he knew the political problems they had caused his Orange relations. His actual policies (the material available means that the following account is largely limited to Brandenburg) were more akin to those of other contemporary mercantilist rulers and ministers such as Louis XIV and Jean-Baptiste Colbert, and to the ideas of such German cameralist writers as Johann Joachim Becher (1635–

82).[67] All stressed that the ruler should encourage population growth to provide a larger workforce and to pay taxation, and that he should also foster agriculture and establish domestic industries, especially ones needed by the army. A ruler should similarly promote domestic and foreign trade, while excluding foreign manufactured goods to protect native ones and to conserve bullion.[68] Frederick William told his Privy Council in 1683 that establishing industries would not only 'benefit trade' but also ensure that 'the country does not lose gold to foreign nations'.[69] Throughout his reign, therefore, he was to try repeatedly to prohibit a range of imports, including iron, copper and brass ware, plate glass, tin and salt, as well as millstones, refined sugar, tobacco and coarse textiles. But inadequate policing and high domestic demand meant that most continued to be imported, except for salt which was a state monopoly.[70]

On the whole, native merchants and entrepreneurs in the Hohenzollern lands and Germany were indifferent to establishing their own industries. Their attitude was summed up by merchants in the Imperial free city of Augsburg, who observed in 1677: 'manufactures require knowledge, continual experience and much capital. Any merchant can invest his money better and with more certainty in commerce; it is more fitting for the public interest so to employ itself than the private individual.'[71] In any case Frederick William intended the initiative should come from him. Even where his own bourgeoisie existed in significant numbers, as in Cleves and Königsberg, he did not appreciate their economic worth and distrusted them because of their ties with the political groups and institutions which constantly vexed him.[72]

For most of his reign Frederick William himself undertook rather haphazard initiatives to try to establish a number of enterprises; at the very end of his life he was to act more systematically, often using expert foreigners and refugees. In 1654–5 he was instrumental in setting up a copper foundry at Neustadt-Eberswalde, a glass works at Grimnitz and an ironworks at Peitz in Brandenburg. Attempts in 1662 to re-open old ironworks and to find iron-ore deposits in the electorate failed because of lack of native expertise. However, similar efforts in the 1660s and 1670s to develop existing ironworks in the Rhenish county of Mark did succeed and iron began to be exported, including large amounts to England. Industries of similar military importance, such as lead, also in Mark, and saltpetre in Halberstadt, were helped too. Iron and copper works were both monopolies of the crown, as was all metal mining in Mark,

Magdeburg and Halberstadt. Far less successful were the three sugar-cane refineries Frederick William helped to establish in Berlin between 1660 and 1670 to satisfy the growing demand for sugar and to skim off profits for the crown. The refineries failed, as they could not match the quality or price of sugar from western Europe.[73] Undeterred, between 1676 and 1678 Frederick William had his master of the mint set up workshops in Brandenburg to produce shoe leather, tin plate and scythes. In 1678 two of the officials involved in the administration of his domains, Stephani and Esich, were ordered to open a large enterprise in Berlin to handle the sale of woollen goods produced by domestic workers. Although all were protected by tariff privileges and export bans, these schemes fared no better than previous ones. Set up in a hit-or-miss way and under-funded by the crown, they soon collapsed. In 1679–80, however, Stephani and Esich, this time with private funds, went on to found the first Brandenburg joint-stock company, another sugar refinery in Berlin. The Elector invested in this and encouraged ministers and courtiers and, unusually, the Berlin burghers Bartholdi and Senning to join in. The latter were evidently felt trustworthy enough to be allowed to start their own venture in 1681 to cure tobacco, receiving a monopoly throughout Brandenburg and Pomerania for twenty years. None the less, all these schemes of the late 1670s and early 1680s proved just as ephemeral as the previous ones. An exception was a works set up by the crown in the last decade of the reign to manufacture plate and decorative glass: the raw materials, sand and timber, were of course plentiful in Brandenburg, and the Elector provided much of the demand.[74] Another success, and a very profitable one, was in Halle in Magdeburg, when Frederick William in 1681 used the crown's salt monopoly to extend the workings there.

This flurry of state-inspired industrial activity in the late 1670s and 1680s was accompanied by a typically mercantilist attempt at economic planning, the creation of commercial councils or colleges. In 1677 a Monetary and Commercial College (*Müntz- und Commercien-Collegium*) was founded for Brandenburg, with Stephani and Esich and some privy councillors as members. Although this was short-lived, a new Commercial College replaced it in February 1684 with administrative and judicial powers over trade, especially tariffs, and similar colleges for Prussia and Pomerania were created at Königsberg and Kołobrzeg. While earlier economic measures had been rather improvised, from the mid-1680s tighter administrative control was exercised, especially by the evolving General War Commissariat. Now efforts were made to ensure high quality through state monopolies or intervention in various industries. Previously wool from Brandenburg's extensive flocks had been mainly exported to western Europe, but in the 1680s the General War Commissariat, with its interest in military uniforms, began to supervise the manufacture of cloth. By 1687 even the inmates of the gaols at Spandau and Magdeburg and of the poor house at Potsdam were having to spin wool.[75] Now almost all Frederick William's infantry was kitted out in blue cloth manufactured in Stendal, Berlin and Frankfurt an der Oder. The detailed edicts issued in 1684 and 1687 to regulate the textile industry,[76] tax cloth imports and prevent the export of wool, were probably modelled on those of Louis XIV's minister Colbert, and a Frenchman was given overall supervision as inspector general. The regulations were usually enforced by the General War Commissariat's officials in charge of the urban excise. These officials, and the excise tax itself in Brandenburg in the 1680s, were useful mercantilist instruments to oversee all goods manufactured in the towns.

Similar regulations were to be imposed, together with protective tariffs, by the Commissariat on the new industries developed by the Huguenots. These were to put all Frederick William's previous industrial enterprises in the shade. Very few Huguenots were peasants; instead they had a variety of professional, entrepreneurial and artisan skills. The range of manufactories they set up was vast and included paper, glass, leather, soap, candles, tobacco, watches, carpets, clothing accessories such as hats, gloves, stockings and wigs, and all kinds of fine textiles from tapestries, silks and lace to printed cotton. Possibly half the Huguenot artisans were involved in textiles of one kind or another, or in allied trades such as bleaching and dyeing.[77] There were surgeons, apothecaries and printers, and also many market gardeners, who introduced such French delicacies as lettuce, asparagus and artichokes: a whole sandy suburb of northwest Berlin was settled by them and given the biblical name Moabit.

Unfortunately many of the new luxury industries of the 1680s not only lacked raw materials and capital, but the poverty and overwhelming peasant society of Brandenburg itself meant customers outside the court were few, and markets had to be found elsewhere. The manufacturing needs of the majority of the population of the Hohenzollern lands were met, at least in Brandenburg and Prussia, directly by the Junkers' industries on their manors. The role of

The skill s.t not the demand

industry and trade under Frederick William was of course hardly significant compared with that of agriculture. Even the bonus of the Huguenots probably had little real or long-lasting effects on Brandenburg's industrial development. This is evident from how Frederick William I and Frederick the Great had to build their monarchy's industry from scratch.[78]

In welcoming and granting privileges and monopolies to foreigners, who he hoped would generate future revenues and benefit the state, the Elector probably further harmed his own artisans, manufacturers and merchants. While his building in Berlin and Potsdam may have benefited the immediate neighbourhoods, the gain is unlikely to have trickled out to the other towns and countryside, which remained as poor as ever. Even the expansion of the army, with its fortresses and magazines, was of doubtful general economic benefit. The financial burden had to be paid for by the population as a whole, and while food, uniforms and some weaponry were bought locally, the heavy guns, as well as most of the ships for the navy and merchant marine, had to be purchased abroad.

It is probable that the Great Elector had more success in developing the infrastructure of Brandenburg than in setting up industries. After the Thirty Years War he had tried to improve its communications, to persuade foreign traders to use its roads and rivers and to pay him tolls to do so. In 1647 he lowered the tariffs, and ships sailing between the commercial centres of Hamburg and Leipzig began to appear on the Spree. Frederick William's ultimate goal was to use this river and the Havel to provide a navigable waterway across Brandenburg from the Elbe to the Oder. In the early 1650s parts of the Havel were dredged and cleared of driftwood, but little else was done till 1662. Then he ordered a canal to be dug to the south-east of Berlin to join the Spree to the Müllrose Lake. Over the next five years Philippe de Chièze constructed this 10-kilometre channel, later called the Frederick-William Canal, using Dutch techniques and assistants. They had to cut through sand ridges 40 metres high and build eleven locks. Costs were kept down by using soldiers for labour and the electoral forests for timber. Frederick William funded it all himself, to make sure it was completed.[79] Goods could now be shipped all the way between the North Sea and Wrocław/Breslau in Silesia and then overland into the rest of the Habsburg territories and Poland, without having to pay to use the Danish Sound and Swedish Szczecin. Berlin itself became a minor port and commercial centre, acting as a transit point between the two great German rivers, with warehousing and quay facilities paid for by Frederick William.

The new canal was to prove far more important in developing Brandenburg's commerce than all the Elector's later overseas trading ventures, and it has been called 'the first great act of a German territorial prince in the economic sphere'.[80] While there were other attempts to improve communications, they were not on the same scale. The harbour at Kołobrzeg, the only significant port in East Pomerania, was improved in 1660 and again in 1681–2. In the 1680s work was carried out at the Prussian ports and larger ships could dock directly at Königsberg. Road transport was also not neglected. In March 1669 an edict ordered the circle commissioners in Brandenburg to repair roads, bridges and embankments. However, the one measure so dear to the embryonic liberal economists of the next century, abolishing internal tolls to encourage trade, was not even considered. For tolls were a source of crown income, free from interference by the Estates and far too valuable to lose.

The success of the Frederick-William Canal was matched by the creation of a Hohenzollern postal service. In 1649 Michael Matthias was put in charge of the Brandenburg post and eventually that of the other possessions. Three years later Frederick William could already boast to the Emperor: 'My post is ordered with such pains that it is an encouragement for all posts to follow a similar good and fast system'.[81] Contemporaries were impressed enough by its speed and reliability to dub it the 'flying' post. Operating twice a week, carrying private and official mail, it linked all the Hohenzollern lands from Klaipeda/Memel to Cleves, with relay stations every 22.5 kilometres. It was a very effective way of bringing Berlin closer to all Frederick William's lands, taking six days to Cleves and five to Königsberg. But Matthias went further: by using his own couriers and making agreements with other services, he developed a postal network across the whole north-German plain, reaching Hamburg, Leipzig and Warsaw. The service proved highly profitable, bringing the Elector annual revenues of 40,000 thalers by 1688.

Frederick William's efforts to improve his backward lands have impressed historians more than contemporary foreign observers, especially those from Louis XIV's France. In 1662 the French envoy in Berlin wrote: 'Money is very scarce in this country and the coin is so bad that twenty-five is lost for every hundred in exchanging them for good money ... The Elector's subjects are also very poor and his palace appears the most ruined that I have seen in

Germany.' Two decades later, in 1681, Rébenac remarked about the electoral lands: 'It is unbelievable, sire, how much they are ruined. The villages are deserted and the lands for the most part left fallow, except for those of Magdeburg and Halberstadt.' In 1687 he reported that the country 'is so exhausted' that the Elector was surviving by reducing the troops' wages and increasing billeting. Rébenac added that the coinage was being debased, which was likely to destroy Brandenburg's trade because other countries would reject its coin.[82]

. . .

IMMIGRATION

Throughout his reign Frederick William tried to attract immigrants to expand the sparse population of his eastern lands and to make up the losses caused by the Thirty Years War. This was part and parcel of his more general mercantilist policies. Once again Waldeck's hand can be seen in encouraging 'efforts to get subjects into the country'.[83] The Elector always wanted settlers to be Protestants, preferably Calvinists, and tended to acquire them indirectly, rather like mercenary soldiers, through agreements with contractors who had local links and funds. After the Peace of Westphalia he was to attract hundreds of Dutch and German immigrants into Brandenburg and smaller numbers into Prussia. For example, in January 1649 two contractors agreed to settle eighty Dutch Frisian families near Werben in the Altmark on abandoned marshy land belonging to the crown. Their villages were to be self-governing on the Dutch pattern, with Calvinist churches and ministers. Each family was to lease 60 acres and to be exempt from rent and taxes for three years. They were to receive free timber from the electoral forests and the whole enterprise was loaned 10,000 thalers for nine years. The settlers did not have to perform labour services, and their children could marry without the consent of their lord, the Elector. This and other contracts, such as the one with two Dutchmen to settle 200 people at Gramzow in the Uckermark in 1651, show Frederick William realised he would not attract colonists from the freer social climate of western Europe if they faced the burdens of his own peasants.
Frederick William always believed western immigrants could turn his wastes, fens and sandy tracts into fertile lands, and he put this on a wider and more systematic footing by edicts of 1650 and 1661.

Foreign peasants willing to take over abandoned farms were offered long leases, six years' freedom from rent, tax and billeting, as well as gifts of timber, seed and tools. Artisans were also encouraged to settle in towns, with promises of citizenship and guild membership. Special projects, such as the rebuilding of Berlin's defences after 1658 or the Frederick-William Canal in the 1660s, demanded skills only found abroad. His envoys in the Dutch Republic were therefore always looking out for craftsmen, including drainage engineers and millers to renovate and build windmills. His agent in Amsterdam, Matthias Doegen, reported as early as 1653, during a slump there: 'Every day in these wretched times bricklayers and joiners come to ask if Your Electoral Highness has any work. They are willing to pay their own travel expenses.'[84] Despite the effort put into all this, only a trickle of artisans entered Brandenburg before the Huguenot flood in the 1680s. By 1685 about 4,000 immigrants, mainly Dutch and Frisian peasants, had been persuaded to enter.[85] As they were usually Calvinists, all sections of Lutheran society were hostile, and their economic influence was probably marginal. Even their farms were not very successful, which was hardly surprising, given the wastelands they were expected to cultivate. Their western farming practices also seem to have had little influence on the native cultivators and 'almost no impact on the structure of rural society'.[86]

Immigrant numbers were to increase dramatically in the last years of the reign because of a fresh bout of religious persecution by some Catholic rulers. A few Calvinist burghers had fled to Brandenburg in the late 1670s to escape the Emperor Leopold's repression in Hungary.[87] By 1677 there were already 100 French refugee families in Berlin, and Louis XIV's mounting attacks on his Calvinist Huguenots, culminating in the 1685 Revocation of the Edict of Nantes, led to mass flight. Frederick William had immediately responded by issuing his own Edict of Potsdam, promising lands and building materials with the usual rent and tax exemptions. The Brandenburg envoy in Paris, Spanheim, tried to provide immediate relief, and staging posts were set up to help the refugees cross France and Germany. In 1686 all Brandenburg was invited to contribute to a relief fund. As Frederick William's Lutheran subjects did not respond, the invitation was changed to a demand. Between 1685 and 1688 7,000 Huguenots entered Brandenburg, and by the end of the century at least 10,000 had found refuge there. This influx was also accompanied in the late 1680s by a smaller one of a few hundred peasants into the Havelland and Ruppin from the Swiss Calvinist cantons. There were also 7,000 Protestant immigrants from the Palatinate between 1680 and the end of the century. While most of these newcomers stayed, the Protestant Waldensians, who came in 1688 because of persecution from the Duke of Savoy, immediately returned home once he changed his policies. These southerners liked Brandenburg no more than any other part of Germany, claiming that 'God has not created us to drink beer'.[88] Because most of these refugees in the 1680s were Calvinists, they extended Calvinist influence for the first time significantly outside the electoral court. As with the earlier Dutch immigrants, the cost of settling them was high and the advantage to the local population problematic. To settle some of the Palatines in Magdeburg cost a huge 150,000 thalers.[89]

Even less popular with the native population was another group of immigrants Frederick William encouraged, the Jews. While there were few restrictions on Jews in Cleves-Mark, they had been expelled from Brandenburg in 1571 and had also been outlawed from Prussia. The Elector, however, did not share the prejudices of most of his contemporaries. In 1683, when the Havelland circle deputies had asked for Jews to be expelled, Frederick William insisted that: 'It is known that cheating in trade takes place among Christians as well as Jews and with more impunity.'[90] In the 1640s and 1650s he had used Jews extensively in Cleves and Mark in various financial dealings.[91] In these same decades he had also allowed a few to enter Brandenburg temporarily to attend fairs, and when Emperor Leopold expelled them from most of his hereditary lands, Frederick William seized the chance in 1671 to let fifty of the richest families settle in Brandenburg 'for the furtherance of trade and traffic'.[92] When the outraged Estates there complained in December 1672, the Elector insisted that 'the Jews do no harm to the country, but rather appear to be useful'.[93] He now felt strong enough to override objections and allow Jews to open shops and market stalls. Although forbidden synagogues, they could worship in private and employ their own rabbis and a kosher butcher. In Landsberg/Gorzów, for example, the Jewish population rose from under half a dozen families in 1671 to twenty-one in 1690.[94] Like many German rulers, including even Emperor Leopold, if on a smaller scale, Frederick William used Jewish contractors for loans and to supply his army, such as Israel Aaron in Prussia during the War of the North. In Prussia itself the power of the diet made direct toleration more difficult, and in the agreement with it in 1663 Jews were expressly forbidden there. Frederick William, however, did protect a few individuals: in the 1680s and 1690s the very successful merchant Moses Jacobson de Jonge lived in Klaipeda/Memel under crown protection, despite constant complaints from the Estates. He had extensive trading links with Poland-Lithuania and Holland and by 1694–5 he was paying almost double the customs duties of all the other merchants in the port.

· · ·

OVERSEAS EXPANSION

Frederick William's successful, if rather prosaic, ventures in communications and the postal service have not caught historians' imagination in the same way as his far less rewarding undertakings in overseas trade. This is understandable because the latter seemed to anticipate Germany's development as a naval and colonial power under Kaiser William II, even though the early schemes were to collapse and remain in abeyance for two centuries.[95]

From the beginning of his reign the Elector was attracted by plans, often utopian ones, to participate in extra-European trade and even to build his own navy. Like so many of his contemporaries, he was bewitched by Dutch success, and we find him at various times using language similar to that of an edict of January 1686, that 'navigation and trade are the principal pillars of a state, through which subjects, by sea and by manufactories on land, earn their food and keep'.[96] The opportunities seemed there because Brandenburg was so close to the rich Baltic market and because Pomerania and Prussia had their own sea coasts. Unfortunately the prospects for success were really nil because of the dominance of Anglo-Dutch shipping and Sweden's grip on the outlets of the major German rivers. The latter made it seem even more vital for Frederick William throughout his reign to gain the Pomeranian port of Szczecin and the mouth of the Oder. As Szczecin continually eluded him and the tiny Pomeranian port of Kołobrzeg lacked the same natural advantages, he was forced to adopt unsatisfactory substitutes. Königsberg was an obvious, existing port, but it was overshadowed by neighbouring Gdańsk, and its trade was always to remain chiefly in Dutch and English hands. The independent-minded Königsberg merchants never showed any interest in the Elector's schemes,[97] which he did not want to share with them in any case.

As early as 1647–8, when the Elector could not even afford to send ambassadors abroad, he was none the less listening to a scheme to found a company in Prussia to trade with the East Indies. Then in 1651, though no native Brandenburg or Prussian ship had passed through the Sound for three years, he persuaded Denmark to charge any hypothetical Hohenzollern shipping the same rates as the Dutch. Ten years later, in July 1661, he signed a commercial treaty with Charles II, giving his equally hypothetical merchants most favoured nation treatment in English ports. In 1664, however, he actually had two ships built in Holland, the *Duchy of Cleves* and *County of Mark*, hoping to send Dutch crews under his flag to trade between Baltic ports and Spain. Unfortunately, this coincided with the Second Anglo-Dutch War, and the vessels were captured by the English off Falmouth with a load of Norwegian timber bound for Cadiz. The whole enterprise then collapsed, with financial loss by the Elector who had owned the cargo.

Frederick William's enthusiasm ebbed after this mishap, and it took a decade to revive. In 1675, however, the Dutchman Benjamin Raule (1634–1707) arrived in Berlin. He was a Zeeland merchant, who had suffered heavy losses during the French invasion and occupation. Clearly persuasive, he soon became a particular favourite of the Elector, who valued his commercial and maritime experience and contacts in the Republic. Frederick William encouraged him to acquire ships in Holland and build some in East Pomerania and Prussia. This small fleet assisted the Pomeranian campaign in the late 1670s, when it seemed Szczecin could be annexed. The ships, sixteen to eighteen small craft, at first belonged to Raule himself, and were leased to Frederick William, who eventually bought eight of them in 1684. After the conclusion of peace, in 1680 the Elector let Raule send six frigates from Prussia to prey on Spanish shipping off western Europe in a vain attempt to force Madrid to pay 1.5 million thalers arrears of subsidy from the war. Raule, who was now appointed *Oberdirektor* of the navy, had orders 'to arm as many vessels as possible, to seize and bring back all the ships and goods of Spanish subjects at sea'.[98] The squadron, commanded and crewed by Dutchmen, sailed as far south as Cape St Vincent in a bungled plan to seize some of the silver fleet. A minor scrap there in October 1680 was the Hohenzollerns' only naval battle till the twentieth century. The fleet had had one success, however, in previously capturing the Spanish 28-gun *Charles II*, with a valuable cargo of lace and linen, off Ostend. This vessel was renamed *The Margrave of*

Brandenburg and became flagship of the tiny navy. Although such pro-French ministers, as Meinders, Grumbkow and Fuchs, supported the policy because of its anti-Spanish aspect,[99] others were not in favour, especially Jena. The latter confided to an English envoy that the Elector 'did not at all understand sea affaires, and that he had been put upon them by some, who sought their owne interest in it more than his'.[100]

Privateering was only part of Raule's activities. Like many of his countrymen, he wanted to breach the monopoly of the great English and Dutch trading companies in the Americas, Africa and the Orient. After joining Frederick William's service he soon convinced him of the feasibility of dispatching a fleet to the Guinea coast to muscle in on the West African gold, ivory and slave trade.[101] In autumn 1680 two ships, financed by Raule and other Dutchmen, sailed from Prussia, with Dutch crews, on the five-month voyage for Guinea. The Elector merely provided twenty musketeers and the Hohenzollern red-eagle standard. By May 1681 a treaty was negotiated with some African chiefs in what is now western Ghana, granting Brandenburg a monopoly of trade and allowing a coastal factory to be built. The Dutch West India Company, however, was enraged at Dutch interlopers' using a Brandenburg flag of convenience. They managed to seize one ship on the return voyage, although the other reached Prussia safely in August 1681 with a small cargo of gold and ivory. Frederick William was delighted, used the gold to mint commemorative coins and was determined to proceed. He insisted the Dutch company had no claim to areas it had not occupied, and in March 1682 he founded the Africa Company, a joint-stock one, at Baltiysk/Pillau to trade with those parts of the west-African coast unoccupied by Europeans. As none of his own subjects would invest,[102] he provided 8,000 thalers, his ministers 2,000, and Raule and his Dutch partners 24,000. In July two ships set sail again with forty-two soldiers. Early in 1683 they landed and built a factory and small fort with ten guns, close to the Dutch base of Elmina (also in modern Ghana). Despite attacks from malaria and Africans, the fort, named Groß-Friedrichsburg, survived and was reinforced from home during the year. The company's headquarters were meanwhile strengthened by moving to the North Sea port of Emden in East Friesland in May 1683. Brandenburg troops had occupied the city the previous November with the agreement of the East-Friesland Estates because of a quarrel between them and the Regent Christine Charlotte.[103] In 1684 and 1685 the company made further agreements with local chiefs to erect forts east of Groß-Friedrichsburg at Accada and Taccarary, places previously abandoned by the Dutch company.

If the Brandenburg Africa Company was to break into the lucrative Atlantic slave trade, it needed a base in the West Indies to sell its human cargoes, since the established European companies would never buy from it.[104] Consequently in 1685 Frederick William bought land on St Thomas, one of the Virgin Islands, from the Danes, who retained the sovereignty. Although a few warehouses were built, no regular trade was established with Africa. The whole African venture itself was hardly a success and has been described as a 'fiasco'.[105] Raule was no commercial genius and his master lacked the capital and the political and military clout to break into the closed market. Raule summed up the problem in an impeccably mercantilist letter to Frederick William in 1684:

> when one intends to populate a province or a city and to introduce manufacturers, the State must assist. Your Highness's lands are . . . well-placed for trade, yet there exists not the faintest inclination there towards commerce and navigation. What could not be accomplished in seafaring, shipbuilding, and manufacturing if only one could get one hundred thousand ducats? If Berlin, Colberg [Kołobrzeg], Königsberg, and Memel [Klaipeda] had each only eight or ten merchants who would push maritime enterprise with intelligence and energy[,] . . . one could move mountains. But for my part I fail to see how anything worthwhile can be accomplished unless Your Highness takes advantage of these troublous times, when religious persecution is rife in neighbouring countries, and imports groups of foreigners from England, France and Holland . . . into your lands and cities, so nearly destitute of good merchants. Such aliens are almost always merchants and traders.[106]

The Brandenburg ships were continually harried and seized by the Dutch company, which occupied Accada and Taccarary in 1687, returning the former in 1690 after Frederick William's death. Altogether about fifty ships sailed to Africa under the Brandenburg flag between 1682 and 1709. Almost all the voyages lost money and had to be paid for from the Prussian tolls and from leasing domain lands. In 1688 the Marine Chest (set up two years before) had an annual income of 60,000 thalers but debts of 220,874 thalers.[107] Most of the goods taken to Africa and those brought back were bought and sold in Dutch ports. Some of the new merchant fleet were also bought there, but fourteen were built in Pomerania and Prussia in the 1680s under Raule's direction with Dutch workmen.

He and his partners provided the finance and Frederick William the timber. By 1695 Königsberg had a fleet of seventy-six ships, mostly coastal vessels sailing to Gdańsk or Stockholm. Despite the limited successes, Frederick William himself was not put off, being described a few months before his death by the Imperial ambassador as 'infatuated with commerce and seeking all feasible ways to expand it'.[108] He had received little support from his ministers for his colonial ventures. None of them, from Schwerin to Jena, Meinders and Fuchs, was in favour.[109] The Africa Company itself was to struggle on for thirty years after the Great Elector, largely because King Frederick I knew how much it had meant to his father. His less sentimental grandson, King Frederick William I, however, sold the company and its factories as a job lot to the Dutch West India Company in 1721, saying: 'I have always regarded this trading nonsense as a chimera'.[110]

. . .

NOTES AND REFERENCES

1 Isaacsohn, II, pp. 122ff.
2 Hüttl, p. 278.
3 Isaacsohn, II, p. 254.
4 Waddington, *Prusse*, I, p. 376.
5 G. Schmoller, O. Hintze et al., eds, *Acta Borussica: Die Behördenorganisation und die allgemeine Staatsverwaltung Preußens im 18. Jahrhundert* (Berlin, 1894), I, p. 87.
6 Breysig, I, p. 37.
7 Dorwart, p. 16; Opgenoorth, *Friedrich Wilhelm*, I, pp. 245f.
8 Dorwart, p. 116, and see Tümpel, p. 115.
9 Philippson, III, p. 70.
10 Opgenoorth, *Friedrich Wilhelm*, II, pp. 293f.
11 Macartney, p. 254.
12 Waddington, *Prusse*, I, p. 347.
13 Droysen, part 3, III, p. 287.
14 Spannagel, *Minden*, pp. 193, 197.
15 An English observer as early as 1681 believed the excise discouraged trade in Frederick William's lands: 26 February o.s., Berlin, 7/17 June 1681, Halle, Poley to Conway, BL, Ad. Ms. 37,986.
16 See R. Braun, 'Taxation, socio-political structure and state building: Great Britain and Brandenburg-Prussia', and W. Fischer and P. Lundgreen, 'The recruitment of administrative personnel', both in

C. Tilly, ed., *The Formation of National States in Western Europe* (Princeton, NJ, 1975).

17 Carsten, *Origins*, p. 199.

18 Nachama, pp. 44, 98.

19 Carsten, *Origins*, p. 266; J. Kunisch, 'Kurfürst Friedrich Wilhelm und die Großen Mächte', in Heinrich, ed., *Ein sonderbares Licht*, p. 21.

20 Isaacsohn, II, p. 335.

21 Carsten, *Origins*, p. 266. Between 1674 and 1688 he received altogether 2,712,000 thalers – 57,000 from Denmark, 467,000 from Spain, 503,000 from France, 912,000 from the Dutch and 973,000 from the Emperor and Empire. He also borrowed 700,000 over the same period. Fay, *The Rise*, pp. 43f. Detailed figures are in Breysig, II, p. 578.

22 The Swedes above all had shown how to use war commissioners effectively. See T. Ertman, *Birth of the Leviathan* (Cambridge, 1997), p. 249.

23 Jannen, p. 173.

24 See especially Opgenoorth, *Friedrich Wilhelm*, I, p. 312.

25 J. Kunisch, 'Der Nordische Krieg von 1655–1660 als Parabel frühneuzeitlicher Staatenskonflikte', in H. Duchhardt, ed., *Rahmenbedingungen und Handelsspielräume europäischer Außenpolitik im Zeitalter Ludwigs XIV*, Zeitschrift für Historische Forschung, Beihefte 11 (Berlin, 1991), p. 28.

26 C. Jany, *Geschichte der königlichen preußischen Armee* (Berlin, 1928), I, p. 210.

27 Carsten, *Origins*, p. 263.

28 Hahn, 'Landestaat und Ständetum', p. 60.

29 Carsten, *Origins*, p. 200.

30 Ibid., p. 250, and see same author's *Princes and Parliaments in Germany from the Fifteenth to the Eighteenth Century* (Oxford, 1959), p. 303.

31 For this see O. Büsch, 'Die Militärisierung von Staat und Gesellschaft im alten Preußen', in Schlenke, ed., *Preussen*, p. 48.

32 See H. Schmidt, 'Militärverwaltung in Deutschland vom Westfälischen Frieden bis zum 18. Jahrhundert', in W. Paravavini and K.F. Werner, eds, *Histoire comparée de l'adminstration: Actes du XIVe colloque franco-allemand* (Munich, 1980), p. 570.

33 For full descriptions of the army, besides Jany, passim, see Opitz, pp. 31, 69, and H. Bleckwenn, *Unter dem Preußen-Adler* (Munich, 1978), passim.

34 Droysen, part 3, II, p. 174.

35 Jany, p. 151.

36 Jany, pp. 148f. Another Frenchman, des Noyers, the Polish Queen's secretary, was also impressed, describing the army as containing 'the best troops in the world': des Noyers, p. 11.

37 G. Heinrich, *Geschichte Preußens, Staat und Dynastie* (Frankfurt am Main, 1984), p. 112.

38 Jany, pp. 178, 341, and Luvaas, ed., *Frederick the Great*, p. 61.
39 Jany, pp. 169, 173.
40 Platen worked hard to achieve this. Opitz, pp. 67f.
41 *Urk. u. Akt.*, XIV, part 2, p. 79, Fernemont to Leopold I, Cölln, 28 March 1658.
42 Dietrich, ed., *Die politischen Testamente*, p. 199.
43 Opgenoorth, *Friedrich Wilhelm*, I, p. 199.
44 See note 41.
45 Fay, 'The beginnings', p. 773.
46 G.A. Craig, *The Politics of the Prussian Army, 1640–1945* (Oxford, 1955), p. 2, note 1, for the German original.
47 The English envoy, Vane, said of this force, 'the Elector payes these troupes he has very well, and . . . has good officers as any prince in Germany': 29 December 1665/8 January 1666, Cleves, Vane to Charles II, PRO, SP 81/56.
48 Those working on the fortifications there in 1665 were said to be 'fresh and sound, well-clad, and their needs seen to'. *Urk. u. Akt.*, XIV, part 2, p. 219, Goess to Leopold I, Berlin, 13 March 1665.
49 H. Prutz, *Aus des Großen Kurfürsten letzten Jahren* (Berlin, 1897), p. 30.
50 Jany, p. 261.
51 Waddington, *Prusse*, I, p. 405.
52 In 1680 Frederick William told William III during his visit that he then had '31,000 men and officers in pay, whereof 13[000] being necessary for his garrisons, he can march 18,000 men wherever he pleases': 14/24 October 1680, Berlin, Southwell to Jenkins, PRO, SP 81/83.
53 Jany, p. 281.
54 Heinrich, *Geschichte Preußens*, p. 113.
55 Carsten, *Origins*, p. 273, for examples in 1678 and 1678.
56 Philippson, III, p. 51.
57 See P.H. Wilson, *German Armies: War and German Politics, 1648–1806* (London, 1998), pp. 29, 66, 162; Jany, p. 278; Carsten, *Princes*, p. 239.
58 See M.S. Anderson, *War and Society in Europe of the Old Regime, 1618–1789* (Leicester, 1988), p. 83. For details of the Imperial army, see T.M. Barker, *Double Eagle and Crescent: Vienna's Second Siege of Vienna and its Historical Setting* (Albany, NY, 1967).
59 Carsten, *Origins*, p. 273.
60 F. Schevill, *The Great Elector* (Chicago, 1947), p. 235.
61 G. Schmoller, 'Die Entstehung des preußischen Heeres von 1640 bis 1740' [1877], reprinted in O. Büsch und W. Neugebauer, eds, *Moderne Preußische Geschichte, 1648–1947: Eine Anthologie* (Berlin, 1981), II, pp. 749ff.
62 Opgenoorth, *Friedrich Wilhelm*, II, p. 275. The burden was also increasing in such German states as Bavaria and the Brunswick duchies. S. Ogilvie, ed., *Germany: A New Social History* (London, 1996), II, p. 251.

63 D. Stutzer, 'Das preußischer Heer und seine Finanzierung in zeit-genössischer Darstellung, 1740–1790', *Militärgeschichtliche Mitteilungen*, 24 (1978), p. 39; Heinrich, *Geschichte Preußens*, p. 112.

64 P.-M. Hahn, *Fürstliche Territorialhoheit: Die herrschaftliche Durchdringung des ländlichen Raumes zwischen Elbe und Aller, 1300–1700* (Berlin, 1989), pp. 236–8.

65 Kunisch, 'Kurfürst Friedrich Wilhelm', pp. 25, 29.

66 The best account (and largely used by most authorities) is still that of 1927 by Hugo Rachel, 'Der Merkantilismus in Brandenburg-Preußen', reprinted in Büsch and Neugebauer, eds, *Moderne Preußische Geschichte*, II, pp. 951ff.

67 For the German cameralist/mercantilists, see I. Bog, 'Mercantilism in Germany', in D.C. Colman, *Revisions in Mercantilism* (London, 1969), pp. 162ff. Another influence was Frederick William's brother-in-law, Duke James of Courland, who developed the commerce of this Polish fief (now in modern Latvia), using the Baltic port of Liepaja/Libau. For him see A.V. Berkis, *The Reign of Duke James in Courland, 1638–1682* (Lincoln, NE, 1960).

68 See F.-W. Henning, *Landwirtschaft in ländliche Gesellschaft in Deutschland, Vol. I, 1800–1750* (Paderborn, 1977), p. 230.

69 *Urk. u. Akt.*, X, p. 613, 2 April 1683, Potsdam, Frederick William to Privy Council.

70 Rachel, 'Der Merkantilismus', p. 954.

71 Bog, 'Mercantilism in Germany', p. 170.

72 Nachama, p. 136 – 'the realm itself took on the role of the bour-geoisie, without having to pay the political price'.

73 Waddington, *Prusse*, I, p. 282; Opgenoorth, *Friedrich Wilhelm*, II, pp. 54, 299ff.; Philippson, III, p. 92; Kellenbenz, p. 275.

74 *Der Große Kurfürst: Sammler*, pp. 81f.

75 H. Eichler, 'Zucht- und Arbeitshäuser in den mittleren und östlichen Provinzen Brandenburg-Preußens', *Jahrbuch für Wirtschaftsgeschichte*, no volume number (1970), p. 135.

76 Macartney, pp. 265ff. prints one.

77 *Der Große Kurfürst: Sammler*, p. 84.

78 See the pessimistic conclusion in Ogilvie, p. 196, for their reigns as well: success 'was minimal: not a single industrial region developed in the central and eastern province of [Brandenburg-] Prussia before 1800'.

79 Schultze, *Mark Brandenburg*, V, p. 46.

80 Rachel, 'Der Merkantilismus', p. 294.

81 Schultze, *Mark Brandenburg*, V, p. 45.

82 Waddington, *Prusse*, I, pp. 405f., Prutz, p. 398.

83 As Waldeck himself said in 1653. Menk, *Waldeck*, p. 104.

84 W. Volk, 'Die Stadterweiterungen Berlins im 17. und in der ersten Hälfte des 18. Jahrhundert', *Jahrbuch für Geschichte*, 35 (1987), p. 19.

85 S. Wolffsohn, *Wirtschaftliche und soziale Entwicklungen in Brandenburg-Preußen, Schlesien und Oberschlesien in den Jahren 1640–1853: Frühindustrialisierung in Oberschlesien* (Frankfurt am Main, 1985), p. 29.

86 R. Vierhaus, *Germany in the Age of Absolutism* (Cambridge, 1988), p. 16.

87 See O. Krauske, 'Der Große Kurfürst und die protestantischen Ungarn', *Historische Zeitschrift*, 58 (1887), p. 493.

88 T. Kiefner, 'L'Accueil des Vaudois du Piémont en Allemagne', offprint from 1989 Torre Pellice Conference kindly provided by Dr C.D. Storrs.

89 Hahn, *Fürstliche Territorialhoheit*, p. 235.

90 *Urk. u. Akt.*, X, p. 613, Frederick William to Privy Council, Potsdam, 2 April 1683.

91 J.I. Israel, *European Jewry in the Age of Mercantilism, 1550–1750* (Oxford, 1985), p. 102, and see pp. 148ff. for Frederick William's liberal policies towards Jews. And see F.L. Carsten, 'The Court Jews: prelude to emancipation', in his *Essays in German History*.

92 L. Kochan, *Jews, Idols and Messiahs: The Challenge from History* (Oxford, 1990), p. 42. For the Jews in Berlin under the Great Elector, see Kochan, pp. 40ff.

93 Lackner, p. 288.

94 Israel, *European Jewry*, p. 169.

95 The major work on Brandenburg colonialism was keen to draw the analogy, R. Schück, *Brandenburg-Preußens Kolonial-Politik unter dem Großen Kurfürsten und seinen Nachfolgern, 1647–1721* (Leipzig, 1889), I, pp. xiff.

96 Philippson, III, p. 91.

97 Schück, I, pp. 41ff., 111.

98 Philippson, III, p. 221.

99 *Urk. u. Akt.*, XIV, part 1, p. 953, Berlin, Lamberg to Leopold I, 28 July 1680.

100 6/16 November 1680, Berlin, Poley to Jenkins, PRO, SP 81/84.

101 For the African venture see especially E. Schmitt, 'The Brandenburg overseas trading companies in the 17th century', in L. Blussé and F. Gaastra, eds, *Companies and Trade* (Leiden, 1981); Schück, pp. 134ff.; and W.O. Henderson, *The German Colonial Empire, 1884–1919* (London, 1993), pp. 9ff.

102 For Prussian merchants' lack of interest see 18/28 January 1681, Berlin, Poley to Jenkins, PRO, SP 81/84.

103 M. Hughes, 'The East Frisians: the survival of powerful provincial estates in N.W. Germany in the 18th century', in *Album François Dumont* (Brussels, 1977), p. 140.

104 The English envoy had realised this weakness earlier: 23 October/2 November 1680, Berlin, Southwell to Jenkins, PRO, SP 81/83.

105 Schmitt, p. 174.
106 O.H. Richardson, 'Religious toleration under the Great Elector and its material results', *English Historical Review*, 25 (1910), p. 108.
107 J. Ziechmann, ed., *Panorama der Fridericianischen Zeit: Friedrich der Große und seine Epoche* (Bremen, 1985), p. 119.
108 Philippson, III, p. 96.
109 Opgenoorth, *Friedrich Wilhelm*, II, p. 311.
110 Schevill, p. 242; and see Schück, p. 288.

Chapter 8

'THE SHREWDEST FOX IN THE EMPIRE',[1] 1660–1679

. . .

BALANCING BETWEEN THE POWERS

In 1661 Louis XIV of France began his personal rule at the death of his first minister, Cardinal Mazarin. The French King was to make all the running in European politics for the next half century: his army was the largest and best and his diplomatic service the most sophisticated. The weakness of the Emperor, the decline of Spain, and Dutch attempts to withdraw from continental commitments allowed Bourbon France to advance to a position almost of hegemony. Louis was above all determined to decide the future of the Spanish monarchy and the German Empire, and he soon embarked on enlarging Mazarin's territorial conquests and network of client states, especially the League of the Rhine.[2] This presented the German princes with a choice between the seemingly irresistible French and the far weaker Emperor, who was also having to deal with growing, and eventually persistent, rebellion in Hungary and the threat of further advance by the Turks in the Balkans.

Gaining the sovereignty of Prussia had made Frederick William a sovereign European prince, but this did not change the fact that he was still very much a minor one, with poor resources and faced by potential foreign policy problems in all parts of his dispersed territories. His main aim was to preserve his independence and escape being absorbed into one of the European power groupings. For a second-rate power, independence entailed trying to avoid permanent friendships or antagonisms. Consequently, during most of the 1660s, Frederick William wanted to avoid tying himself too closely to either Louis XIV or Leopold. He also saw that, for the moment, expansion in Pomerania or Jülich-Berg had to take second place to consolidating his position with his Estates and protecting his vulnerable and scattered lands. While this policy was essentially defensive, it was clearly not the passivity continually urged by his Estates. In his advice for his successor in his *Political Testament* of 1667, he warned: 'It is quite certain that if you sit still and believe the conflagration is far from your borders, then your lands will become the stage for the tragedy.' He also dealt specifically with the problem of the Spanish-Austrian Habsburg and Franco-Swedish power blocs, advising that it was best to follow the example of the Italian princes and to shift allegiance from one to another, 'so that you can always keep a true balance between them'.[3] As a newly sovereign European prince with a growing number of diplomats at the important courts, he hoped to exploit the powers' differences and to exert some influence in his own right. Yet from the beginning he knew he was vulnerable himself and that in any conflict he would need foreign subsidies.

The way the northern peace settlement had been imposed on Frederick William inevitably made him enter the 1660s hostile towards Sweden and her French protector. He also realised the dangers of France's increasing predominance earlier than most of his fellow German princes. In July 1660 he wrote to Schwerin that he would rather depend on the Turks than on France.[4] Then in November 1661 he warned Gladebeck, the envoy of the Brunswick Duke of Celle, that France intended to decide everything in the Empire before reducing the princes to 'slavery'. It is not surprising, therefore, that he was to reject repeated French invitations to join their satellite League of the Rhine, and he told Gladebeck that he was 'neither Imperial, Spanish, French nor Swedish, but purely and simply *reichisch* [i.e. loyal to the Empire as a whole]'. At the same time, however, while valuing Imperial support against a resurgent Sweden, he wanted to prevent the revival of the Emperor's power in Germany: he had also boasted to Gladebeck that 'he owed the Emperor nothing in the world except the safety and defence of the Empire, and if the Emperor . . . were to threaten this, then he would be the Emperor's worst enemy'. In the same vein, six years later, he warned his successor to 'take care of the good of the Empire, of the Protestants and of yourself and surrender nothing to the Emperor which harms the Protestants or decreases German liberties'.[5]

In the event French strength and the Emperor's weakness meant that Frederick William had gradually to accept that his own ability to play any role in European politics 'stood and fell with relations with France'.[6] For their part, the French always kept the door open for Brandenburg to join their anti-Habsburg League of the Rhine. In March 1661 Louis XIV had written to Gravel, his envoy at the Imperial Diet: 'It should certainly be enlarged by such a considerable prince, provided we can detach him genuinely from his engagements with the Emperor.'[7] Over the next two years the French continually made offers to Frederick William, but he proved elusive. It was not till March 1664 that he would ally with Louis and agree to join the League of the Rhine. Although the King guaranteed all the Hohenzollern possessions, including the sovereignty of Prussia, Frederick William managed to limit his commitments to promising diplomatic support and to delay his formal accession to the league for a further year, by which time it was disintegrating. The signature of the Franco-Brandenburg treaty itself brought typical French largesse to Berlin: Electress Louise Henrietta received 'a green velvet bed, with gold inlay, matching chairs, fine hangings, a fine mirror and a silver table with two pedestal tables, and a silver chandelier'. The French envoy, Colbert de Croissy, reported that she and her husband were very pleased, often going 'to admire' the furniture. The electoral ministers, especially Schwerin, also received money from Louis, but as their master knew about this it probably had little political influence on them.[8]

At a time of obvious French ascendancy in western Europe, the alliance with Louis and membership of the League of the Rhine gave Brandenburg some security from the King and his allies, especially the Swedes. Frederick William may also have hoped to paralyse the league, for, as he told an Imperial envoy in March 1665, 'The more of us are in it, the weaker it will be'.[9] In any case he had no intention of becoming a French vassal: throughout his reign he was often forced into French alliances, but he was also to be eager to escape them. There was little real warmth between France and Brandenburg at this time, and the alliance of 1664 was not a great gain for Louis XIV. The Elector had also made sure it gave him far more freedom of manoeuvre than similar ones concluded by France with other German princes. In the one made concurrently with Saxony, Elector John George II had promised 'to do nothing . . . prejudicial to the King or his crown, and . . . to vote [in the Imperial Diet] in everything . . . according to the good intentions of the King'.[10]

The area of Europe where Frederick William was above all determined in the mid-1660s to maintain his independence from France was Poland. He had become increasingly suspicious of French designs in Warsaw, where the actions of the energetic and half-French Queen Louise Maria gave them an opportunity to interfere. She hoped to strengthen the monarchy of her husband, John Casimir, by having his successor elected during his lifetime. As they had no children, the Queen had to look elsewhere, eventually finding a candidate in the Duke d'Enghien, son of the French military hero Prince Condé. Louis XIV naturally welcomed this scheme: it could turn Poland into a client state and destroy Habsburg influence there. But all this alarmed Frederick William, who did not want a French puppet for a neighbour. He also feared that a revival of the Polish crown might threaten his sovereignty in Prussia, which had to be confirmed by each new Polish king. For a while in spring 1661 he had even toyed with declaring himself a candidate for the throne, since this might appeal to the Calvinist magnates in Polish Lithuania. He wrote to his envoy in Warsaw, Hoverbeck, in April 1661, that if such a union came about, 'what power could match it?' But he soon realised it was not feasible unless he became at least a nominal Catholic. And he was not willing 'to alter my religion because of it, to hear a couple of masses and then believe what I want, since how could I be true to them [Poles] when I was not true to my God'.[11] The only realistic way to prevent Louise Maria's schemes, therefore, was to encourage the Polish nobility to oppose them.

Louis XIV realised from the start that his alliance with Frederick William of spring 1664 would not help him in Poland. In the September the King informed his envoy in Warsaw that the Elector had refused to 'engage himself to anything for Polish affairs, so we ought to observe towards him the same reserve and the same circumspection [over Poland] as before this treaty'.[12] But Louis was to find Frederick William also acted very much as a free agent when a crisis developed in the Rhineland in autumn 1665. In October, six months after the outbreak of the Second Anglo-Dutch Naval War (1665–7), the bellicose, Catholic Bishop of Münster, Bernhard von Galen (known as *Kanonbernd*), attacked the Dutch Republic, using English subsidies to pay for his considerable army. As the Republic kept few troops on foot and it was widely believed that the Spanish and Austrian Habsburgs had incited Münster, Louis XIV dispatched a small force to the Meuse to defend the Dutch, still nominally his allies. By frightening off the Bishop, he hoped to deter Habsburg intervention and show the German princes that France, not the Emperor, would now settle all disputes within the Empire. Although

Bernhard did not make peace, he withdrew his troops, and by the end of the year the crisis seemed over.

This outcome did not suit Frederick William. He suspected the Catholic Habsburgs would soon assist the Bishop and he was convinced Bernhard's motives were primarily religious. Even though he was wrong in this instance, religion still had a strong influence on the policies of the German states in the generation after the Thirty Years War.[13] In late October 1665, therefore, he came to Cleves from Brandenburg, ordering troops to follow. As in Prussia ten years before, he clearly intended to protect his own territories in case a wider conflict developed and to pick up what he could for himself.[14] But he was also concerned to uphold Dutch independence and their Protestant religion, even though the republican and anti-Orange Regents were in power in The Hague. He told his Privy Council on 1 December: 'Firstly, as an elector, I have a duty to preserve peace in the Empire; secondly, religion is the chief reason for not wanting to see the States [Dutch] destroyed; they are surrounded by Catholics; to stay neutral would be like a worm which lets itself be eaten.'[15] Ignoring the fears of his leading advisers, Schwerin and Jena, of being dragged into war, he offered the Republic full military support. However, the Dutch Pensionary, De Witt, was uninterested, realising Frederick William would want subsidies, the removal of Dutch garrisons from Cleves and, probably, promises for the future of the young William of Orange.[16] He even told the French ambassador, 'We would rather die than concede to His Electoral Highness what would be neither useful nor glorious to the state, since we can depend on your King'.[17]

By the end of 1665 Frederick William had assembled 12,000 troops in Cleves, but it did not seem that he would be able to use them: the Bishop of Münster's army was continuing to withdraw and no wider religious conflict had developed. Then at the turn of the year an English envoy arrived in Cleves, Sir Walter Vane. He first offered Brandenburg a subsidy for an alliance with Charles II and Münster against the Dutch, and then, off his own bat, a subsidy just to stay neutral.[18] The Elector immediately saw he could use these offers as a lever to scare the Dutch to pay for his troops. He could then threaten the Bishop, force him to peace and increase his own prestige. Even so De Witt remained indifferent, and it was only to please Louis XIV that he changed his mind. By the first months of 1666 the King wanted to withdraw his troops from the lower Rhine to prepare for an early attack of his own on the Spanish

Netherlands. He also judged it wise to keep Frederick William sweet in case he offered his troops to the Spanish or Austrian Habsburgs. His foreign minister, Lionne, believed him 'the most powerful Elector of the Empire'.[19] Consequently, in mid-February Louis persuaded the Dutch to pay Brandenburg a subsidy to bring Münster to peace. Force was not necessary, and by April Frederick William presided over a settlement at Cleves between the Dutch and a suitably chastened Bishop Bernhard. The Dutch swallowed their pride enough to strike a medal celebrating Frederick William as their 'truest ally'.[20]

The peace was certainly a diplomatic triumph and increased the Elector's standing in Germany. Its most immediate result was that he could use his troops, paid with Dutch money, to frighten the city of Magdeburg into admitting a garrison and acknowledging him as heir to the secularised bishopric of Magdeburg.[21] A further effect of this new prestige was a series of alliances with other German princes, including the Emperor. Once more showing himself independent of Louis XIV, Frederick William was beginning to develop his own diplomatic position in Germany and even trying to restrict the King's influence there and in Poland. In Vienna the Imperialists were quite grateful for his actions in the Rhineland, as these had led to the French withdrawing from the Meuse. In May 1666, therefore, Leopold renewed the Brandenburg–Imperial alliance of 1658 and also smoothed the way for a surprising rapprochement between Frederick William and the Duke of Pfalz-Neuburg.

The dynastic feud between Hohenzollerns and Pfalz-Neuburgs over Cleves-Jülich had caused two recent spats and seemed a fixture in the diplomatic landscape. Yet in the mid-1660s both sides came to see the value of a final compromise settlement. What produced this change was the deteriorating situation in Poland. During 1665 it was becoming clear that King John Casimir intended to abdicate, but that his wife still wanted d'Enghien elected. This led to a revolt by the Grand Marshal Lubomirski, partly financed by the Elector. Although some magnates were urging Frederick William to declare an interest and to convert to Catholicism, he refused, telling a French envoy, Millet, in 1667: 'I shall never waver in my religion: I am happy as I am. Even if the crown of Poland were at my feet, I would leave it there. The King of Poland is the slave of his subjects, a mere dispenser of favours . . .'.[22]

The sensible alternative was to find a candidate who would look on him as a protector and appeal to the magnates as a weak ruler. In casting around for someone, he discovered that Philip William of Jülich-Berg, who had succeeded his father as duke in 1653, was willing. With seventeen children to place, Philip William needed a wider field than his Rhenish lands. The Elector therefore seized the chance to produce a pliant king in Poland by settling their dynastic quarrel. In doing so, he acted, as in the earlier attacks on Berg, mostly on his own initiative and against his ministers' advice. After four months of talks a definitive settlement was reached in Duisburg in September 1666. This essentially confirmed the territorial and religious *status quo* in Cleves-Jülich. The Elector also promised to support Philip William in Poland, while the Duke agreed, if elected, to protect Protestants there and to guarantee Frederick William safe access to Prussia through Poland.

During 1667 Frederick William was obsessed with the reach of French power across Europe, and in May he warned the Polish envoy in Berlin that success in Poland would bring Louis closer to 'universal monarchy'.[23] When the French King in the same month invaded the Spanish Netherlands, beginning the War of Devolution with Spain (1667–8), Frederick William let the French envoy, Millet, know his 'extreme displeasure'.[24] Three months later, he replied to Waldeck, who had written to him, still emphasising the Habsburg danger:

> Every good German should always adjust his counsel and conduct to preserve German freedom and protect the fatherland ... At one time this house [of Habsburg] was suspected of pursuing universal monarchy. Now the tables are turned and there is little to fear on that score. France, however, has become too powerful and assumes the *Arbitrium* in everything.[25]

He warned Elector John George of Saxony that the invasion of the Southern Netherlands was a prelude to Louis's seizing the Dutch Republic and the Empire itself, with the electors reduced to marshals of France.[26] He was so angry with Louis XIV that Schwerin feared his fiery temper might lead him to intervene directly in the Southern Netherlands: during the year his army had been raised to 24,000 men, which was more than Spain herself had there.

Angry or not, Frederick William would not risk acting alone. Instead he wanted to stimulate a broad front against France. There was little to be expected from the other German princes, as too many, such as Saxony, were in Louis's pocket. But the signature of peace between the English and Dutch in July 1667 made him hope, despite his Privy Council's lack of enthusiasm, that he could join a wider coalition. He assumed that the Dutch and the Imperialists would take the initiative and hoped they would pay him to lead an allied army to rescue the Southern Netherlands, where the Spaniards were crumbling before the French. Unfortunately, Vienna did not respond: Emperor Leopold, despite his own dynastic interest in the future of the Spanish monarchy, listened to his chief minister Auersperg's insistence that their financial and Balkan problems made it impossible to confront Louis XIV. Auersperg feared that the sickly child Charles II of Spain (1665–1700) might die during the present war and that Louis would seize the whole Spanish inheritance. He preferred agreement with France over a future partition, and a treaty for this was signed in January 1668.

With the Emperor out of the game, the only power able to stem French advance in the Southern Netherlands was the Dutch Republic. The Dutch were already working for an alliance with their recent English enemies to contain Louis. Although Frederick William was eager to be included, De Witt was very cautious. He wanted to avoid actual war with France and saw Brandenburg's role in an Anglo-Dutch alliance as a junior partner subsidised by Spain. As the Spanish administration in Brussels had no cash, this effectively ruled out Brandenburg involvement. De Witt in any case preferred Swedish help,[27] and an Anglo-Dutch-Swedish treaty was negotiated during autumn 1667 and signed in January 1668. He intended this Triple Alliance to exert diplomatic pressure to bring Louis to a compromise peace with Spain. For his part, Frederick William would have nothing to do with this new grouping. He was exasperated with the Dutch and suspicious they might get him to commit himself against France and then leave him in the lurch. In the last months of 1667, therefore, the Elector backed away from challenging Louis XIV. Instead he once more turned turtle.

By now the French had come to see Brandenburg as the keystone of a potential hostile German-Dutch-Spanish coalition. The Elector had become nuisance enough to be bought off, and in the autumn Louis decided to make him an offer he could not refuse. In return for Brandenburg neutrality during the present Franco-Spanish war, the King promised to support the Pfalz-Neuburg candidacy in Poland. By tying Poland and the Spanish Netherlands together in this way, Louis brought Frederick William to an agreement signed in Berlin on 15 December 1667. Although Frederick William claimed[28] he had 'kept a completely free hand', the French looked on this treaty as a significant success in further neutralising the German princes and the Emperor. By taking out the Elector and then making the partition treaty with Leopold the next month, Louis had destroyed all danger of a broad European coalition against him. The Berlin treaty also came cheap. Money was merely distributed among the Brandenburg ministers. Schwerin received 10,000 écus from Louis via Philip William of Pfalz-Neuburg, and a similar sum indirectly through a banker in Gdańsk. The other ministers were paid much less, about 2,000 écus each.

During the first months of 1668 Frederick William, like the Emperor, maintained a benevolent neutrality towards the French campaign in the Spanish Netherlands, despite his recent outbursts about French ascendancy. He continued to cold-shoulder the Triple Alliance and its attempts to mediate. Instead he urged Louis in February to make his own peace with Spain, 'so as to mortify this rabble of Dutchmen who wish to lay down the law to great kings'.[29] In May Louis did make peace with Spain at Aix-la-Chapelle/Aachen, receiving minor gains in Flanders. Although the Elector welcomed this, he had played no part in it. None the less, he was rewarded with a subsidy of 50,000 thalers from Louis and, more importantly, a further promise of cooperation in Poland.

The main purpose of Frederick William's recent manoeuvring had been to solve his problems over the Polish monarchy. And in this he seemed successful. The death of Queen Louise Maria in May 1667 had already weakened d'Enghien's candidacy and now Louis XIV had also ostensibly ditched him. In May 1668 even Sweden came out openly in favour of Philip William, realising he was likely to prove a weak ruler.[30] Then in September John Casimir brought matters to a head by abdicating. Frederick William immediately moved to Königsberg to concentrate on a year-long campaign to have Philip William elected. He spent his own money on building a Pfalz-Neuburg party, which now appeared certain of French, Swedish and even Imperial support. Unfortunately there was little enthusiasm within Poland for this German prince, and, just as important, the French had not given up the notion of running their own candidate. As d'Enghien withdrew, they secretly backed his father Prince Condé, knowing he would attract support from several Polish magnates, including John Sobieski. In May 1669 the Brandenburg envoy in Paris, Blumenthal, discovered Louis was sending money underhand to Warsaw on Condé's behalf: this caused the French Foreign Secretary, Lionne, to act 'ashamed and embarrassed'.[31] At the same time Vienna was found to be underwriting another candidate, the Imperial general Charles of Lorraine. None the less, Frederick William felt confident enough to prepare for Philip William's triumphal procession through Prussia for his coronation in Poland.

In the event all the foreign pressure and bribes to Polish magnates had no effect: 50,000 minor nobles turned up for a noisy and confused election on the banks of the Vistula in June 1669 and forced through the election of a native Pole, Michael Wiśniowiecki. His unimportance – the magnates mocked him as 'the monkey'[32] – ensured that Poland and its monarchy would remain feeble. The Brandenburg envoys in Warsaw were therefore not too disappointed, writing: 'the business is not exactly to Your Electoral Highness's prejudice, and the *Respublica* [Polish Commonwealth] is not strengthened'.[33] And Frederick William himself, despite his annoyance at Louis's and Leopold's deceit, quickly realised he had little to fear from King Michael (1669–73). The new king soon became involved in wars with Turks, Tartars, Cossacks and his own magnates, and he needed to conciliate the Elector.[34] Even the kidnapping of the Prussian dissident Kalckstein by electoral agents in Warsaw in 1670 (see pp. 142–3) only led to cool relations for a year, and in July 1672 Michael confirmed Frederick William's sovereignty in Prussia.[35] In effect the Elector gained more from Michael's election than any other power. No foreign satellite had been established on his borders, and a weak Poland strengthened his own control over Prussia and allowed a successful showdown with the opposition there in the 1670s (see pp. 143–4).

. . .

LOUIS XIV'S DUTCH WAR AND BRANDENBURG'S VICTORY OVER SWEDEN

After the War of Devolution Louis XIV's power and prestige continued to grow, as they did for the rest of Frederick William's life. The peace with Spain in 1668 gave the Sun King merely pause for breath. He blamed the Dutch for his limited gains in the Spanish Netherlands and now sought to destroy them. Charles II of England was recruited in 1670 for the assault, but just as important, and almost as successful, was Louis's quest for German allies to back an invasion of the Republic across its eastern border from the lower Rhine. Inevitably Berlin was on his calling card and he possibly hoped to use Frederick William's differences with the Dutch republicans as a pretext for war. In spring 1669 Lionne assured the Brandenburg envoy that his King knew:

> how the gentlemen in The Hague have treated the Elector; that he will not allow them to tread on his [Elector's] toes: if they do, you only need to hint for us to provide very powerful help against any wrong or injury. For God's sake, your master must have his cities in Cleves back [those with Dutch garrisons] and we must try to make the Prince of Orange great.[36]

The suggestion that the traditional quasi-monarchical role of the house of Orange in the Republic should be restored under Prince William could be expected to appeal to Frederick William, especially given De Witt's insulting indifference during the recent Franco-Spanish conflict. But it appeared at first to the Brandenburgers that Paris was planning a new war against the Spanish monarchy rather than a direct attack on the Republic. During spring and summer 1669 the French envoy in Berlin, Vaubrun, made tentative offers of subsidies and the part of Spanish Gelderland bordering Cleves for help in a future strike against the Spanish Netherlands. Negotiations with the French were taken up in earnest in September, and there is little doubt that Frederick William himself was keen to align himself more closely. Desire for subsidies for his standing army played a part, but equally important was his growing irritation with the Imperialists. He blamed his failure in the Polish contest chiefly on Emperor Leopold, who had quickly established close relations with King Michael. On 29 September Frederick William wrote to his ministers Schwerin and Jena, who were in charge of the talks with Vaubrun, that these were 'not for the money, but he had to be sure of the King of France's friendship, particularly as the Emperor had forgotten all he had done for him, wished to injure him and to satisfy him in nothing'.[37]

The French were delighted with this, hoping eventually to persuade the Elector to further their ultimate goal of destroying the Dutch Republic. His growing reputation and strategic position on the lower Rhine made him a key potential ally. Lionne wrote to Louis XIV on 1 October 1669: 'it is important above all to gain the Elector of Brandenburg, whatever the price. Almost as important as the King of England . . .'. The Foreign Minister believed they might not even need active English help if Louis could 'engage the Elector of Brandenburg with the Bishop of Münster and other Imperial electors and princes in the design of attacking the Dutch'. Consequently talks in Berlin progressed smoothly, especially as nothing was said as yet about a Dutch war. The Elector showed the most enthusiasm and had to drag along his ministers, who did not want far-reaching commitments: Schwerin wished to avoid further war, while Jena was 'very pro-Dutch'.[38] By the first week of 1670 a ten-year Franco-Brandenburg treaty was signed. In this secret alliance Frederick William promised to lead 10,000 men to help Louis conquer the Southern Netherlands on Charles II of Spain's death, which was thought imminent. Louis was to pay him a pension of 10,000 livres[39] for the first year and then 50,000 every year for the next nine. Once the Spanish Netherlands were conquered, Frederick William was to receive Gelderland. Louis also promised to press the Dutch to remove their garrisons from Cleves and to urge the Emperor to restore the former Hohenzollern fief of Jägerndorf/Krnov in Silesia. A pension and the chance of small territorial gains were evidently now more important than the Elector's earlier worries about French expansion in the Spanish Netherlands. In any case, he had become convinced once more that Emperor Leopold was the more immediate danger, and in the alliance he also promised to support French policy in the Empire. He was particularly angry at recent savage attacks by Imperial troops on Protestants in Hungary. On 2 April 1670, he wrote to Schwerin in a rage:

> The devil must be at large in Vienna; what is happening in Hungary is very bad and it disgusts me; if God gives me my life and my health, then I will try to avenge this, since it is intolerable. That's the thanks I get for putting the crown on his [Leopold's] head. Perhaps one day I can take it off him and put it on the head of someone more deserving.[40]

In signing his alliance with Louis XIV, Frederick William was far from unique. He was joining several German princes, including the Bavarian and Saxon electors, who had accepted Louis's money, passed into the French camp and turned their backs on the Emperor. Commitment to a war against the Dutch, however, was a different matter, and his alliance had not mentioned this. None the less, the French believed Frederick William was now their man and could be edged this way. On 6 January 1670, only two days after the secret treaty was signed, Lionne's roving ambassador in Germany, Wilhelm von Fürstenberg, reached Berlin. He disclosed to an astonished Schwerin a scheme to partition the Republic, offering Brandenburg Dutch Gelderland and Zutphen as well as the expulsion of the Dutch garrisons from Cleves. Frederick William was probably even more surprised. Despite his hostility to the present Dutch regime, deep down he still saw the Republic, whatever its government, as a bulwark against both Catholicism and the hegemony of Bourbons or Habsburgs. Therefore, to avoid being dragged into war with the Dutch, he sent an experienced diplomat, Krockow, to Paris in February to press Louis to keep the peace. This was useless, as the French court was set on war. Attempts at the same time to persuade the Dutch to accept Frederick William's mediation were no more successful. De Witt suspected his motives, believing he was tied to the French – he knew about the earlier treaty, if not the recent secret one. Above all, the Dutch Pensionary refused to believe an invasion would happen, and he remarked, as late as 1671, '[the King] will not attack us because he is afraid we will harm him . . . a war with us will destroy France's maritime trade'.[41] Moreover, to prepare for a war on land by building up the army would have strengthened the Orange party which always advocated this. The Dutch republicans much preferred to buy troops from the Danes or German princes, although they unfortunately misjudged how long it would take to assemble these.[42]

Given the attitude of the Dutch and French, Frederick William throughout 1670 had no answer to the problem of the approaching war. This depressed him, and the Imperial envoy Goess found him in late March uncharacteristically gloomy.[43] He was really in a cleft stick: he was on poor terms with the Dutch, he felt cheated by the Imperialists over Poland and believed they were indifferent to western Europe, and he was allied to Louis XIV, whose expansion he was in danger of furthering at Dutch rather than Spanish expense. The French King was also paying him a subsidy which he needed to keep the Brandenburg army on foot.

French pressure to recruit Brandenburg for an invasion of the Republic mounted throughout 1670, since Louis hoped to launch it the next year. He believed it was merely a matter of getting the price right, and in April 1671 he sent a new envoy, Verjus, to Berlin. Already sure of Münster, Cologne and England for the coming assault, the King asked at least for benevolent neutrality. This depressed the Elector further: over the following month Verjus found him 'despondent and irresolute',[44] especially as war seemed likely within weeks. At this time Frederick William wrote to Schwerin:

> Verjus is pressing for an unambiguous declaration of neutrality, which means I will not have a free hand. I have experienced neutrality before: even under the most favourable conditions, you are still treated badly. I have vowed never to be neutral again till I die . . . This has kept me awake all night . . . I believe it will be best . . . to play for time to see the first results of the war.[45]

In this way he would not risk a French attack or lose her subsidies. As the Republic was refusing to help itself, there was little else he could do. In this he was no different from those German powers who were not in actual military alliance with France. The Emperor Leopold, who had no love for the Protestant Dutch and was more concerned with his Hungarian rebels, even signed a secret neutrality treaty with Louis in November 1671, promising to keep out of any war not involving the Spanish monarchy or German Empire.[46]

In the event Louis XIV put off the invasion in 1671, but he was determined to go ahead in spring 1672. This meant Frederick William still had to stand apart or take sides. The choice became no easier because of the continuing hostility of De Witt's government, its lack of allies and refusal to raise a proper army. Not surprisingly, Louis XIV himself was beginning to lose patience with Berlin. The King warned Krockow in autumn 1671: 'I know the Elector's good sense too well to believe he would be rash enough to side with those facing the ultimate fate.'[47] In January 1672 yet another new French envoy to Berlin, the young and highly regarded Count de St Géran, once more asked for a clear promise of neutrality, trying to put the heat on the Brandenburg court as well by mentioning that Louis was negotiating in Stockholm for an alliance.

Frederick William was still evasive, but he had almost decided by now that he would have to help the Dutch. He seems above all to have begun to consider Louis XIV as great a threat to Protestantism as the Emperor Leopold. The King was increasingly pressing his own Calvinists, the Huguenots, to convert, and there were disturbing rumours from London about Charles II's intentions. On 6 January 1672 St Géran wrote from Berlin that the Elector's ministers were claiming 'this is a religious war, that you [Louis XIV] have informed Rome that the King of England will become a Catholic after the Dutch war'.[48] Worries about the fate of Protestantism weighed more with the Elector than the prospect of territorial gain or the destruction of Dutch republicanism and the restoration to power of the Orange family, in the person of his nephew William.

Although St Géran believed the whole Brandenburg court was pro-Dutch, this was hardly true. The Dutch party in Berlin was not that strong. Frederick William's Dutch wife, Louise Henrietta, had died in 1667, and his German second wife, Dorothea (see pp. 233–4), did not have her family ties. The Elector's personal valet, as well as his Master of Horse, Pöllnitz, who owned a Dutch regiment, were certainly pro-Dutch, and some of the generals, including Derfflinger, were keen to fight the French. But in the Privy Council only Dohna and Friedrich von Jena had Dutch sympathies and even they were cautious about committing Brandenburg and risking war with France. The most influential minister, Schwerin, wanted to avoid further conflict and was often considered pro-French. Whatever their misgivings, all the ministers, including Schwerin, agreed with Frederick William that it would be prudent to raise more troops, if only for defence. Recruiting, therefore, began in earnest over winter to expand the army to 15,000 men. Unfortunately, foreign subsidies were needed to keep up such numbers. These did not seem in the offing from the Dutch, who were still reluctant to negotiate seriously. Despite the imminent danger of invasion, De Witt's special envoy, Amerongen, only reached Berlin after St Géran. His instructions showed little urgency, almost implying that the Republic was honouring Frederick William by letting him help. In February he merely offered to return one Cleves fortress and to pay meagre subsidies for only half the troops the Elector was willing to supply. Most of the Elector's ministers therefore cautioned against being drawn into a disaster. During March Schwerin kept away from court, claiming to be ill; even the pro-Dutch Jena wrote to his master on 12 April, warning that allying with the Republic would cause:

> very grave danger for him and his house; the other electors and princes have decided for the other [side] or accepted those conditions [for neutrality] Brandenburg was offered but refused; the previous conduct of the States [Dutch] hardly inspires much confidence; and it is very doubtful if they will keep up [subsidy] payments; most Brandenburg lands are poor and exhausted ... in these inauspicious circumstances the Elector's military renown could easily be harmed ...[49]

Despite all this contrary advice Frederick William himself by now was set on helping the Dutch. This resolve was strengthened when popular pressure forced the republicans to appoint William of Orange captain general of the army in February. Even so, discussions dragged on with Amerongen till early May, when French troops were already massing in the Rhineland. Frederick William no longer insisted the Dutch evacuate his fortresses: these could now help protect Cleves. He also agreed to raise 20,000 men and have them in Westphalia within two months of receiving subsidies. The Dutch were to pay for only half these troops; Louis had previously offered double the subsidies just for Brandenburg's neutrality. Although both sides promised not to negotiate or make peace separately, the poor deal over the subsidies made it almost certain that Frederick William's active role in the conflict would be short-lived.[50] Given Louis's military power and the clear intention of the Emperor and German princes to keep out, the Elector's single-handed support for the Dutch seemed rash and courageous. However, he probably did not expect the French campaign, which opened Louis XIV's Dutch War (1672–9) in June, to prove so swift and triumphant. The Dutch also seemed likely, on their past showing against the Spaniards, to tie down the new invaders in a war of sieges. Though Louis XIV had paid Sweden in April to put 16,000 men into her German lands to intimidate Frederick William, the weak and greedy regime in Stockholm was expected merely to pocket the cash.

Unfortunately, in June and July the French army and its Münster and Cologne allies occupied all the Dutch Republic except for the major coastal towns. At the same time they seized and plundered all Cleves, restoring the Catholic mass to Protestant churches. The Elector could only watch and recruit furiously. As the Dutch money was paid promptly, he managed to raise 23,500 men by mid-July. Their quality and mobility seem, however, to have been poor, and cash was very short. Schwerin wrote at the time to the Prussian Stadtholder, Croy: 'The campaign will open in a few days, and if I were asked for 2,000 thalers I would not know where to find them. My hair stands on end just thinking about it.'[51] Moreover Frederick William could not risk attacking the massive French invasion force in the rear with his own modest army. Although William of Orange, who assumed direct control in the Republic in August when an Orange mob killed De Witt, pleaded for this, it would have been suicidal. The Brandenburg troops advanced no further than Halberstadt, while Frederick William himself stayed in Berlin during the summer, crippled by another attack of gout. The only military solution seemed to be to persuade the Emperor and other

German princes to join Brandenburg in a diversion further south on the middle or upper Rhine.

Such a diversion at last appeared possible because the scale of French success had even moved Leopold to sign a treaty with Frederick William in late June. They agreed to field a joint army to safeguard the borders of the Empire established by the Peace of Westphalia. But the Imperial contingent could not be ready before September and Leopold intended it to protect the Empire from France not to save the Dutch. His main concern was still further rebellion in Hungary and possible Turkish intervention there. In any case he did not trust Frederick William, believing him 'a man to keep a foot into two stirrups'.[52] In the Council (*Konferenz*) on 30 August Leopold's ministers even wondered if Frederick William's actions were a 'Calvinist ploy to get His Imperial Majesty directly involved against France for the sake of Holland'.[53] The Imperialists were concerned enough even to assure the French ambassador covertly that their army on the Rhine would stay on the defensive.

By allying with Leopold, Frederick William had effectively shackled himself militarily to Vienna. This soon became clear when 16,000 Imperial troops under Montecuccoli arrived in Halberstadt in September to join up with 12,000 Brandenburgers there. Frederick William accompanied his troops, but he put his brother-in-law, the Prince of Anhalt, in command instead of the more experienced and capable Derfflinger, probably because of precedence and Anhalt's close relations with the Imperial court. A more serious problem, however, was the Imperial army. Though Montecuccoli was one of the greatest generals of the age, having smashed the Turks at St Gothard in 1664, and Frederick William had worked well with him during the War of the North, he came with private orders 'to avoid a rupture [with France] if possible and to do nothing to provoke it'.[54] He therefore would not disrupt the French campaign in the Dutch Republic by a diversionary offensive on the Rhine. Instead he insisted on leading the joint army south along the right bank of the river, to deter any move into the Empire by a large French force under Turenne, who was shadowing the Germans on the opposite bank. Scared of breaking the alliance with the Imperialists and reluctant to challenge a general of Montecuccoli's reputation, Frederick William felt he had to fall in. By early November the allied army, sodden from heavy autumn rains, had crossed the Main and stayed put there for a month, living off the minor German states.

The normal campaigning season was now well over, and at a council of war in early December it was decided to withdraw the joint army to Westphalia. The march northwards was once more in pouring rain along flooded roads and fields. Stricken by disease and suffering from Anhalt's weak discipline and careless provisioning, the Brandenburgers were on the point of collapse. Their pay was also well in arrears. Frederick William's revenues had been badly hit by the occupation of Cleves and Mark by France and Münster, and the Dutch subsidies arrived irregularly, drying up by the end of the year. The Dutch had been angry that the autumn campaign had done nothing to help them, and the new Pensionary, Fagel, compared it to 'the journey of the Jews from Egypt to Canaän, who when they had reached the frontiers of the promised land returned to Egypt'.[55] Worse was to follow.

In January 1673 Montecuccoli, disgusted by the role forced on him, pleaded ill health as an excuse to resign. Within a month his successor, Bournonville, was outflanked in the county of Mark by Turenne, who had followed the allied army. Imperialists and Brandenburgers now had to retreat. Frederick William was thoroughly dejected and ordered his men back to Halberstadt, intending to leave the war as soon as possible. He was above all disappointed that the other German princes had not intervened and the Emperor had undermined the campaign. In mid-February he informed his Privy Council that he would have to ask for a truce, at the same time writing to the Emperor, 'I fear the French will follow us and ... my lands be totally ruined and my fortresses lost, and I will have to conclude a humiliating peace'.

The French saw little point in pursuing the Brandenburgers and preferred a separate peace. Louvois, the French Secretary of State for War, wrote to Turenne on 14 March that, although their master would have liked to punish Frederick William, 'to teach him and the German princes ... not to interfere outside the Empire, he knows well enough, however, it is more important to settle German matters, so that he can unite all his forces finally to defeat the Dutch'.[56] Both sides, therefore, accepted the offer of Duke Philip William of Pfalz-Neuburg to mediate. On 26 March Frederick William, who was still with his army, wrote home to Berlin, blaming the Dutch for not paying any subsidies for five months and the Imperialists for their inactivity: 'Otherwise His Imperial Majesty and the States [Dutch] could be assured I would not abandon the common cause; but they must give me the time and the means to prove, at less risk, my attachment to the good party. For my ruin would benefit no one.'[57] In April Louis finally ordered Turenne to conclude a truce, and Frederick William could then leave his troops and return to Berlin.

Inevitably the allies were upset. William of Orange denounced his uncle, claiming he 'has thrown away his honour, has shamefully broken the treaty with us'.[58] In Vienna they cynically blamed Brandenburg for the collapse of the last campaign, and it was openly said that 'it would be better not to let the Elector of Brandenburg expand further; it would be far better to see him humiliated'.[59] This criticism was unreasonable, given Frederick William's real difficulties, and it would be fairer to judge him in the light of his actions later. In any case the criticism did not deter him from negotiating with France for peace throughout the spring. His increasingly influential minister Meinders, who had had the thankless task of funding the recent campaign, was sent to the French court.[60] Here Brandenburg was encouraged to desert the allies by revealing the secret Franco-Imperialist treaty of 1671 and Vienna's assurances of the last summer that their Rhine campaign would be merely 'pretence and appearance'.[61] A peace treaty was eventually signed at Louis XIV's camp at Vossem on 26 June. In this Frederick William promised not to help 'the enemies of His Majesty, whoever they might be', with the proviso that 'His Electoral Highness keeps a free hand over the Empire, in case anyone should attack it'.[62] The French handed back most of the Cleves fortresses and promised to pay the Elector 300,000 livres at once and 100,000 annually for the next five years, money he desperately needed. Fortunately for Frederick William, Louis XIV still viewed him as an irritant that he could remove in his usual way with German princes, by giving him a pension. Although the Elector had been chastened and was now heavily in debt, the outcome of this first stage of the Dutch war was less a disaster than it could have been. What it had shown, however, was that he alone was far too weak to check French expansion or to play the kind of balancing role between the western and central powers he had managed between Poles and Swedes in the War of the North.

Louis XIV did his best to confirm the new relationship by dispatching some money within a month. At the same time his envoy in Berlin, Verjus, handed out 5,000 écus each to Meinders and Jena. Although Schwerin refused the 10,000 offered, saying he had spoken against accepting foreign pensions in the Privy Council, Verjus believed he would soon weaken, as he did. The Electress Dorothea does not seem to have been given anything, even though Frederick William had asked outright 'Is there nothing for my wife?'[63] He almost certainly knew about the gifts to his ministers. While both Meinders and Schwerin over the next months pressed to maintain peace with Louis XIV, they did so primarily because of the lesson of the recent campaign rather than because of his money. In any case it was Frederick William who decided policy, and from the start he was unhappy with what he had been forced to do. The reports of the Dutch envoy, Brasser, in June and July show the Elector was distressed at having had to abandon William of Orange and was hinting he would return to his nephew's side when he could. On hearing in July that Leopold was sending another army to the Rhine, Frederick William exclaimed, clearly upset, 'Oh, why didn't you decide to do this before'.[64] Throughout the summer Verjus found the Elector 'could hardly bear to see or meet anyone and all felt he was ashamed and confused'.[65] He kept away from Berlin, spending even more time hunting. The French envoy believed that Calvinism and family connections with the house of Orange meant Frederick William would always be sympathetic to the Dutch. He also found that among the ministers only Meinders and the old and increasingly sick Schwerin were not pro-Dutch. Verjus wrote home in the autumn: 'I am at a terrible court, where I see the Prince filled with indecision and his ministers divided. At bottom things are not well for us and will be difficult to change.'[66]

Verjus's main disappointment was his failure, despite strong support from Meinders, to develop the Peace of Vossem into a proper alliance. This was not only because of Frederick William's Dutch sympathies but also because of the situation within the Empire over the summer and early autumn. Here an anti-French coalition and wider conflict were developing. Louis XIV had increasingly bullied the German princes, and the Emperor realised he had to act decisively: at the end of August Leopold allied at The Hague with the Dutch and Spaniards. A very successful Imperial campaign followed on the Rhine under Montecuccoli, which by November 1673 had even forced Louis to begin to withdraw his troops from the Dutch Republic. From now on the King was to switch the focus of the war from the Dutch to trying to expand directly into the Spanish Netherlands and to repel the military threat from the Emperor on the Rhine. By early 1674 several German princes had allied with Leopold and in May the Imperial Diet declared war on France.

Frederick William viewed all this with growing impatience and resentment at his own ties to Louis XIV. In September 1673 he had already begun to complain to Schwerin about France's 'tyrannical' behaviour in the Empire.[67] Added to this was annoyance at receiving only part of the promised subsidy, and even some of this had been in letters of exchange, which he had refused to accept. On 24 October he wrote angrily to Schwerin:

> It is obvious no money will come and that they are playing games with me. So much the better, for if they break their promises, I do not have to keep mine. When Verjus comes to see me, I will tell him straight: the King is trying to get me to conclude further treaties and offering me large sums, even though he cannot pay the little promised . . . this is . . . chicanery . . . [and] I will act accordingly.[68]

From the beginning of 1674 it was really only a matter of when Frederick William would rejoin the alliance against France, especially as this was now developing along the lines he had hoped for in vain two years before. He still had around 15,000 troops on foot but needed subsidies to maintain or use them. Understandably, the Dutch and Imperialists did not fall over themselves to sign him up. The Dutch suspected he would use their money to pay his army and then do nothing. In February, when a new Dutch envoy reached Berlin, it was with what amounted to an invitation to hire the alliance 12,000 Brandenburgers rather than to join as a principal. Frederick William, however, wanted to participate fully with more troops and to have the Dutch settle subsidies outstanding from 1672. In March he became even keener when Louis XIV's troops overran and destroyed much of the Palatinate. He wrote furiously to Schwerin that 'everyone will consider this French action worse than anything else they have done'. Now none of his ministers, including Schwerin, talked of neutrality. Yet negotiations to re-enter the war dragged on throughout the spring. As other German princes were offering troops, the Emperor Leopold was very wary of bringing back the Elector. The Imperial diplomat Lisola wrote from The Hague on 3 May: 'except in dire circumstances I would not advise arming any heretical prince at our expense, especially the Elector of Brandenburg. I do not expect anything good, or fear anything bad, from him, since I know his temper [*Geist*], which always tries to fish in troubled waters.' The Venetian envoy in Vienna also observed: 'Brandenburg . . . pledges herself as easily to one party, as she frees herself from it . . . and the Court has no confidence in her present disposition'. The Imperialists were right to be wary. As Frederick William recruited an army of 20,000 troops and talks with the allies to pay for them continued, he wrote to Schwerin on 14 May: 'If the negotiation with Holland fails, we will have to deal with France.'[69]

In the event Frederick William did not get what he wanted from the allies, but he decided to stick with them, partly because of a French victory at Sinzheim on the Rhine in mid-June but also because of what was happening in Poland. Here in May John Sobieski was elected king, following the death of King Michael the previous November. He had been a pensioner of Louis XIV and was married to a Frenchwoman, and his election was a triumph for the French party. It had also been such a foregone conclusion and so rapid that Frederick William and the Imperialists could not interfere. Even so, it was not till early July that Brandenburg signed a final treaty with the Dutch, the Emperor and Spain. Here the Dutch liquidated their arrears with a lump sum of 200,000 thalers and Frederick William was admitted to their alliance as a principal. But he was to contribute only 16,000 men and to receive subsidies from the Dutch and Spaniards for just half of them. As the Danes also joined, Frederick William felt that they, and the threat of a Dutch fleet, would deter any Swedish attack. He was confident enough to boast to Verjus in mid-July that he wanted 'to teach kings the respect they ought to have for the electors of the Empire'. The Frenchman was not impressed, and he was more amused than awed when Frederick William assembled a sword, pistol, musket and arquebus for his own use: 'When he puts them on, it will not be to retreat or to advance; they are so heavy, he will be rooted to the spot.'[70]

On 20 August 1674, Frederick William, Electress Dorothea and Crown Prince Charles Emmanuel left Potsdam to join the Brandenburg army assembling in Thuringia. Because he had insisted on entering the war as a principal, the force was a self-contained unit, able to act alone rather than as just a contingent of the Imperial army. The Elector himself also considered it 'a very fine army, . . . well disciplined and not causing any complaints [from the local communities]'.[71] It was 20,000 strong, ten infantry, fourteen cavalry and two dragoon regiments, this time commanded by the capable Derfflinger. In October they crossed the Rhine and joined the Imperialists in Alsace, where Frederick William assumed nominal command of the total allied force of around 50,000. He hoped for a rapid campaign to defeat Turenne's weaker opposing army before the onset of winter. Victory here would relieve the Dutch and Spaniards in the Southern Netherlands, where they were facing the main French army. Unfortunately, Bournonville, who was once more leading the Imperialists and acted as real commander of the allied force, was far more cautious. In a council of war, the Imperial generals rejected the Brandenburgers' tactical plans. This caused Derfflinger to storm out, and the Elector wrote that the Imperialists dismissed their suggestions as 'ridiculous, and I was laughed at'.[72] An eventual allied attack on Turenne at Saverne/Zabern, where Derfflinger led the initial assault, seems to have been ruined by Bournonville's refusal to follow through. Instead he insisted on staying put, making Frederick William fume that they 'could have destroyed him [Turenne], but for that rogue, Bournonville'.[73] As the allied army lacked the sophisticated supply system of Louis XIV, the longer it stayed in one place the more difficult it became to feed from local resources. In November and December the Imperial troops were resorting to wide-scale looting and their army was rapidly deteriorating from hunger and disease, although the Brandenburgers were more disciplined under Derfflinger and better fed through Meinders' efforts.[74] The whole campaign was turning into a disaster and should really have been abandoned because of the winter. Turenne finished it off in early January 1675 by a brilliant manoeuvre in the Vosges, culminating in an attack on the allies at Türkheim. Although the actual battle, in which Frederick William fought alongside his musketeers, was indecisive, the allied position had become untenable. They had to abandon Alsace completely, recross the Rhine and enter winter quarters. While the Imperialists were largely ruined, the Brandenburg regiments were still intact. Frederick William was especially grateful to Derfflinger, giving him 10,000 thalers and saying: 'I would be unlucky to lose him: I don't know where I would find someone else who understands his trade from the bottom up.'[75]

Yet another German campaign had been lost in the Rhineland, and the chance to regain Alsace had gone with it. Louis XIV had a medal struck, which boasted, with not too much exaggeration, 'Sixty-thousand Germans driven across the Rhine'. Inevitably the blame for the defeat was put on Frederick William as nominal commander, and he was ridiculed in Vienna and The Hague for twice leading his army against the French only to retreat. Frederick William himself took the criticism badly, and he was at a low ebb physically and emotionally. It was made far worse because his eldest son, the twenty-year-old Charles Emmanuel, who was a promising soldier, died from dysentery during the campaign in early December. A final blow was news that the Swedes had invaded Brandenburg.

The government of the young Charles XI of Sweden had so far resisted being drawn into the war. But their desperate need for French money during 1674 led them to give way to Louis XIV's demands and put 14,000 troops into Pomerania to threaten his enemies in Germany. As Sweden could not pay for this army from home, 'the only escape from the financial strain seemed to be to move them with all speed into foreign territory'.[76] In January 1675 the elderly Karl Gustav Wrangel ignored contrary orders from Stockholm and led his starving men into Brandenburg, more to feed them than to attack Frederick William. He demanded contributions in cash, grain and meat and ominously set up supply bases, showing he planned to stay. His troops were also ill-disciplined and were soon looting. There was little organised resistance, since the Prince of Anhalt, who had been left as stadtholder, concentrated his few troops on holding the main towns and fortresses. When he summoned the militia, the nobility were apathetic, though the peasantry surprisingly responded well, especially in the Altmark.

The Swedish invasion proved a blessing in disguise for Frederick William, and he quickly grasped this. On hearing of it, while still in Alsace, he told the officers around him: 'I can use this to get all Pomerania.'[77] And he was to write to Schwerin early in 1675: 'I am determined to revenge myself on the Swedes . . . I shall persist, come what may, in ridding myself of their neighbourhood.'[78] If nothing else, he intended to seize Szczecin, so that he could build a fleet there. Instead, however, of answering desperate appeals to rush home, he took his time in preparing his army in quarters already assigned to him by the Emperor in Germany. He also worked hard to persuade his allies that expelling the Swedes from Germany would undermine France's ascendancy. But they tended to look on his new struggle almost as a personal one, irrelevant to the main war in western Europe. The Imperialists in particular felt they had enough on their hands with Louis XIV and a continuing rebellion in Hungary. Leopold wrote to his own envoy at The Hague that he did not want the Swedes 'on his neck', while the Swedish envoy in Vienna was even told that the Elector had no treaty to defend him from attack.[79] Fortunately the Dutch were more understanding, once Sweden showed she intended to occupy Brandenburg, and they agreed to persuade the Emperor and other German states to help. But more delay followed, as Frederick William was ill for weeks with another severe attack of gout. He was not well enough to go to The Hague till mid-May, when a treaty was signed between Brandenburg, the Dutch, the Emperor, Spain and the Brunswick dukes of Celle and Wolfenbüttel. The Dutch agreed to send a fleet to the Baltic, while the Emperor pledged a small force to help in Brandenburg. Frederick William in turn promised not to make peace separately from his allies.

While the allies had now given their blessing to Frederick William's withdrawal from the Rhine campaign and to expelling the Swedes, they provided little immediate practical help. He would have to save himself, and the prospect was becoming more daunting as the months passed by. Throughout the winter and spring of 1675 the Swedes had been tightening their grip on Brandenburg and their numbers had grown to 20,000 men. Their veteran commander, Karl Gustav Wrangel, was considered on a par with Turenne, Condé or Montecuccoli, but his poor health meant that his brother Waldemar had most direct responsibility. The latter was a weak disciplinarian, and he condoned widespread looting. A report from Prenzlau of early May showed that the horrors of the Thirty Years War were recurring:

> every day our poor town has to hand over to the Swedish army 120 casks of spirits, 40,000 pounds of bread and 100 oxen, as well as contributions in cash. They also continue to plunder villages and churches, causing fires here and there and driving the cattle away everywhere. They behave just as tyrannically towards the people. They stab them in the hands . . . Some are [tortured, hanged and broken on the wheel, others] buried up to their necks, [and] innocent children are murdered for sport . . .[80]

The Brandenburg army had spent the winter and spring in the minor states in Franconia, living at the expense of the communities there. At the beginning of June Frederick William took command of 13,000 foot, 7,000 cavalry and 1,100 dragoons. The horses had been fed on the lush spring grass and the whole army marched 300 kilometres in under three weeks to reach Magdeburg on 22 June. Meanwhile in the electorate the Swedish army was once more under the direct command of Karl Gustav Wrangel, who had spread his troops loosely along and to the east of the River Havel. He himself held Havelberg in the north at the junction of the Havel and the Elbe; a regiment occupied the fortress and bridge at Rathenow in the centre; and the bulk of the army was to the south in the town of Brandenburg under Waldemar Wrangel. Defence should have been easy, but poor intelligence meant that they were unaware that Frederick William and his army were 17 kilometres away at Magdeburg. The Elector managed to keep this element of surprise, when he and his commander, the 69-year-old Derfflinger, decided on a rapid move to split apart the Swedish line on the Havel. They set off immediately with 7,000 cavalry, taking 1,000 musketeers with them on carts to get there faster. Although it was raining heavily, and soldiers often had to push and drag the carts through deep mud, the downpours helped disguise their advance. Early in the morning of 25 June, the Brandenburgers surprised the Swedish regiment at Rathenow, destroying and dispersing it for the loss of fifteen of their own men.

The whole Swedish line on the Havel had now been ruptured. To remedy this and reach his brother in Havelberg, Waldemar led his troops some way to the east of the meandering, sluggish river. He needed to cross one of its tributaries, the Rhin (sic), at Fehrbellin to skirt round the Brandenburgers at Rathenow and then join the rest of the Swedes. Unfortunately for him, the countryside he chose to march into, the Havelland, was treacherous fenland, linked by narrow causeways. By the time Waldemar reached Fehrbellin he found the bridge over the Rhin had already been destroyed by cavalry sent ahead by the Elector. It was obvious that the Brandenburgers would soon be upon him, so he set up battle positions. He had 11,000 men and 24 guns, which he deployed in an orthodox fashion, with the 7,000 infantry in the centre and 4,000 cavalry on the wings. When Frederick William and Derfflinger arrived, they had only 6,200 cavalry and dragoons and 12 guns, having moved too fast for the infantry and rest of the artillery to keep up. While Derfflinger would have preferred to wait for these, Frederick William insisted on an immediate attack, declaring: 'We are so close to the enemy, that he must lose his hair or feathers.'[81] As the Swedes had double his numbers, it was a very risky decision.

The Brandenburgers attacked during heavy showers in poor light on the morning of 28 June. The decisive action was the seizure by their dragoons of a few sandhills in front of the Swedes' left flank. Guns were set up here and pounded the whole enemy line. Continual Swedish attacks on this position were repulsed: Frederick William himself led his dragoons in hand-to-hand fighting, 'at one stage being surrounded and having to be hacked out by his men. Two hours after the battle began, Waldemar had had enough and fell back on Fehrbellin while his centre and left flank were still intact. He stayed there for the rest of the day and night: the Brandenburgers were too tired and lacked the infantry to force him out. The next day, however, reinforced by the arrival of 2,000 foot, they renewed the assault, although less vigorously, as the demoralised Swedes crossed the Rhin by the bridge they had managed to repair. Although most Swedes escaped, several hundred were captured with all their baggage and seven guns. Over the two days they had lost 2,500 killed and wounded compared with 500 Brandenburgers. The Elector said he had taken few prisoners on the first day 'because little quarter was given'.[82] His exhausted troops did not pursue the Swedes, who fled through the fens, although the local peasants attacked and butchered more than had fallen in the battle. When Waldemar joined up with Karl Gustav's force a few days later, the Swedish army had been ruined and only 7,000 managed to flee into Mecklenburg on 2 July. Most of their German mercenaries deserted.

Immediately after the victory a song was published in Strasbourg (still a German city till 1681), celebrating Frederick William as the 'Great Elector' (*Große Kurfürst*).[83] His own publicists quickly took this up, although the name was not really to stick till after his death, when it was used in the title of a biography written by Pufendorf. It was certainly justified as he was undoubtedly the greatest of the electors of Brandenburg. The battle of Fehrbellin itself was the first he had fought and won without foreign help or interference, and it was one where he took huge risks, including personal ones: a cannon shot killed an officer at his side. Afterwards he was rather disappointed that he had not annihilated the Swedes. Had he waited for the infantry, as Derfflinger wanted, this might have happened, but the enemy might also have escaped. The Brandenburgers in any case were soaked through and exhausted from their marches. It is also hardly surprising that cavalry alone could not break infantry in prepared positions. The numbers involved meant that Fehrbellin itself 'can hardly be called a battle',[84] but it had considerable psychological, strategic and political importance. Sweden's field army had been effectively destroyed and no sizeable force could be shipped across the Baltic for the rest of the war. Her military reputation, second only to that of France in Europe, had been shattered and was not restored till the reign of Charles XII, a generation later.

More immediately, the victory freed the electorate from the Swedes, and it encouraged the Danes to invade the Swedish mainland, the Brunswick Duke of Celle to fall on Bremen and the Dutch to send their fleet to the Baltic. The Elector of Bavaria also abandoned plans to enter the war on Louis XIV's side. Turenne had written to Louvois on hearing of the Swedish defeat: 'all Germany will change its thinking'.[85]

In July Frederick William took his army into Mecklenburg. This was not to follow the Swedes, who quickly moved into their coastal enclave of Wismar, but to live off his Mecklenburg neighbour's towns and villages. Subsidies from the Dutch and Spaniards were in arrears, and his troops went unpaid, leading to looting and even mutiny. Although he hanged the ringleaders, he admitted to William of Orange: 'One cannot live on air.'[86] It was not till the arrival of some Imperial and Danish troops in October that he could concentrate at last on the ultimate objective of his war against Sweden – West Pomerania. By the end of the year, he had conquered most of it except the coastal towns, including Szczecin. The garrisons there were still being supplied by sea, and contrary winds had kept the Danish and Dutch fleets at Copenhagen. One naval success, however, was the capture of islands in the mouth of the Oder with the help of a tiny Brandenburg squadron.

The following year, 1676, should have seen the Swedes expelled from all Pomerania. They were faced by a Danish invasion of southern Sweden; Bremen and Verden fell to a mixed force of Danes and Brunswickers; and the defeat of their fleet in June by the Dutch and Danes cut off the Pomeranian ports. But the inevitable did not happen, and the Swedish commander, Königsmark, conducted a skilful campaign with only a few troops. Although Frederick William had an army of 20,000, including a few thousand Imperialists, his repeated and costly assaults failed to reduce Szczecin. As Frederick the Great later pointed out, this was not helped by the lack of a competent engineer in the Brandenburg army.[87] Money was also more scarce than ever: Dutch subsidies had finally dried up; and the Emperor was making difficulties over winter quarters for the Brandenburg troops in minor German states. Frederick William complained to Schwerin in February 1676 that the Imperialists 'seem intent to ruin me and to force me into desperate measures'. And a little later he wrote to him that 'the water has now risen up to my mouth'.[88] The Dutch and Imperialists of course were more concerned with the main struggle with France in the west.

The burden of the Pomeranian campaign fell chiefly on Brandenburg itself. Here at the beginning of 1677 a novel poll tax was levied on all, including Junkers, ranging from 1,000 thalers for the Elector to 8 groschen for labourers. It proved very profitable, raising 268,000 thalers, but such a 'revolutionary' step was taken only because of the war emergency.[89] Even then lack of cash delayed the 1677 campaign till June. Huge efforts had been put into assembling an impressive artillery train of 150 cannon and 24 mortars, brought mostly by water from as far away as the Rhineland: Frederick William was determined to take Szczecin before his allies made peace and possibly sacrificed his gains. Tentative Franco-Dutch talks had already taken place at Nijmegen at the end of 1676, causing him to warn the Republic's envoy, van der Tocht, that if the Dutch were 'attacked again, I will not be the one to help them. While I will be harmed [by peace], they will suffer as well in the long run.'[90] Consequently, he renewed the siege of Szczecin desperately in July with heavy bombardments. It was a formidable undertaking because of water channels, swamps, a moat and walls. Derfflinger directed operations, but the Elector, gout-ridden as usual, and even the Electress Dorothea, appeared in the batteries. When an officer remonstrated with him about the danger, he answered: 'Did you ever hear of an elector of Brandenburg who was killed?'[91] In the event the garrison surrendered only when the walls were breached in the last days of the year. Frederick William entered the city on 6 January 1678, clearly intending to stay there for good and make it the focus for Brandenburg's future maritime trade. Tax concessions were given to the citizens and a trade council established.

Even the fall of Szczecin did not end the Pomeranian campaign, since the Swedes still held Stralsund and other enclaves. In June 1678 Frederick William began to reduce these, with a massive army now 45,000 strong – 31,000 foot, 9,700 horse and 3,400 dragoons. By the end of November, he had taken them all. Unfortunately, events elsewhere made all this irrelevant. The previous January, months before this final campaign in Pomerania, the Dutch envoy had urged Frederick William to send his troops against France instead. He warned that if France continued to advance in the Spanish Netherlands, the Elector could find himself in 'a situation in which his conquest of Pomerania would be of little help to him'.[92] But Frederick William had no intention of being diverted from Pomerania. This was a mistake, and he might have done better to have listened to the elderly Schwerin, who wanted an agreement with France and Sweden before it was too late. As Schwerin feared, the fate of Pomerania was not being decided in the batteries before Stralsund, but in western Europe. Here by the turn of 1677–8 the anti-French coalition was collapsing as the Dutch and Spaniards decided to end the war. In late summer 1678 both states made peace with Louis XIV at Nijmegen. One reason why the French King himself also wanted peace with them was that he felt honour-bound to rescue his northern ally. On 10 January 1678, Louis had written that 'satisfying Sweden . . . is what I attach the most to'.[93] In the Peace of Nijmegen, the Dutch and Spaniards were to agree that all Sweden's German territories should be restored.

France could not enforce these terms immediately, since Emperor Leopold continued the war along the Rhine till the end of 1678. Throughout the year the Imperialists had pressed Frederick William to join them. He would not do so, not just because of his obsession with Pomerania, but also because the protracted campaign there had allowed a French-inspired plan to mature for an attack on Prussia. In October 1678 12,000 raw Swedish troops under General Horn invaded Prussia from Livonia and began to pillage the duchy. If Horn had been more daring he might well have seized Königsberg. The Stadtholder, Croy, only had the militia to defend it, and the citizens were indifferent because of the heavy taxation being imposed. Fortunately, Horn's timidity, harsh weather, sickness and hunger among his men held him back north of the city. This delay allowed Frederick William to act. Immediately after the last Pomeranian fortresses fell, he decided to deal with this new invasion himself, declaring that he could not let 'the one he had driven out of his nest now settle down in his own'.[94] In mid-December he sent 9,000 men and 34 guns ahead, following with his wife and second son Frederick, now Crown Prince, early in the new year. On 26 January the electoral family and the army reached Königsberg, after crossing the frozen southern lagoon of the Vistula on carts and sledges. The news frightened the Swedes into retreating across the ice of the more northerly lagoon. Although Frederick William was suffering from bronchitis, he followed with his army and nearly caught them near Tilsit/Sovetsk in early February, capturing their baggage. Horn fled inland across the frozen Polish-Lithuanian wastes, his army a disintegrating rabble. Thousands perished in the cold and only 3,000 frostbitten soldiers reached Riga. Frederick William sensibly did not risk destroying his own army in pursuit.

This brief winter campaign in Prussia rounded off five successful years of war against Sweden. None the less, it did not alter the fact that Brandenburg was still a minor power in a Europe where others made the ultimate decisions, as they had twenty years before at the Peace of Oliwa. In February 1679 Emperor Leopold concluded peace with France, agreeing that all Sweden's German lands should be restored, including West Pomerania and Szczecin. The decision to abandon Frederick William had been an easy one, encouraged by the other German princes, who all believed he would have deserted them as readily. Leopold's Council during 1678 had concluded that 'the day the King of France hands him Stettin [Szczecin], he will lay aside his arms and his anger'.[95] The Emperor moreover preferred a weak Sweden in Pomerania than a strong Brandenburg. His Court Chancellor, Hocher, told the Danish envoy in November 1678 that they 'would not like to see the rise of a new king of the Vandals [i.e. Frederick William] on the Baltic'.[96]

Emperor Leopold had good grounds for suspicion, since Frederick William had also been negotiating with the French at Nijmegen since June 1678. Meinders had been sent there, with orders to return Stralsund and Greifswald for the rest of Pomerania with Szczecin. He was also to try to win Louis XIV over by offering to abandon the allies and to support France in the German Empire. Frederick William told Schwerin at this time that if Louis agreed, 'not only will I change my conduct, but the King's interest will be mine, and I will join all my forces to his'. Some months later, in November, he remarked over dinner to the young French Count de Rébenac, who had been captured with the Swedes at Stralsund and could be counted on to inform Paris, that his troops would help Louis 'against everyone without exception . . . if the King abandons the Swedes'.[97] A day or two afterwards one of his ministers, Fuchs, proposed to Rébenac a separate peace and an alliance, in return for Szczecin and Pomerania up to the River Peene, even offering to let Sweden have Minden in exchange.[98] Fuchs added that the Elector 'had only one natural enemy, the Emperor, who was the King's as well. He will act against him: there are sound enough reasons'.[99] Similar offers were being made to the French during the autumn and early winter through Meinders in Holland and then in Paris. He was even told to propose that Sweden be given 'some tons of gold' for Pomerania and troops to use against the Danes who also were still at war with her.[100] Of course, while all these offers were being made to France, Frederick William, true fox that he was, was urging Leopold to continue the war.[101]

Louis XIV proved indifferent, especially once the Imperialists became willing for peace. He was determined to stick by Sweden, believing his 'glory' (*gloire*) demanded it. He even refused to mediate a settlement between her and Brandenburg, declaring, 'How can I act as a mediator, since I am biased?'[102] In March 1679 French patience finally snapped. The War Minister, Louvois, threatened Meinders that France was ready to attack the Hohenzollern lands: 'first we will take Lippstadt [an enclave of the county of Mark], Minden will cause us no trouble, then Halberstadt and Magdeburg will fall to us one by one, and finally we will reach Berlin'.[103] Frederick William wriggled desperately to escape, even offering the duchy of Cleves just for Szczecin. When Meinders proposed this to the French Foreign Minister, Pomponne, he was told icily that the Swedes would no more lose Szczecin than Stockholm itself.[104]

At the beginning of May Frederick William was still declaring: 'We are resolved to wait for the *extrema* and face the consequences rather than agree to such conditions.'[105] But the next month, as 30,000 French plundered their way through Mark and then besieged Minden, he accepted it was all over. On 29 June 1679 Meinders signed the Peace of St Germain, surrendering all Swedish Pomerania for a few minor concessions: Sweden returned the tolls on the East-Pomeranian ports and all but one of the enclaves on the right bank of the Oder. However, this brought Frederick William neither free navigation of the river nor access to the sea. A more positive gain was that Dutch garrisons were not allowed back into Cleves. And as a gesture of goodwill Louis also promised to pay the Elector 300,000 thalers over two years, which would go some way to clearing his debts of three times this sum.

By this Peace of St Germain 'Frederick William had suffered the worst political defeat of his career'.[106] The main problem was that his ambitions had far outrun his true position as a minor power. He was bitterly disappointed at the outcome and, quite unreasonably, blamed it all on his allies' deserting him, especially the Imperialists. He now concluded that the way ahead lay in alliance with France. He told the Danish envoy openly a few days after the Peace of St Germain: 'I want to separate France from Sweden and I would like us [Brandenburg and Denmark] to accommodate with France for our safety and to revenge ourselves on those who have deserted us so disgracefully.'[107]

. . .

NOTES AND REFERENCES

1 This was how the French envoy in Vienna, Grémonville, described the Elector in 1672. Prutz, p. 159. Much of the material for this chapter has been used in my 'Small-power diplomacy in the age of Louis XIV: the foreign policy of the Great Elector during the 1660s and 1670s', in R. Oresko, G.C. Gibbs and H.M. Scott, eds, *Royal and Republican Sovereignty in Early Modern Europe* (Cambridge, 1997), pp. 188ff.

2 See J.T. O'Connor, *Negotiator out of Season: The Career of Wilhelm Egon von Fürstenberg, 1629–1704* (Athens, GA, 1978), pp. 23f.

3 G. Schöllgen, 'Sicherheit durch Expansion? Die außenpolitischen Lageanalysen der Hohenzollern im 17. und 18. Jahrhundert im Lichte des Kontinuitätsproblems in der preußischen und deutschen Geschichte', *Historisches Jahrbuch*, 104 (1984), p. 24; Opgenoorth, *Friedrich Wilhelm*, II, pp. 72f.; and Dietrich, *Politischen Testamente*, p. 190.

4 Opgenoorth, *Friedrich Wilhelm*, II, p. 78.

5 Pagès, pp. 23f., 65–7.

6 Opgenoorth, *Friedrich Wilhelm*, II, p. 77.

7 Droysen, part 3, II, p. 53.

8 Pagès, p. 100.

9 Ibid., p. 102.

10 Droysen, part 3, II, p. 62.

11 Meinardus, 'Kurfürst Friedrich Wilhelms', pp. 63f.

12 Pagès, p. 99.

13 W. Kohl, *Christoph Bernhard von Galen. Politische Geschichte des Fürstbistums Münster 1650–1678* (Münster, 1964), p. 208.

14 The French minister, Pomponne, believed 'The Elector came to Cleves not so much to defend his lands as to get what he could from whoever needed his help'. Droysen, part 3, II, p. 127.

15 Hüttl, p. 339; Philippson, II, p. 63.

16 Frederick William, like Charles II of England, was a guardian of the prince, the future William III.

17 Philippson, II, p. 57.

18 This unauthorised offer caused Chancellor Clarendon to explode: 'God forbid the Crown of England should fall so low as to give the elector of Brandenburg money to do us no harm.' K. Feiling, *British Foreign Policy, 1660–72* (London, 1930), p. 161.

19 *Urk. u. Akten*, II, p. 300, Lionne to Colbert de Croissy, 26 March 1666.

20 Opgenoorth, *Friedrich Wilhelm*, II, p. 93.

21 Although his succession to the incumbent Saxon Administrator, Augustus, had been laid down in the Peace of Westphalia, the city magistrates had so far not agreed. Magdeburg was to pass peacefully to Brandenburg at Augustus's death in 1680.

22 Philippson, II, p. 127.
23 Opgenoorth, *Friedrich Wilhelm*, II, p. 100.
24 Philippson, II, pp. 104f.; Pagès, p. 162.
25 Philippson, II, p. 96.
26 Ibid., II, p. 121.
27 See Rowen, pp. 699f.
28 In a letter to his mother-in-law Amelia of Solms, Hüttl, p. 356.
29 Rowen, p. 768.
30 Wójcik, p. 268.
31 Droysen, part 3, II, p. 265.
32 Waddington, *Prusse*, I, p. 479.
33 Philippson, II, p. 157.
34 See Kamińska, pp. 7ff.
35 King John Sobieski did so in 1677 and again in 1688 at Elector Frederick III's succession.
36 Droysen, part 3, II, p. 253; Philippson, II, p. 228.
37 Philippson, II, p. 229.
38 Pagès, pp. 207, 214.
39 There were about 3 livres to 1 thaler.
40 Droysen, part 3, II, p. 364; Pagès, p. 200. A further Political Testament drawn up around this time included a plan to conquer Silesia if the Austrian Habsburgs died out. It was unconnected with the problem of the Hungarian Protestants but caused by Leopold's serious illness in January 1670 when he had no male heir. If his line died out, then Saxony, or even Sweden, might seize Silesia. The plan was not a forerunner of Frederick the Great's invasion and was meant for the exceptional circumstances of the time: it was not mentioned again. See Opgenoorth, *Friedrich Wilhelm*, II, p. 105; Redlich, p. 101; and Schöllgen, 'Sicherheit durch Expansion?', pp. 25f.
41 Droysen, part 3, II, p. 326.
42 Rowen, pp. 728f.
43 Philippson, II, p. 233.
44 Pagès, pp. 256f.
45 Reconstructed from Droysen, part 3, II, p. 370; Philippson, II, p. 238; and Waddington, *Prusse*, I, p. 484.
46 Redlich, p. 106.
47 Philippson, II, p. 244.
48 Pagès, p. 276.
49 Droysen, part 3, II, p. 387.
50 Opgenoorth, *Friedrich Wilhelm*, II, p. 126.
51 Pagès, p. 290.
52 19 June, old style, 1672, Vienna, Gascoigne [English envoy] to Arlington, PRO, SP 80/12.
53 Philippson, II, p. 275.

54 Redlich, p. 112. The Swedish envoy to Vienna wrote at this time: 'Brandenburg is considered a wild unbroken horse that needs another tame and docile beast harnessed to it, to prevent its bolting headlong into something harmful to the Empire.' Waddington, *Prusse*, I, p. 493.

55 W. Troost, 'William III, Brandenburg, and the construction of the anti-French coalition, 1672–88', in J.I. Israel, *The Anglo-Dutch Moment: Essays on the Glorious Revolution and Its World Impact* (Cambridge, 1991), p. 304.

56 Philippson, II, pp. 288, 290.

57 Pagès, p. 311.

58 Klopp, I, p. 335.

59 Philippson, II, p. 293.

60 For these negotiations see A. Koller, *Die Vermittlung des Friedens von Vossem (1673) durch den jülich-bergischen Vizekanzler Stratmann* (Münster, 1995), pp. 133ff.

61 Droysen, part 3, II, p. 446.

62 Ibid., p. 443; Waddington, *Prusse*, I, p. 501.

63 Pagès, p. 333; Prutz, pp. 49ff.

64 Philippson, II, p. 300.

65 Prutz, p. 43.

66 Erdmansdörffer, *Deutsche Geschichte*, p. 582; and see Pagès, pp. 340f.

67 Opgenoorth, *Friedrich Wilhelm*, II, p. 148.

68 Pagès, p. 343; Orlich, appendix, p. 13.

69 Philippson, II, pp. 312–15.

70 Pagès, p. 360.

71 Droysen, part 3, II, p. 491.

72 Erdmannsdörffer, *Deutsche Geschichte*, p. 604.

73 Philippson, II, p. 325.

74 Opgenoorth, *Friedrich Wilhelm*, II, p. 159.

75 Philippson, II, p. 330.

76 M. Roberts, *Essays in Swedish History* (London, 1967), p. 228.

77 Philippson, II, p. 341.

78 Schevill, p. 330.

79 Philippson, II, p. 345.

80 Hüttl, p. 403.

81 Philippson, II, p. 357.

82 Erdmannsdörffer, *Deutsche Geschichte*, p. 622.

83 Hüttl, p. 41.

84 M. Immich, *Geschichte des europäischen Staatensystems von 1660 bis 1789* (Munich, 1967, reprint of 1905 original), p. 85.

85 Droysen, part 3, II, p. 536.

86 Philippson, II, p. 365.

87 Luvaas, p. 63.

88 Pagès, p. 365.

89 Opgenoorth, *Friedrich Wilhelm*, II, pp. 180f.
90 Philippson, II, p. 382.
91 Waddington, *Prusse*, I, p. 524.
92 Troost, p. 309.
93 P. Höynck, *Frankreich und seiner Gegner auf dem Nymweger Friedens-kongress* (Bonn, 1960), p. 111.
94 Droysen, part 3, II, p. 655.
95 Klopp, II, p. 160.
96 Orlich, p. 158.
97 Pagès, pp. 376, 388.
98 Waddington, *Prusse*, I, p. 522.
99 Pagès, p. 388.
100 Philippson, II, pp. 415f. Meinders' offer caused even Frederick William's apologist, Philippson, to admit that 'the Elector was no more honest [ehrlicher] than his allies'.
101 Höynck, p. 160.
102 Philippson, II, p. 417.
103 Droysen, part 3, II, p. 667.
104 Philippson, II, p. 426; Waddington, *Le Grand Électeur*, II, pp. 423–5.
105 Philippson, II, p. 424.
106 Opgenoorth, *Friedrich Wilhelm*, II, p. 194.
107 Pagès, p. 411.

Chapter 9

THE FINAL YEARS, 1679–1688

. . .

FRICTION WITHIN THE ELECTOR'S FAMILY

In July 1667 Frederick William's first wife, Louise Henrietta, died
from pneumonia. She was forty and had been in poor health for ten
years, her many pregnancies having taken their toll. The Berliners
had disliked her as a foreigner and Calvinist, and her corpse was
even insulted during the lying in state.[1] Her death left her dis-
traught husband with three young sons, Charles Emmanuel (Karl
Emil), aged thirteen, Frederick eleven, and Louis two. The children
were badly affected by her death. She had been a caring mother
and the choice of her friend Schwerin as the boys' tutor was hers,
although Frederick William certainly approved. There is a touching
letter from him to Schwerin, written from Königsberg in December
1662, commenting on the minister's decision to move the children
from Berlin to the fortress at Spandau to escape an outbreak of
plague. Frederick William observed: 'It troubles me a good deal
that the children will suffer terribly from the cold there.' He suggested Schwerin take them to Potsdam, which was 'smaller and
warmer'.[2] It was as much because of the boys' misery at their
mother's death, as well as Frederick William's own, that he decided
to remarry quickly. As he wrote to one of his sisters: 'I must have
someone to look after my own [family], if I fall ill.' Nine months
after losing his wife, the 48-year-old Elector had chosen another,
the widowed Duchess Dorothea of Brunswick-Hanover (1636–89).
By birth a Holstein-Glücksburg princess, she was thirty-two, and
had been married for over ten years, with no children. She agreed
to convert from Lutheranism to Calvinism, and the couple married
quickly and quietly in June 1668. The Elector's Orange relatives,

233

especially his mother-in-law, were unhappy, but as he explained to one of them, Johann Moritz of Nassau: 'I am so lonely, that I had to do it for companionship.'[3]

On a personal level Frederick William's choice was a lucky one, and he was probably happier with Dorothea than with his first wife. Although she was rather plain, lacking Louise Henrietta's intelligence and charm, she was far more robust, enjoyed hunting and drinking with her husband and accompanied him on campaigns. She proved an ideal companion and looked after him during his sick old age. While she influenced him a lot, it was more over personalities than policies. Foreign envoys were always very careful to give presents to her and her ladies-in-waiting, and Dorothea was not backwards in asking for them. She received many from the French envoy, Rébenac, and in August 1682 the Imperial envoy, Lamberg, asked for money to 'distribute among the Electress's ladies'.[4] Her husband knew all about the gifts and felt they were her due.

Dorothea's companionship was especially valued in the years after the Dutch War, when Frederick William increasingly isolated himself with a few courtiers at Potsdam. This withdrawal was from a court in Berlin which had developed quite impressively since the 1660s. Gaining the sovereignty of Prussia had of course turned Frederick William from a German elector into a sovereign European prince, if a secondary one. His victories over the diets also meant he could now spend more of his personal revenues. This was reflected in the very lavish furnishings of his palaces, the grander tone of the court and the adoption of a more stylised ceremonial. The model was the Orange court; the more obvious example of Louis XIV with his life of public display, in Paris and then at Versailles, attracted Frederick William less than other German rulers, although he did begin to wear the long wigs made fashionable by the French King. Close relations with France in the early 1680s brought little change. Frederick William remained convinced of the superiority of the Dutch world, and the artists and craftsmen he employed continued to be mainly from the Netherlands. Although these were joined by French Huguenots at the very end of his reign, the latter's real influence was to be on his successor's court.

The grander style, more fitting for a sovereign prince, was also apparent as he travelled outside Brandenburg in the 1670s and 1680s. On his visits to Cleves and Königsberg, as well as to other north-German courts, he was accompanied by at least 200 horses. Returning to Berlin from the winter campaign in Prussia, he was met by 'eight triumphal arches and magnificent displays of homage'.[5] When his nephew, the Prince of Orange, visited the Berlin *Schloß* in October 1680, this produced the kind of spectacle found in no other German court outside Vienna, and it even impressed the snobbish Rébenac. William III was greeted by twenty-four trumpeters and forty pages, and the electoral servants glittered in new livery with gold and silver braid. Another Frenchman, Reymond, who was in Berlin during 1682, wrote that 'the electoral court is more lavish than any other in Germany' and was royal in all but name.[6] Both Rébenac and his Dutch rival, Amerongen, complained about how expensive it was to live there. But what was grand in German terms was still very small beer compared with Louis XIV's court and its later German imitations. Above all there was not the money for a French-style court, and Brandenburg also lacked great nobles to live there and perform ceremonial duties. As government was still associated with the Elector's own household, his ministers had to take on a dual, and secondary, role as court officials when necessary – for example Schwerin was Lord High Chamberlain besides all his other posts. The court also remained rather provincial and essentially a family affair, particularly in its fairly simple pleasures. There were carriage rides in summer and sleigh rides in winter; ceremonial fanfares and hunting music were preferred to concerts and ballets; and the peak of entertainment was the *Wirtschaften*, popular throughout Germany, including the Imperial court in Vienna. These were masquerades, where guests dressed like peasants in a country inn.

Dutch influence is apparent in the residence at Potsdam where Frederick William retreated more and more during the 1680s. This village, set in a pleasant spot on the Havel among lakes, low hills and many trees, was some 24 kilometres from Berlin. After the War of the North it had become a favourite place for Frederick William to hunt. Over the next two decades a hunting lodge there was transformed into a small horseshoe-shaped palace with a few state rooms in the Dutch style. The work was carried out by Memhardt and Chièze and was the only extensive building undertaken during the reign. Because of the open aspect beside the river, there was space for a large park with red deer, geometrical-shaped gardens, fishponds, a vineyard and tree-lined avenues. By the end of the 1660s the palace could accommodate the Elector and some of his court for weeks at a time. In 1672, however, the French envoy, Vauguion, was not impressed by it, considering it little more than a farm house.[7]

It was certainly neither on the scale of any of Louis XIV's buildings nor of that of Frederick the Great's Potsdam palace of Sanssouci.

In the 1680s the residence in Potsdam effectively became the Great Elector's home and he spent as little time as possible in Berlin. (Frederick the Great was to do much the same, particularly after the Seven Years War.) The English envoy, Southwell, commented about Potsdam: 'there is no tollerable accomodation but for himself [the Elector], and wch makes the Councillors for the most part returne back the same day they go thither'.[8] While the Privy Council and other bodies stayed in the Berlin *Schloß*, one or two councillors (especially Fuchs in the 1680s) worked with the Elector permanently in Potsdam. The old way of governing together with his Council was now long past, although the body continued to meet and was occasionally summoned to Potsdam.

During the years after the Dutch War Frederick William, who was sixty in 1680, became infirm and immobile, often unable to climb stairs or even to stand. Heavy jowls, pencil moustache, prematurely lined face and large paunch had been there since his early fifties, and both bronchitis and gouty arthritis had troubled him for twenty years. These became far worse as he grew 'very corpulent',[9] and he proved increasingly tetchy, preferring the company of his wife and his valet, a Dutchman, Kornmesser. His health was particularly bad in winter and spring, improving in summer. By about 1683 the Elector himself, as well as many observers, seems to have accepted he had not long to live, especially as he was now suffering frequent bouts of pain and fever from kidney stones. To try to cure these, he drank vast amounts of tea, thirty or forty cups every morning in 1684.[10] This was said to have caused dropsy which developed in his feet, stomach and chest, although this was more likely a symptom of heart or renal failure.

Despite his illnesses, if his foreign policy demanded it, he would occasionally welcome other rulers to the Berlin or Potsdam *Schloß*. William of Orange in 1680 was followed by the Elector of Saxony in 1681 and the Duke of Brunswick-Hanover in 1682, and in summer 1686 Frederick William made a supreme effort to travel all the way to Cleves to meet William again. The 1680s were also a time of almost continual diplomatic activity and of numerous domestic edicts. Frederick William was closely involved in all this and refused to spare himself, trying to work as hard as ever. He still rose at six, prayed, and ate a sparse breakfast, with tea or coffee instead of the beer soup of his earlier years. He then worked on his papers and consulted councillors all morning. After the usual heavy German midday meal, he would struggle to ride or at least walk in the afternoon, till a few months before his death. The evenings were spent talking or playing cards with his family.

Frederick William's health and family problems (see pp. 238–40) in the 1680s were not helped by the complexity of the international situation he faced. His response to this was not unlike that at the start of the War of the North, when he was between two camps and a false move could have brought disaster on him. As in the 1650s, indecision and rapid shifts of policy were the order of the day, especially as he became aware of his own physical weakness. Rébenac said of him in April 1684: 'The Elector is a prince of 65, who in truth is disposed to war, to plan and carry it out, but he spends three quarters of the year in his bed or chair.'[11] To make matters worse, his advisers seem to have been more factious than previously, dividing into pro- and anti-French camps. No one of Schwerin's stature had emerged after his death in 1679. Although Schwerin's influence had declined towards the end, Frederick William always considered him his most dependable minister and continued to entrust him with the education of Louise Henrietta's sons after she died. In January 1676 he wrote to him: 'I wish you had two bodies, so that one could be here with me, and the other at Cleves with my children.'[12]

Outsiders saw the court as very disunited. In October 1685 Rébenac wrote that '[the] ministers ... are never agreed among themselves'.[13] Frederick William, however, continued to keep the threads of policy in his hands and may have found the impression of feuding ministers useful: he could often explain to foreign envoys that a course of action he had abandoned was the fault of a particular minister. While it has been suggested[14] that the overall morality of the electoral ministers declined as they came to expect foreign gifts as their right, the Elector knew all about these, and probably considered them a supplement to his ministers' meagre salaries.

The one constant in Frederick William's difficult, final years was his wife, who was always there when he was confined to his room or could manage to go out and hunt. Dorothea certainly proved a devoted wife and equally devoted mother to the seven children (three girls and four boys) of their marriage. Unfortunately, this was not true with Frederick William's sons by his first marriage. She showed them no affection and had resented the interference of their Orange relatives. Especially wounding had been the attempt by Frederick

William's brother-in-law, Anhalt, to prevent her acting as the boys' guardian if their father died. Both Dorothea and her husband were very upset over this, and her relations with her stepchildren were permanently soured, especially with the elder ones, Charles Emmanuel and Frederick. This did not matter too much at first because Frederick William himself was very fond of Charles Emmanuel, who had inherited his vigour and hot temper. The Prince's death at twenty from dysentery during the 1674 Rhine campaign was a bitter blow, and it cannot have been softened by rumours that Dorothea helped him on his way. The new crown prince, Frederick, born in 1657, was reserved, sensitive, rather prickly, and crippled from a fall as an infant – an English envoy described him at nineteen as 'low and something crooked, and does appear to want sense'.[15] Although he had been Louise Henrietta's favourite, his father had little time for him, even telling Rébenac in January 1681, 'my son is good for nothing'.[16] Relations between Frederick and Dorothea were just as bad. She acted like the proverbial wicked stepmother, thinking entirely of her own children and their interests. Close observers such as Rébenac believed she 'uses her influence . . . to get her husband to be continually cold to the children of his first marriage'.[17] The Crown Prince in his turn hated Dorothea, and this hatred soon became paranoia. He was convinced that she, or her friends, had poisoned Charles Emmanuel and intended to kill him as well, so that her children could succeed. His father, of course, had feared Schwarzenberg in the same way, and there were many in Berlin, including Frederick's close friend and tutor, the Dutchman Danckelmann, who fed these fears. While Dorothea would have liked one of her own children to inherit, this almost certainly went no further than wishful thinking and pleadings to her husband to provide for them after his death. During the 1680s her own health was so poor, and the Elector's so visibly collapsing, that this can never have been out of her thoughts.

Adding to Frederick's worries were his suspicions about the contents of his father's wills. The Hohenzollern lands had been declared indivisible by earlier family compacts, particularly one in 1598. Contemporaries, however, tended to believe such agreements did not cover new acquisitions, and it was accepted that rulers should provide for younger children so they could make suitable marriages and produce heirs in case the main line died out.[18] As soon as Frederick William had more than one son, he began to think of giving the younger ones minor territories as fiefs, and over the years he drew up seven wills. The fiefs were not intended to diminish the power of the main heir who was to receive the bulk of the territories, since he was still to control their foreign policy and their fortresses and could impose military contributions.[19] In a will of 1664 Frederick, then the second son, was to receive Halberstadt;[20] in that of 1680 Louis, now second son, was to have Minden, while Dorothea's eldest son was to have Halberstadt, and the younger three Ravensberg, Lębork/Lauenburg, Bytów/Bütow and Drahim/Draheim. Although Crown Prince Frederick was asked to endorse this 1680 will, he was not shown the contents and only discovered them through Rébenac, who knew because Louis XIV was an executor. Nor was Frederick shown the provisions of a similar will of January 1686. It seems that, although the Great Elector himself was moving, probably unwittingly, towards his eighteenth-century successors' concept of a unitary state (*Einheitsstaat*), he remained essentially a patrimonial ruler, concerned about his dynasty and family.[21]

Despite Frederick William's misgivings about Frederick's suitability as his heir, he did try, unlike his own father, to give the prince some experience of the business of ruling. These gestures, however, could not disguise the obvious coldness within the family, especially as Frederick and his first wife, Elizabeth Henrietta of Hesse, lived away from court at their own palace of Köpenick outside Berlin. She died in 1683, and the next year he married the sixteen-year-old Sophie Charlotte of Brunswick-Hanover. This marriage led to even frostier relations with his father and stepmother, who were pointedly unkind to the girl. Matters came to a head in April 1687, when Frederick's younger brother, Louis, died at twenty-one from scarlet fever. The doctors had failed to diagnose this and were at first mystified, even suspecting poison. All Frederick's worst fears seemed confirmed, and he was all too aware only he stood between his half-brothers and the throne. He was sure he would be murdered next, especially as he suffered frequent stomach upsets: Rébenac explained these by 'the many powders and antidotes he took'.[22] Not surprisingly, Frederick wanted to get far away from his stepmother, especially as Sophie Charlotte was wrongly believed pregnant. The Elector himself made matters even worse by an aside that 'the girl was indeed pregnant but only God knew by whom'. In June 1687, therefore, the couple fled to Sophie Charlotte's family in Hanover. They refused to return home and Frederick wrote to his father that 'it was not safe for him to be there, since it plainly appeared that his brother had been poisoned and that by the niece of the Electress'.[23] (This woman, Louise-Charlotte of Holstein, was his main suspect.) Frederick William therefore stopped his allowance and threatened to cut him out of the succession. Fortunately the Emperor Leopold and William III pressed the Elector to forgive and reassure his son, and his own ministers wanted the same. After Frederick William told everyone that he would not let the couple be murdered, they returned to Berlin in November. The last months of his life were then passed with an uneasy quiet in the family.

. . .

THE FRENCH YOKE

Frederick William's health and family worries can never have been far from his mind during his final years. By the time he had chased the Swedes from Prussia he was entering his sixtieth year, and signs of ageing were clear to all. It is not surprising, therefore, that after the hard lessons of the 1670s his foreign policy had an increasingly cautious edge. His main concern seems to have been to prevent major war in the German Empire and to allow his successor to inherit in peacetime.[24] His standing army was now kept at around 20,000, which made foreign subsidies essential. Until 1685 the necessary cash as well as security for his territories appeared to lie in alliance with Louis XIV, who now seemed invincible. From 1685, however, Frederick William had to accept that the King must eventually be resisted, in part because of his relentless pressure on his neighbours but mainly because of his threat to European Protestantism. Frederick William's attitude towards Sweden also changed in these years. The main aim again was probably defensive: to separate Sweden and Louis XIV and to keep the Swedes from deploying dangerous bodies of troops on the southern shores of the Baltic. While the Elector certainly did not abandon his ambition to conquer Swedish Pomerania, this would only be considered seriously if the Brunswick dukes and Danes helped and if Louis himself did not exploit the disruption in Germany. Once the French threat to Protestantism and the German Empire became overwhelming in the late 1680s, Frederick William recognised Sweden's value as a Protestant ally.

After the Dutch War Louis XIV was at the height of his power and almost immediately embarked on further expansion. This was through his *Réunion* policy of annexing neighbouring territories, especially in the Spanish Netherlands and the German Empire, which he claimed were feudal dependencies of the French crown. These gains were then used by his engineer Vauban to construct an iron barrier of fortresses round France. To disable the Emperor and the Empire, it was essential to bully or bribe the German princes into alliances.[25] Most of the princes proved willing, including Frederick William.

It was the Great Elector's own decision to approach Louis for an alliance soon after making peace with him in 1679. Clearly he had no love for France, and there is some disagreement over why he did so. Earlier biographers thought he was above all alienated from his recent Dutch and Imperial allies and saw the chance to reconquer Szczecin by usurping Sweden's role as France's northern ally. Ernst Opgenoorth, however, has argued more convincingly that Frederick William used the relationship with France essentially as a temporary expedient to protect Brandenburg and that he soon dropped his hostility to the Emperor and Dutch. Security was to prove more important than Szczecin: he had been rattled by France's success in 1679 in turning such German princes as Saxony and Brunswick-Celle against him. In early August 1679 he summarised his views in a letter to Schwerin, shortly before the *Oberpräsident*'s death:

> Our essential aim has been ... to separate ... France from Sweden. ... Moreover, as most of the princes, and especially all our neighbours, have declared against us, we cannot find any security, besides divine protection, except in the power of the King. You know how the Emperor and the Empire have treated us, and since they were the first to leave us defenceless before our enemies, we no longer need consider their interests unless they agree with ours. As to France we have no reason to have any special affection for her; even less to further her expansion, because the French yoke is well known to us. However, ... France already has the *Arbitrium* in her hands ... so that ... no one will find his security and advantage except in the friendship and alliance of France.[26]

A few weeks before this, Frederick William had ordered Meinders, the minister most associated with the new direction of policy, to negotiate 'a very close alliance' in Paris to provide subsidies to pay for his standing army and for a dozen frigates.[27] Although the French let him sweat for a while, at the end of October a secret Franco-Brandenburg alliance was signed. This protected the Elector from attack; in return he promised to vote for a French candidate in a future Imperial election and to let French troops cross his territory. They also agreed to cooperate at the next Polish election and Louis promised to press the Elector's claims in Vienna to the Silesian fief of Jägerndorf/Krnov. As for subsidies, Louis was to pay an annual pension for ten years of 100,000 livres. This was such a small sum that Pomponne, Louis's Foreign Minister, considered it a token of friendship rather than a subsidy. None the less, the treaty brought immediate security, and, as Meinders put it, was 'the beginning of something more'.[28]

The French at first probably attached no more significance to this alliance than to an almost identical simultaneous one with the Saxon Elector. At the end of 1679, however, Louis XIV appointed Colbert de Croissy his Foreign Minister. The latter, together with the War Minister, Louvois, wanted to press ahead with the *Réunions* and saw Brandenburg as pivotal in a protective network of relationships with German princes. In January 1680 Count Rébenac was sent back to Berlin, where he had recently enjoyed his comfortable captivity. Young and ambitious, Rébenac was very much a grand seigneur, writing on one occasion, 'because corn is dear, I see no reason to eat less bread'.[29] Like many of Louis's diplomats, he was a skilful courtier and dispenser of bribes, and he soon established good personal relations with the Elector and Electress. He also began to turn ministers and courtiers into French pensioners, some receiving more from him than from their electoral office. Meinders' share was 47,000 livres and Fuchs's 32,500. In April 1680 Rébenac gave Jena and Grumbkow 6,000 livres each, the Electress's favourite, Fräulein von Wangenheim, 4,000 and even the Elector's valet, Kornmesser, 2,000. In February 1681 Jena also received 4,000 thalers from the Imperialists, and he flitted between supporting the pro-Habsburg Anhalt and Dörfflinger and the pro-French Meinders and Fuchs at court.[30] The Electress Dorothea was particularly cosseted by Rébenac and soon became a partisan of the French alliance. Her greed was proverbial: William III warned an English envoy going to Berlin that she 'bore it very ill to be forgot'.[31] Consequently, Rébenac provided an expensive diamond brooch and earrings in 1680. These went down well and were followed two years later by a silver dressing table and a Gobelins tapestry, worth 100,000 livres. (Rébenac's wife had to show her how to use some of the accessories for the dressing table as these were unknown in Berlin.) Frederick William himself accepted 100,000 livres as a personal gift in November 1683. Presents were undoubtedly given to Rébenac in return by the Elector, and Louis XIV was sent a fine amber dressing table with crystal mirrors.

Frederick William's dilemma after making the alliance with Louis XIV is shown by conversations in spring 1680 with the perceptive English ambassador Southwell, who of course knew nothing of the secret agreement. While the Elector had 'nothing but reproaches' against the Emperor and the Dutch, he also told the Englishman that 'no man sees clearer into the [French] design of bringing the Bastile into Germany . . . or would more cordially oppose it . . . , if he could get partakers of equal resolution'. He further explained that he 'must be kept in armes, in spight of all his wants [i.e. of money]', because the Swedes, whose 'enmity . . . must be immortal, . . . [are] but two days distance', the Brunswick dukes and Saxony had 'old grievances of neighbourhood' against him, and King John III Sobieski of Poland was guided by France. He also pointed out that Saxony,[32] Bavaria, and the Brunswick Duke of Hanover in the last war 'lost nothing by their neutrality, and that therefore he that was the first before ought now to sit still or be the last to join'. Southwell believed, none the less, that 'he has some fits of kindness for the Prince of Orange, and is often heard to say, that if Holland could make him any tollerable satisfaction [over past subsidies], he would forget all and esteeme their friendship'. A few months later the envoy concluded that the Elector 'has a good army wch he is able to support, and so lives as with his bridge drawn up . . . after his death [the power of Brandenburg] will shrink and prove a quite different thing. But for the present, tis certain he makes a brave and great figure.'[33]

During summer 1680 Frederick William worked to strengthen his relations with Louis XIV, continued to be hostile to the Emperor and became involved in a minor privateering war with the Spaniards (see pp. 188–9). The French King was responsive and a further secret alliance was concluded in November, when the Elector's good behaviour was rewarded by trebling the subsidies to 100,000 thalers a year. Both rulers promised to defend each other's territories, as well as their rights and claims, from attack, even if this was provoked. In Louis's case these rights and claims included those 'which he enjoyed or ought to enjoy by virtue of the said treaty [Nijmegen]',[34] and this was clearly an attempt to tie Frederick William to support the King's *Réunion* claims. On the other hand, as the Elector would eventually discover, Louis had no intention of supporting Hohenzollern claims against Sweden.

There seemed no alternative to the relationship with France, but Frederick William showed more resignation than enthusiasm for it. In December 1680 Rébenac reported hearing he had remarked that 'the wine was poured and would have to be drunk'.[35] Visits by Imperial emissaries to Berlin changed nothing, and that by the Emperor's War Minister, the Margrave of Baden, in June 1680 merely put the court in a panic. Terrified by an outbreak of plague in the Habsburg lands, they forced Baden to douse himself with so much perfume it was almost impossible to eat at the same table.[36] Meanwhile relations with the Dutch remained cool because of how the last war ended and because of unpaid subsidies. These became glacial in summer 1681 when the Dutch West India Company seized a Brandenburg merchant ship off Africa (see p. 189). Consequently, there was no serious criticism from Berlin of Louis's *Réunion* demands in the Rhineland in 1680 and 1681, and three days after the news that France had seized the Imperial city of Strasbourg in September 1681, Frederick William assured Rébenac that 'his opinion of Louis . . . had not altered'. He then gave him a sword set with diamonds, causing him to write home in delight: 'these are the rocks they throw at me here'.[37]

The Great Elector was also prepared to ignore Louis's piecemeal expansion into the Empire, despite the general outcry there, because of friendly noises from Rébenac over Pomerania. This was a response by France to a worrying shift in Swedish policy towards alliance with the Dutch and the Emperor.[38] Charles XI of Sweden had been affronted because Louis had seized, among his other annexations, the German principality of Zweibrücken at the death of its ruler. Charles had expected to inherit this himself, and in October 1681 he allied with the Dutch to limit further French expansion. Louis, therefore, encouraged Frederick William's hostility towards Sweden as a way of putting pressure on Stockholm. Over the next few years Frederick William's ambitions in Pomerania were to be kindled and then damped down, as it suited France. Autumn 1681 was a time to let his hopes rise, and Rébenac found this easy enough. As he wrote to his father, the French ambassador to Sweden, Frederick William thought of invading Swedish Pomerania 'day and night', and 'If our King gives me powers to conclude, I promise to have the Elector inside Pomerania in two months'.[39]

What Louis XIV intended is clear from his own correspondence with Rébenac. At the end of 1681, while telling him 'to flatter the

244

Elector's hopes concerning Sweden', he added: 'let this prince imagine all the advantages he can hope from the mischievous con-duct of Sweden without agreeing to further his designs to profit from it'.[40] Despite Charles XI's fickleness, the French King con-tinued to prefer Sweden as his ally in the north to anyone else.[41] None the less, Rébenac was ordered to offer Frederick William yet another secret alliance. Believing all Pomerania was once more in his grasp, Frederick William needed little persuading to make a further ten-year treaty with France in January 1682. This recognised France's existing *Réunion* gains in the Empire, including Strasbourg. The annual subsidies were raised to 133,000 thalers in peacetime and 300,000 in wartime, and Louis promised to assist the establishment of Brandenburg trade in West Africa.

Louis XIV had been prepared to spend more in Berlin because opposition had been hardening elsewhere in Germany. The *Réunions* and his gradual erosion of German territory were pushing the Bavarian and Saxon Electors and the Duke of Brunswick-Hanover towards Vienna. The Emperor Leopold himself was also listening more to ministers who wanted to resist France and to discount the danger of a new war with the Turks. In February 1682 Leopold joined the recent Swedish–Dutch alliance, which Spain also joined in May. But Frederick William was indifferent to all this. The financial ben-efits from his relationship with Louis XIV had steadily improved and went some way to support his standing army. While having his envoy in Paris, Spanheim, warn Colbert de Croissy in February against further 'robberies' in the Empire[42] and delivering similar warnings throughout the year, he tried to solve the dilemma his relationship with an expansive France had caused him in Germany. Above all he had to prevent war between France and the Emperor, not just because he would have to declare his hand militarily, but also because he was convinced France would win and seize even more. At the Imperial Diet, in June 1682, therefore, the Brandenburg delegate urged the other princes to appease France and accept her gains, since the Emperor's problems in the Balkans meant France could not be resisted. The Elector also showed no interest in the embryonic anti-French coalition William of Orange was promot-ing, being certain it would collapse.[43] He had in any case interpreted the Emperor's joining the Swedish–Dutch Association as a threat to him as well as to the French. In early May 1682 he even warned his own ministers in his Privy Council against criticising his association with France. Adding that he knew some were taking the Emperor's money, he blustered that they would answer with their heads. This was clearly aimed at Jena, who was suitably frightened, although he would die safely in his bed before the year was out.

While trying to prevent war on the Rhine, Frederick William still believed he needed to protect himself from the Swedes, if not actually to undertake a further assault on them. He therefore persuaded Louis to extend their association to Christian V of Denmark, who had kept up his army and his ambitions against Sweden. A Brandenburg–Danish alliance in February 1682 was followed by a Franco-Danish one in March. Throughout the spring Frederick William raised troops energetically, although the pressure for action against Sweden at this time was coming from Copenhagen not Berlin. His instructions to his envoys show he wanted to avoid conflict, since this would merely encourage Louis to seize more German territory. None the less, in June 1682 Frederick William met King Christian in Holstein, where they signed an offensive alliance against Sweden, though without any specific timetable for action. In Frederick William's mind, any war would hinge on further French subsidies and clear support, and there were no signs of these yet.

By the end of 1682 some strains were beginning to show in the Franco-Brandenburg association. In the August Louis's troops had seized William III's principality of Orange, a Protestant enclave in southern France. This infuriated the Elector and the anger was obvious in the changed attitude of his secretary, Fuchs, whom Frederick William was now depending on more than the overtly pro-French Meinders. Previously Paris had also considered Fuchs a friend of France, but he now openly criticised French policy to Rébenac and this essentially reflected Frederick William's own thinking. In the autumn Fuchs drew up a memorandum for his master, setting out the options before them. This showed their main concern was their own security and preventing war in the Empire, and that Pomerania was not the overriding priority. While Fuchs considered the French alliance had financial value and offered a chance to expel the Swedes, he also recognised its drawbacks. If the Turks remained quiet and allowed Leopold and his allies to attack France and Brandenburg, Louis would be tied down on the Rhine and unable to defend Frederick William. Fuchs went on to point out that if Frederick William himself attacked Sweden, he would be opposed by his own neighbours, while France would merely take the opportunity to seize more German territory.[44] Fuchs, none the less, was wary of associating with Louis's enemies: they were weak and divided and Leopold could soon find himself involved in war with both the Turks and France. The best option for Brandenburg, therefore, seemed to be a 'policy of sitting on the fence [*Schaukelpolitik*]'.[45] They should pretend to negotiate with the Dutch, while getting the French to pay more subsidies to help strengthen the electoral army. At the same time they should avoid becoming involved in an assault on Sweden, although they needed the protection of Danish friendship.

The Great Elector was to accept Fuchs's suggestion of a see-saw policy as the basis for his actions during 1683, which is hardly surprising as the secretary probably drew up the memorandum to fit in with Frederick William's views. Consequently, in the first week of the new year Spanheim in Paris was advised that while Frederick William would stick by his friendship with France, 'from now on do not press your negotiation [for subsidies to attack Sweden] especially hard ... but pay close attention and take matters *ad referendum*'.[46] To complement this cooling towards Louis XIV, in the January Schwerin's son was sent to Vienna to urge Leopold to settle with France, so that he could concentrate on the Turks, who were by now clearly intent on war. Frederick William offered military help, but asked in return for some former Hohenzollern fiefs in Silesia. Inevitably, the Imperialists did not want advice from this suspect source and refused even minor concessions. The younger Schwerin's mission, however, did have an effect in France, where Brandenburg anger over the annexation of Orange had already registered. There was also concern there that Emperor Leopold's influence in Germany was recovering. Bavaria, Saxony and Hanover now seemed firmly in the Imperial camp, while even the pro-French John Sobieski of Poland wanted to cooperate against the common Turkish enemy. Louis's response was to play the northern card once more: on 4 February 1683 he ordered his envoys in Berlin and Copenhagen to try to tie Frederick William and Christian V closer to him by appearing willing to sacrifice Sweden. He proposed paying them to attack Sweden and conquer her German territories, if she shipped troops across there. This, of course, was not the green light for them to launch their own war, since Louis did not expect the Swedes would dare to provoke this. In mid-January he had already written to Rébenac: 'My information on Swedish affairs gives me no grounds to believe that this Crown will soon be in a position to move troops into Germany.'[47] However, if the Swedes had moved, in what would clearly have been an anti-French manoeuvre, Louis would probably have urged his allies to act.

Rébenac now proved less cautious than his master and became convinced war was in the offing, even asking Frederick William for a regiment to command against Sweden. The Great Elector himself began to hope that Louis had finally decided to abandon Charles XI and replace Sweden by Brandenburg as his permanent ally in the north. Even so, he and his ministers, including Meinders, were not willing to rush ahead, despite Danish pressure for an immediate assault. Security was still more important than Pomerania. In any case in the first quarter of 1683 a military adventure would have been difficult: Frederick William was in constant pain from kidney stones, and many at court thought he was close to death.

In early May 1683, when the Poles and several German princes were arming to help the Emperor defend his own Austrian lands from a massive Turkish invasion, Rébenac tried to force things to a head in the north. On his own initiative, he signed a French alliance with Brandenburg and Denmark. In this Frederick William and Christian agreed to attack Sweden if she increased her forces in the Empire or tried to send troops through it. If the Brunswick dukes of Celle, Hanover and Wolfenbüttel supported the Swedes, they were also to be attacked. France was to prevent Dutch or Brunswick intervention by dispatching a force to the lower Rhine. The three allies were to defend one another from attack, and France was immediately to pay large subsidies. If it came to war, they were not to make peace till Brandenburg gained Pomerania and Denmark had Bremen, Verden and Wismar. A fortnight later Frederick William himself went further, assuring Christian he would support his reconquest of Scania/Skåne and would not object if he swallowed all Sweden.

For a while in May 1683 Frederick William himself probably believed the opportunity had at last arrived for a new war on Sweden. He spent the month mobilising troops and artillery and fitting out warships and transports in Königsberg. But nothing came of it all, because the Swedes, as Louis XIV had rightly surmised, had no intention of inviting an attack by a false move.[48] Moreover, the King himself had not wanted to unleash his allies against the Swedes. It was more important to him to get general recognition of his *Réunion* gains and to apply direct pressure to the Emperor's friends in Germany, especially the Brunswick dukes. He much preferred Brandenburg and Denmark to attack the Brunswickers rather than the Swedes. On 29 April he ordered Rébenac to 'insist that it is impossible to succeed against Sweden unless one disarms the House of Brunswick first'. When news of what Rébenac had signed in Berlin reached him in May, Louis refused to ratify it, telling him roundly the terms were: 'some – unreasonable, others – impracticable, and several – downright impossible'.[49]

While the Danes were willing enough to please Louis by attacking the Brunswick dukes, this was not popular in Berlin, where these rulers had even been considered as allies against Sweden. Above all, Derfflinger, the ageing hero of Fehrbellin, who still commanded the Brandenburg army, dug in his heels and opposed it. By June Frederick William himself was disillusioned enough to refuse to ratify the agreements of May, believing Louis had intended to involve him in a war he would not join himself. Instead, throughout the summer, he tried to mediate between Denmark and the Brunswickers, even betrothing Crown Prince Frederick to Sophie Charlotte, daughter of Duke Ernest Augustus of Hanover. (They were married in October 1684.)

Although Rébenac blamed Frederick William's various illnesses for making him indecisive and erratic during the summer months, a more likely reason for his ultra caution was the dramatic events in the south-east. Here the Turkish army had actually managed to besiege Vienna. The enormity of the danger posed by Kara Mustapha's two-month siege was leading to dramatic offers of help from many German princes as well as from the Poles. The Great Elector realised he had to do something himself. Believing, as he told William of Orange, that 'Common sense calls for avoiding everything that can irritate France this moment',[50] he urged the Spaniards to concede to the new territorial demands Louis had been making against them in the Netherlands and Luxemburg. He also sent his brother-in-law, the pro-Imperial Anhalt, to Leopold's court which had fled to Passau, while Derfflinger was ordered to assemble 12,000 men on the Silesian border for immediate dispatch. On the last day of July he had told Rébenac: 'keeping the Turks out of Germany is not contrary to the alliance with France or attempts at peace in the Empire . . . My shirt is closer to my skin than my coat: I am an elector of the Empire and must help the Empire in its need.'[51] However, when Anhalt reached the panic-stricken Imperial court on 7 August, his offer to send Derfflinger's force was tied to a settlement over the Silesian fiefs, various financial demands, amounting to 500,000 thalers, and insistence that Leopold appease

France in Germany. As the Emperor was only paying John Sobieski 200,000 thalers for a whole army and the Brandenburg troops were unlikely to arrive before winter, the demands were absurd. Anhalt soon realised this, abandoned them and offered equally absurd terms of his own. He agreed to send the 12,000 men for a mere 100,000 thalers and Brandenburg was to ally with the Emperor and Spain to force France to disgorge her gains once the Turks were defeated. Not surprisingly, the Great Elector recalled Anhalt in disgrace and kept his troops at home. In this moment of supreme danger and ultimate triumph for Emperor and Empire, Frederick William was one of the few German princes to stand aside. His contribution was limited to 1,200 men attached to the Polish relief force.

John Sobieski's victory outside Vienna in September 1683 saved the city and Germany from the Turks. It led, however, to the involvement of Emperor Leopold and many of the German princes in a major war in the Balkans, as Louis invaded the Southern Netherlands in October to force Spain to surrender Luxemburg. With conflicts in the south-east and the west, Frederick William had now even less intention of attacking the Brunswickers for Louis's sake, telling Rébenac at the beginning of October, 'there are already enough wars and troubles in Christendom'. He also appealed to the King to 'keep his general resolution not to increase his power by robbing Germany', especially during the Turkish war. But his need for cash to maintain his troops meant that he could not afford a break with France. In November Rébenac, unknown to Frederick William's ministers, gave him 100,000 livres, and could write home: 'I can assure you that this present has been more agreeable to him than a much larger sum ... through the usual channels.' Electress Dorothea also received a present, and all this helped grease the way to yet another alliance with France. This was signed by Meinders and Fuchs at Potsdam in January 1684: it was to attack the Brunswick dukes if they helped the Spaniards in the Netherlands. Frederick William also promised to get Louis's *Réunion* demands in Germany accepted and 'as far as it depends on him, never to allow the Empire to take a unanimous decision to wage war directly or indirectly against France'. The annual subsidies were raised still further. Although this alliance was secret like the earlier ones, Brandenburg's friendship with France over recent years had been obvious to all, and in December Frederick William had defended this policy in a letter to his minister of a generation before, Waldeck, who was now a close associate of William of Orange. He explained he was trying to 'preserve' the German Empire 'and so far . . . the Empire, despite the present confusion, has survived and is not already in full dissolution or gone up in fire and flames . . . those keenest to mouth the words patriots and fatherland . . . [risk] plunging it into a highly destructive war.'[52]

There was some truth in this explanation, and in fact in his new alliance Frederick William had resisted Louis's requests for direct help in Germany if the *Réunion* gains were not accepted soon. He also seems genuinely to have wanted to prevent the limited Franco-Spanish conflict from spreading eastwards. When Louis offered in February 1684 to make a twenty-year truce with the Emperor and Spain, which would confirm French annexations since the Peace of Nijmegen, Frederick William supported this strongly, as a way of pacifying western Europe. He also found a novel ally in the city of Amsterdam, which was determined to prevent William of Orange from dragging the Republic into war with France. In March 1684 Fuchs visited the Dutch city and encouraged its stand. This led to an angry scene with William, who had spent months trying to persuade the Dutch States General to resist Louis. He declared to Fuchs: '[it] pains me deeply, that the Elector, who has loved me from the cradle like a father, whom I honour as a son, has ranged himself . . . [with] Amsterdam, which prides itself on always opposing me'. None the less, Frederick William, who had hardly left his room all winter because of his chronic ailments, was determined to prevent conflict in the Empire. During spring and summer 1684 he did much to defuse a further crisis in north-west Germany, where the Danes were preparing to attack the Duke of Celle. When the French finally took Luxemburg from Spain in June, going on to seize the Imperial free city of Trier, he wrote furiously to Spanheim in Paris: 'The King will make himself odious and us incapable of working usefully or effectively for his interest.'[53]

Despite these set-backs, by mid-summer 1684 Frederick William seemed to have turned the war crisis in north-west Germany to his own advantage and to feel secure enough to risk moving against Sweden. In August he allied with the three Brunswick dukes, and they agreed secretly to oust the Swedes from Germany: Frederick William was to have West Pomerania, Wismar and Rügen and the Brunswickers were to have Bremen and Verden. Denmark then joined the alliance and was to annex Sweden's satellite, Holstein-Gottorp. By early September the Elector was preparing 12,000 men for action. But when he pressed Louis to increase his subsidies to

the higher war level, so that he and his allies could attack Charles
XI, the King effectively called his bluff by demanding in return
Philippsburg on the Rhine. Inevitably Frederick William had to
abandon the idea of a war, refusing to win land from Sweden 'at the
expense of the Empire'.[54]

Louis XIV in any case had lost interest, for the while at least, in
promoting instability within Germany because all opposition to his
recent annexations had collapsed. Emperor Leopold had decided to
concentrate on full-scale war against the Turks, and on 15 August
1684 he agreed by the Truce of Regensburg/Ratisbon to all Louis's
gains, including Strasbourg and Luxemburg, for twenty years.[55] Spain
and the Dutch Republic quickly followed, seeing resistance was hopeless. As Louis clearly intended the truce to cover all the territories
within the Empire, including those belonging to Sweden, Frederick
William finally realised the King would never allow the expulsion of
the Swedes. This marked the turning point in his relationship with
him and he now began to move step by step into direct opposition.
The next month he protested to Rébenac that 'the King alone has
wrecked my undertaking'.[56]

Louis XIV's German policy, culminating in the Truce of
Regensburg, had been brilliantly successful in terms of territory and
prestige won, but this success was superficial and his gains unstable.
The Emperor and the German princes did not regard the truce as
permanent, since it had been forced on them by the Turkish war. As
soon as the Turks were beaten and the Emperor and his allies felt
strong enough, they would try to reverse the settlement with France.
Louis XIV moreover probably also saw it as a mere breathing space.
Within a year he was to press the claims of his sister-in-law, the
Duchess of Orleans, to parts of the Rhenish Palatinate.

Six months after the truce Frederick William himself realised the
truce had not stabilised the situation in Germany or halted France's
erosion of neighbouring territories. For him at last, enough was
probably enough. Even more important now in shaping his thinking
was the plight of European Protestantism. In France Louis's persecution of his Calvinist Huguenots was coming to a head, and in the
lands he had annexed in Germany the mass was being restored; in
Hungary and Transylvania, Leopold's armies not only expelled the
Turks but were also imposing Catholicism on the Protestant gentry.
In February 1685 the Catholic James II came to the British thrones;
and then in May the last Calvinist Elector of the Palatinate was
succeeded by the Catholic Philip William of Pfalz-Neuburg. It is

hardly surprising Frederick William now became obsessed with the idea of an international Catholic conspiracy to destroy Protestantism. He had complained in Vienna for years about the treatment of the Protestants in the parts of Hungary already under Habsburg control.[57] Similar protests had been made in Paris about the Huguenots, and in autumn 1684 he appealed to Louis on behalf of the Protestants in those German lands seized by France. An English envoy in Berlin, Poley, had already remarked in 1681 that Frederick William resented the

> ill usage of the Protestants in France . . . so much, that his owne Ministers durst not mention it to him, nor informe him of all ye particulars of it, for feare [of what] his passion might make him say . . . it is certain that his H[ighnes]s does in appearance take nothing so much to heart as ye interest of Religion, and has done me the honour to tell me wth tears in his eyes, that he wished nothing so much as to be able to doe something towards ye settling of it before he dies.[58]

By spring 1685 Louis XIV's instructions to his diplomats show that he no longer believed he could depend on the Great Elector. At the same time William of Orange was to take advantage of the new atmosphere in Berlin. In January 1685 he sent the Huguenot François Gaultier secretly to the Elector to propose a Protestant league. Gaultier was well received, especially because the alarming news of James II's accession arrived during his mission. The previous October the Great Elector had written to his envoy at The Hague: 'If the Duke of York [James II] succeeds, things will get worse, because this Duke will need French help to survive and will therefore have to throw himself into the arms of France.'[59] Now during Gaultier's mission Frederick William suggested that William of Orange, who was married to James II's Protestant daughter and heir, Mary, should invade England and seize the throne before the new king was established, and thus assure English sea power for Protestantism. Then in March 1685, claiming to be 'head of all the Protestant Reformed [Calvinist] powers in Europe', he ordered Spanheim in Paris to abandon any notion of an alliance against Sweden because of

> the important and unexpected alteration in England . . . Protestantism has been dealt its greatest blow since the Reformation, so we intend to negotiate something to enable the Protestant powers to combine to

prevent it or at least to render it harmless . . . [To attack Sweden would] set the Protestant powers against each other and ruin them one by one.[60]

In April Frederick William sent Fuchs, now undoubtedly his most trusted servant, to the Republic 'to discuss . . . the maintenance of the reformed religion and their mutual security'. On reaching Holland, where he stayed some months, Fuchs found that the influx of Huguenot refugees and events in England had made even pacific Amsterdam see that Louis would have to be resisted. Prince William was eager to ally with his Hohenzollern uncle, and there seemed to be a general feeling in the Republic that their fate was bound up with Brandenburg. Even the obstacle of the financial 'satisfaction' Frederick William demanded for past subsidies and the Dutch seizure of an Africa Company ship was removed by a settlement of 400,000 thalers, 150,000 to be paid at once. Then on 23 August 1685 Brandenburg and the Republic allied for fifteen years, clearly against France. They promised to safeguard the peace of Christendom against 'potential disturbers'.[61]

As there were no secrets in the Republic, Louis XIV knew about the treaty and warned Rébenac that it was the basis for a European coalition against him. Equally disturbing had been the visit of an Imperial emissary to Berlin in March and his favourable reception. However, one outcome of this, Frederick William's promise in late August of 5,000 troops for the Balkans, was welcomed by Rébenac, since anything which prolonged Leopold's involvement with the Turks could only benefit France. None the less, by autumn Louis felt he had to try to stop the rot. In October he demanded the Great Elector declare he would 'enter no future engagements without the knowledge and direct participation of France'. When this was discussed in the Privy Council Knyphausen assured the Elector they could find the money from their own revenues to make up for the French subsidies (see p. 161). Although Frederick William himself wanted to tell Rébenac outright that he was accountable only to himself for his actions, the Council feared an immediate breach with Louis. Consequently Fuchs and Meinders tried to pacify Rébenac, while the Elector wrote to the King, assuring him of his good intentions and explaining he could not give the declaration asked 'as a sovereign prince . . . without a stain on my honour'.[62] These were mere delaying tactics, especially as Louis's own actions within France meant that relations were moving inescapably to breaking point. At the end of October 1685 he revoked the Edict of Nantes, removing all Huguenot rights. The Great Elector responded immediately, and spontaneously, on 8 November, with his own Edict of Potsdam, throwing open his territories to the Huguenots and forbidding Catholics to hear mass in the French and Imperial ambassadors' homes. Much to Louis's irritation, the Brandenburg embassy in Paris began to shelter dozens of Huguenot families and to help them escape; in October the zealous Calvinist Spanheim rented a larger house to accommodate them all.

Despite these events in the last months of 1685, the break with France was not yet final. Frederick William wanted subsidies paid as long as possible: in December he wrote to Louis personally, assuring him his Dutch alliance was innocuous and that he would observe his treaties with the King 'exactly'.[63] (The French even began to pay subsidies again that month, after withholding them in the autumn, and these were continued throughout 1686, if fitfully and in arrears.) But this was all less important than other events. In Berlin all Rébenac's friends were disappearing, and even Meinders had abandoned him by the end of 1685. On 4 January 1686 Frederick William signed a treaty with the Emperor to provide 7,000 troops for the coming campaign in the Balkans for 150,000 thalers and Leopold's promise to keep the contingent as a separate unit and not to deploy it without its commander's consent. These troops under Schöning were among the best to serve in Hungary and were eventually to play a significant part in capturing Buda from the Turks in the summer. The treaty over the troops was just a preliminary to an alliance, which Frederick William himself now wanted. The same January, known only to Fuchs, he proposed to the Imperial envoy, Fridag, a twenty-year defensive treaty. He also offered to end all alliances incompatible with it and went on to suggest abandoning all his claims in Silesia in return for the poverty-stricken district of Schwiebus/Świebodzin, a Habsburg enclave surrounded by his own Neumark territory. As the Imperial court would not surrender this, Fridag had to find a solution. This came in the person of Crown Prince Frederick, who was desperately short of money and keen for Imperial support in case he had to challenge his father's will when he died. Using the Prince's uncle, Anhalt, as an intermediary, Fridag persuaded Frederick to sign an agreement to return Świebodzin at his accession for 100,000 thalers and an immediate gift of 10,000 ducats. His father fortunately never found out, and when Frederick succeeded in 1688 Świebodzin was handed back.

This meant the Silesian issue was not resolved till the reign of Frederick the Great.

With this problem removed, on 1 April 1686 Fridag and Fuchs signed a secret alliance for twenty years. This was to defend Frederick William's, Leopold's and the new Elector Palatine's states and rights and to defend all the Empire against violations carried out under the pretext of 'Reunions and dependencies'. Frederick William also promised to support Leopold's claims to the Spanish succession and his son's election as King of the Romans.[64] As agreed, Świebodzin was to be ceded in return for ending the Hohenzollern claims in Silesia, and Brandenburg was to be paid subsidies of 100,000 thalers in wartime and two-thirds of this in peacetime.[65] While negotiating with the Imperialists, in February Frederick William also swallowed the bitterest pill of all – an alliance with Charles XI of Sweden, who was now firmly in the Dutch and Imperial camp. The dispute over Pomerania was tacitly put on ice, since both rulers agreed, because of the danger to Protestantism, to defend each other's lands as well as the integrity of the Empire. At the same time as he allied with Sweden and the Imperialists, the Great Elector drew up in his own hand a plan for war against France. Although rather utopian, it shows that illness and sixty-six years had not lessened his talent for the grand gesture. The main thrust of the plan was for William of Orange to march on Paris at the head of 57,000 Dutch and Brandenburg troops, with the expectation that those who had suffered under Louis – Huguenots, the Parlement and princes of the blood – would rally to him. France would then 'be put in such a state, that no one need fear her in the future'.[66] A month later, at the end of May, Frederick William even told Fridag that he would not sleep in his grave if he had not revenged himself on Louis XIV.

Frederick William's relations with the Dutch, and especially with William, had meanwhile drawn even closer after their alliance the previous year, especially as the Dutch paid what was agreed promptly. William also secured his uncle a Dutch loan to rebuild the fortifications at Wesel in Cleves, destroyed in the last war, and persuaded him to station more troops in the Rhineland in the first half of 1686. A personal meeting was also arranged because, as the Elector wrote to William in April, he wanted 'to discuss things with you in a better and more trusting manner'.[67] This eventually took place in Cleves in early August 1686, when they talked at length, often in private. Although there are no records, it is fairly obvious that they discussed a future war against France and William's ambitions in

England. Rébenac, who accompanied the court to Cleves, saw the writing on the wall and believed France had lost the Elector.

Yet Frederick William still did not disown openly what he called in August his 'odious engagements', because he felt he still needed to squeeze as many subsidies from Louis as possible. Even a year later, in November 1687, Spanheim was to ask for arrears from October 1686, amounting to 625,000 livres. The French were actually to pay a further 125,000 in February 1688. This was accompanied, however, by a threatening letter from Louis to Rébenac about the effects of the Edict of Potsdam:

> The Elector must understand that I have enough reasons to complain about his letters and declarations which have induced my subjects of the supposed reformed religion to desert and settle in his lands, that I cannot allow his preventing by force those, who recognising their guilt, wish to return to my kingdoms . . . If this outrage continues, I will be easily driven to decisions, which he will not like.[68]

While there was no complete breach between Brandenburg and France before the Great Elector's death, there was similarly no war between the two hostile camps. All the Emperor's resources, together with help from the German princes, were to be committed to the war in the Balkans, which was becoming almost a new crusade. Meanwhile, William of Orange was still not entirely sure of his ground in the Dutch Republic or his reception in Britain if he ventured across the North Sea. Although the Great Elector was now firmly committed to the anti-French side, he believed, probably till he died, that no serious military action could be taken against France during the Turkish war. Throughout 1687 he urged the Imperialists to disengage in the Balkans, although to no effect. Then in January 1688 he reacted angrily to Louis's latest outrage, to get his dependant, William von Fürstenberg, elected Elector of Cologne. He fumed to Rébenac that this would be like Leopold's installing his own candidate as Bishop of Rheims or Paris.[69] Yet Frederick William, in his last months of life, was still clearly anxious to avoid war. His wife, Dorothea, was constantly ill, and he was becoming much weaker and even more immobile with the onset of dropsy. He wrote to William of Orange at the end of January advising against immediate action. Events, however, were out of his hands. The dispute over the Cologne election was to be the final catalyst for the war which eventually broke out in autumn 1688 between

Louis and Leopold. By the first months of the year, moreover, William of Orange was becoming increasingly determined to invade England. In March Frederick William offered to put 9,000 men in Cleves to protect the Republic's eastern frontiers, presumably to cover William's eventual expedition. For his part, however, William still seems to have distrusted his uncle to the end.[70] About 1 May the exiled Bishop of Salisbury, Gilbert Burnet, who was very close to William's wife, Mary, met the Whig, Admiral Russell, at The Hague and told him the Prince's 'main confidence . . . was in the Electoral Prince of Brandenburg; for the old Elector was then dying. And I [Burnet] told Russell at parting that, unless he died, there would be great difficulties, not easily mastered, in the design of the Prince's expedition to England.' When Frederick William did die on 9 May, William 'was so delighted that he wrote two letters of condolence to the new Elector . . . [and he] looked better than he had for years past'.[71] Although the death was followed by definite Brandenburg commitments to help William[72] and may have been crucial in his decision to risk crossing to England later in the year, Frederick William's survival was not why war was so slow to break out between France and her enemies. To explain the delay in this way exaggerates Frederick William's influence on international relations: Louis, Leopold and William went to war when they were ready, and not before.

. . .

NOTES AND REFERENCES

1 Philippson, III, p. 17.
2 *Urk. u. Akt.*, IX, p. 844.
3 Hüttl, pp. 475, 477.
4 Philippson, III, p. 22.
5 Völkel, p. 219.
6 Philippson, III, pp. 9f.
7 Waddington, *Prusse*, I, p. 414.
8 21 April/1 May 1680, Berlin, Southwell to Sunderland, PRO, SP 81/82.
9 29 November 1681, old style, Berlin, Poley to Conway, BL, Add. Ms. 37986.
10 Philippson, III, p. 7.
11 Prutz, p. 162.
12 Waddington, *Le Grand Électeur*, II, p. 47.
13 Prutz, p. 163.

14 By Prutz, passim.

15 19/29 February 1676, Nimmegen, C. Davenant to Williamson, PRO, SP 80/200.

16 Prutz, p. 183. The English envoy, Southwell, had also not been impressed: 'the Prince his son is not cut out [to] tread in his steps or to make much noise in ye world'. 14/24 May 1680, Berlin, Southwell to Godolphin, PRO, SP 105/49.

17 Prutz, p. 179.

18 For the whole question see Fichtner, pp. 35f.

19 Opgenoorth, *Friedrich Wilhelm*, II, pp. 317f.

20 L. and M. Frey, *Frederick I: The Man and his Times* (Boulder and New York, 1984), p. 39.

21 See especially Hintze, *Die Hohenzollern*, p. 251, and Tümpel, pp. 22, 27.

22 Droysen, part 3, II, p. 837; Prutz, p. 213.

23 Prutz, p. 388.

24 The best guide is Opgenoorth, *Friedrich Wilhelm*, II, pp. 199ff.

25 See D. McKay and H.M. Scott, *The Rise of the Great Powers, 1648–1815* (London, 1983), pp. 36ff.; J. Lynn, *Giant of the Grand Siècle: The French Army, 1610–1715* (Cambridge, 1997), pp. 564f., and *The Wars of Louis XIV, 1667–1714* (London, 1999), pp. 160ff.; and R. Place, 'Bavaria and the collapse of Louis XIV's German policy, 1687–88', *Journal of Modern History*, 49 (1977), p. 370.

26 Pagès, pp. 413f.; Philippson, III, pp. 252f.

27 Waddington, *Le Grand Électeur*, II, pp. 437f.

28 Troost, p. 313.

29 Waddington, *Le Grand Électeur*, II, p. 451.

30 Prutz, pp. 136, 376; Waddington, *Prusse*, I, p. 535. For pensions in French diplomacy, see G. Livet, 'Louis XIV and the Germanies', in Ragnhild Hatton, ed., *Louis XIV and Europe* (London, 1976), p. 75.

31 9/19 March 1680, The Hague, Southwell to Sunderland, PRO, SP 81/2.

32 The Elector of Saxony 'he undervalues . . . as unwarlike; of too little revenue to rayse and support an army tho there be men in plenty. And their religion of Luther sounds to him very little on this side of Popery.'

33 28 April/8 May, 21 June/1 July 1680, Berlin, same to Jenkins, ibid.

34 Waddington, *Prusse*, I, p. 536.

35 Opgenoorth, *Friedrich Wilhelm*, II, p. 213.

36 Pagès, p. 447.

37 Philippson, II, p. 292.

38 See A.F. Upton, *Charles XI and Swedish Absolutism* (Cambridge, 1998), pp. 90ff.

39 Waddington, *Le Grand Électeur*, II, p. 483; Erdmannsdörffer, *Deutsche Geschichte*, I, p. 673.

40 Philippson, III, p. 295; Pagès, p. 487.

41 See especially A. Lossky, *Louis XIV, William III and the Baltic Crisis of 1683* (Berkeley, 1954), pp. 4f.
42 Philippson, III, p. 294.
43 In March 1682 Prince William blamed Frederick William 'alone' 'for the disunity of the Empire'. Klopp, II, pp. 355f.
44 Opgenoorth, *Friedrich Wilhelm*, II, p. 244.
45 Troost, p. 322.
46 Philippson, III, p. 314.
47 Lossky, p. 11.
48 For Swedish policy see Upton, ch. 6. For Frederick William, see Lossky and Opgenoorth, *Friedrich Wilhelm*, II.
49 Lossky, pp. 15, 18.
50 Troost, p. 324.
51 Philippson, III, p. 334.
52 Pagès, p. 511; Philippson, III, pp. 343, 348; Prutz, p. 151; Erdmannsdörffer, *Deutsche Geschichte*, I, p. 690; Waddington, *Prusse*, I, p. 545.
53 Troost, p. 327; Philippson, III, p. 366.
54 Philippson, III, p. 371.
55 A. Schindling, 'The development of the eternal diet in Regensburg', *Journal of Modern History*, 58, Supplement (December 1986), S.69f. (sic), believes Leopold's policy now was to accept French gains to preserve peace in the Empire and unite it under his own leadership.
56 Philippson, III, p. 374.
57 For one protest, which 'had been very ill accepted', see 23 April/3 May 1681, Berlin, Poley to Conway, BL, Add. Ms. 37986.
58 18/28 September 1681, same to same, ibid.
59 Philippson, III, p. 379.
60 Waddington, *Prusse*, I, p. 550; Philippson, III, p. 380.
61 Troost, pp. 328f.
62 Philippson, III, pp. 402f.
63 Ibid., III, p. 410.
64 Leopold's elder son, Joseph, was elected King of the Romans in 1687, allowing him to succeed as emperor without a further election.
65 Redlich, p. 294; Opgenoorth, *Friedrich Wilhelm*, II, p. 265.
66 Philippson, III, p. 423.
67 Troost, p. 330.
68 Waddington, *Prusse*, I, p. 561; Philippson, III, p. 471.
69 Schevill, p. 401.
70 H.L. King, *Brandenburg and the English Revolution of 1688* (Oberlin, 1914), p. 13.
71 S.B. Baxter, *William III and the Defense of European Liberty, 1650–1702* (New York, 1966), p. 225.
72 Troost, p. 332.

Chapter 10

THE GREAT ELECTOR

Frederick William's health finally collapsed in April 1688, although he continued working on his papers and receiving ministers and envoys, despite being in great pain. On 7 May he called together his privy councillors and his son Frederick. After being carried in to meet them, he announced that he was dying. In a scene of great emotion, with tears all round, he thanked them and asked them to serve his successor as well, saying to Frederick,

> Through God's grace I have had a long and happy reign, although a difficult one, full of war and trouble. Everyone knows the sad disorder the country was in when I began my reign; through God's help I have improved it, am respected by my friends and feared by my enemies. I now hand over the government to you and exhort you to conduct it as I have done. Defend and increase the glory I bequeath to you.[1]

The next day, he urged Frederick to look after the Huguenots and to work to prevent Protestants from fighting among themselves. He stayed conscious long enough to bless all his children and beg them to stay Calvinists, and he even apologised to his daughter-in-law, Sophie Charlotte, for keeping on his nightcap. On the 10th he died with great steadfastness and a lot of praying. Rébenac's secretary, Poussin, felt he had 'made a very fine end', while the younger Schwerin wrote that Frederick William's 'family have been able to learn here, how one should die'. His last words were suitably evangelical: 'Come, Lord Jesus, I am ready.'[2] Dorothea, who had suffered from seizures throughout the 1680s, only survived him a year. She lived long enough, however, to see the new elector, Frederick III, ignore his father's wills and compensate his half-brothers with pensions and titles instead of territory. In Frederick's own testament to his infant successor in 1690, he explained he had done this to preserve the Hohenzollern tradition of primogeniture which his father had disregarded 'because of the many lamentations of my stepmother'.[3]

Frederick William had ruled for forty-eight years, the longest of any Hohenzollern, and his reign set his dynasty and state on the road to their future greatness in Germany and Europe. Frederick the Great was convinced that his great grandfather 'certainly deserved the name great, not only because he did everything himself but because he restored the state and created the solid foundations of its greatness'.[4] He also believed that, unlike Louis XIV, who had a Richelieu before him, 'the German hero did more: he paved the way alone'.[5] On the other hand, it seems hardly possible that Prussia would have risen to its later heights without the work of the Great Elector's successors, King Frederick William I and Frederick the Great himself, and also without Napoleon's new order in Germany.[6]

What did the Great Elector achieve? By a policy of practical absolutism, which entailed continual compromise, he established the ruler as the leading political figure in all his territories and ensured that their revenues would be largely applied to his own objectives. The dynasty's own religion had been finally accepted by his subjects, although on the basis of tolerating Lutheranism. The nobles were beginning to be tamed and conditions created which would see them transformed into the service nobility of the next century. A standing army was created, one capable of establishing internal order and defending all the Hohenzollern lands from their neighbours. Frederick William's territories, which were very much separate entities at his accession, were beginning to be ruled as a dynastic whole and the institutions established to create the unitary state or *Gesamtstaat* of the future. It would be far too premature to speak of a unity of his territories under the Great Elector: there was rather 'a coloured palette of solutions'.[7] In the Holy Roman Empire Brandenburg-Prussia was now clearly the leading north-German state and beginning to draw ahead from Saxony and Bavaria. It was already being seen in Vienna as a threat to the Emperor's own influence. In the international arena, although the Hohenzollerns were considered a mainstay of European Protestantism, they could still not pursue policies independent of one of the major power blocs. The frustrations and rapid shifts of Frederick William's policy came largely from this. His motto might very well have been an observation by Pufendorf in 1672 that 'For princes there is but one true and fitting basis of faith, necessity'.[8]

NOTES AND REFERENCES

1 Philippson, III, p. 478. According to Prutz, p. 403, he also said that his success was the result of 'the strength of his arms and the number of his troops' and he advised Frederick 'to increase them still more'.
2 Prutz, p. 403; Droysen, part 3, III, pp. 857f.
3 Dietrich, *Die Politischen Testamente*, p. 211.
4 Ibid., pp. 612f.
5 U. Müller-Weil, *Absolutismus und Aussenpolitk in Preußen* (Stuttgart, 1992), p. 76.
6 See the excellent brief assessment by T.C.W. Blanning, 'Napoleon and German Identity', *History Today*, 48 (1998), pp. 37ff.
7 Opgenoorth, *Friedrich Wilhelm*, II, p. 289.
8 J.H. Burns, *The Cambridge History of Political Thought, 1450–1700* (Cambridge, 1991), p. 586. Pufendorf took it from Bacon.

. . . .
MAPS

Map 1

RUSSIA

ESTONIA

LIVONIA

DEN

COURLAND

BALTIC SEA

PRUSSIA

POLAND

RANIA

BURG

RIAN HABSBURGS'
EDITARY LANDS

HABSBURG HUNGARY

TRANSYLVANIA

OTTOMAN EMPIRE

—·— Borders of Holy Roman Empire

Swedish territories

Frederick William's possessions

Map 2

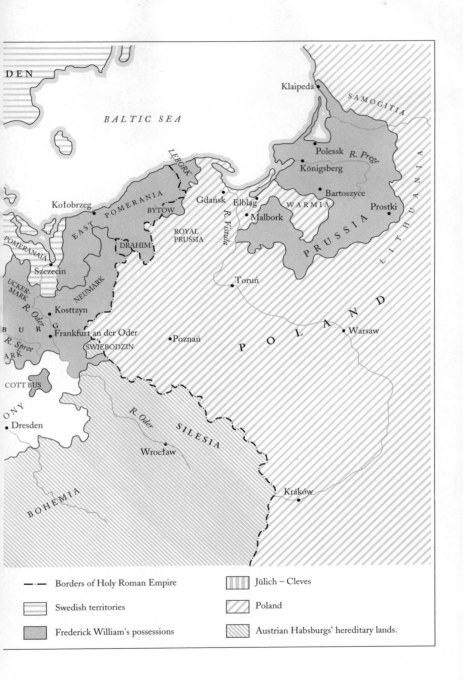

. . . .
FAMILY TREE

HOHENZOLLERN

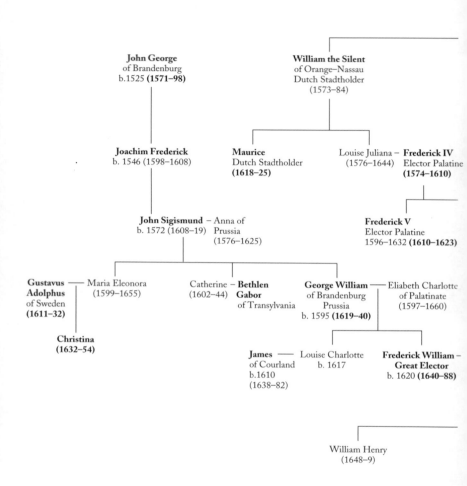

Table 1

ORANGE – NASSAU

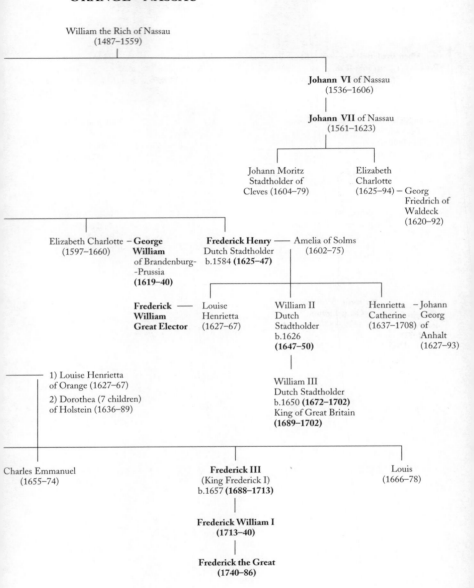

William the Rich of Nassau
(1487–1559)

Johann **VI** of Nassau
(1536–1606)

Johann **VII** of Nassau
(1561–1623)

Johann Moritz
Stadtholder of
Cleves (1604–79)

Elizabeth
Charlotte
(1625–94) – Georg
Friedrich of
Waldeck
(1620–92)

Elizabeth Charlotte – **George
(1597–1660) William**
of Brandenburg-
-Prussia
(1619–40)

Frederick Henry —— Amelia of Solms
Dutch Stadtholder   (1602–75)
b.1584 **(1625–47)**

Frederick —— Louise
William   Henrietta
Great Elector (1627–67)

William II
Dutch
Stadtholder
b.1626
(1647–50)

Henrietta – Johann
Catherine   Georg
(1637–1708) of
Anhalt
(1627–93)

1) Louise Henrietta
of Orange (1627–67)
2) Dorothea (7 children)
of Holstein (1636–89)

William III
Dutch Stadtholder
b.1650 **(1672–1702)**
King of Great Britain
(1689–1702)

Charles Emmanuel
(1655–74)

Frederick III
(King Frederick I)
b.1657 **(1688–1713)**

Louis
(1666–78)

**Frederick William I
(1713–40)**

**Frederick the Great
(1740–86)**

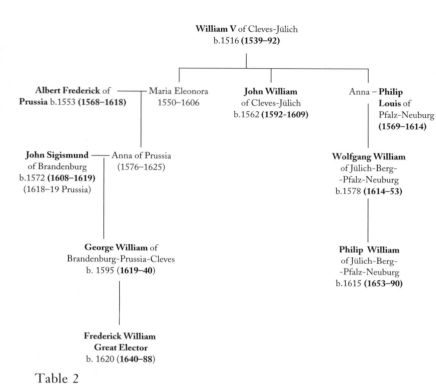

William V of Cleves-Jülich
b.1516 **(1539–92)**

Albert Frederick of —— Maria Eleonora
Prussia b.1553 **(1568–1618)**   1550–1606

John William
of Cleves-Jülich
b.1562 **(1592-1609)**

Anna – **Philip**
Louis of
Pfalz-Neuburg
(1569–1614)

John Sigismund —— Anna of Prussia
of Brandenburg   (1576–1625)
b.1572 **(1608–1619)**
(1618–19 Prussia)

Wolfgang William
of Jülich-Berg-
-Pfalz-Neuburg
b.1578 **(1614–53)**

George William of
Brandenburg-Prussia-Cleves
b. 1595 **(1619–40)**

Philip William
of Jülich-Berg-
-Pfalz-Neuburg
b.1615 **(1653–90)**

Frederick William
Great Elector
b. 1620 **(1640–88)**

Table 2

FURTHER READING

Works in English and French are published in London or Paris, unless indicated.

The material available in English on the Great Elector is very limited. C.E. Maurice's *Life of Frederick William, The Great Elector of Brandenburg* (1926) is very thin, although it possibly has more merit than *The Great Elector* by F. Schevill (Chicago, 1947), which reads like a B-movie script. F.L. Carsten's writings have to be the start for any serious study on Frederick William, particularly *The Origins of Prussia* (Oxford, 1954), *Princes and Parliaments in Germany from the Fifteenth to the Eighteenth Century* (Oxford, 1959), and *Essays in German History* (1985). Because of the author's interests, these are rather restricted to the Elector's relations with his Estates. More rounded, short accounts are the chapter Professor Carsten contributed to *The New Cambridge Modern History, Vol. V. The Ascendancy of France, 1648–88* (Cambridge, 1961), which he also edited, and his article, 'The Great Elector', in *History Today*, 10 (1960). H.W. Koch's *A History of Prussia* (London, 1978) and particularly his 'Brandenburg-Prussia' in *Absolutism in Seventeenth Century Europe* (1990), ed. J. Miller, are interesting. There are fifty pages of relevant documents in C.A. Macartney, ed. *The Habsburg and Hohenzollern Dynasties in the Seventeenth and Eighteenth Centuries* (1970). Much of relevance to Frederick William's reign can be found in an impressive array of modern works on aspects of German or Prussian history. G. Gagliardo, *Germany under the Old Regime, 1600–1700* (1991) has now been supplemented splendidly by P. Wilson, *The Holy Roman Empire, 1495–1806* (1999), *Absolutism in Central Europe* (2000) and *German Armies, War and German Politics, 1648–1806* (1998), all with extensive bibliographies of German monographs. The important works on the agrarian system of Brandenburg and Prussia by William Hagen and Edgar Melton have been detailed in my chapter 5. Very illuminating are R.L. Gawthrop, *Pietism and the Making of Eighteenth-Century Prussia* (Cambridge, 1993) and R.M. Berdahl, *The Politics of the Prussian Nobility, The Development of a Conservative Ideology, 1770–1848* (Princeton, 1988). Important, if unconvincing, is G. Oestreich, *Neostoicism and the Early Modern State* (English trans., Cambridge, 1982). A ground-breaking study on the Hohenzollerns and their conversion to Calvinism is B. Nischan, *Prince, People, and Confession, The Second Reformation in Brandenburg* (Philadelphia, 1994). Although M. Fulbrook, *Piety and Politics: Religion and the Rise of Absolutism and England, Württemberg and Prussia* (Cambridge, 1983) and L. & M. Frey, *Frederick I: The Man and His Times* (Boulder, 1984) concentrate on the years after the Great Elector, they have some relevance to his reign. There is no economic history of early-modern Germany in English, but an important collection of essays is S. Ogilvie, ed. *Germany, A New Social and Economic History, Vol. II, 1630–1800* (1996).

Frederick William has faired much better with French historians than those writing in English. There is a typical, solid pre-First World War biography, concentrating on international relations and based largely on the French diplomatic archives, by A. Waddington, *Le Grand Électeur Frédéric Guillaume de Brandebourg*, 2 vols (1905–8). A more succinct account is in Waddington's *Histoire de Prusse*. Vol. I (1911) G. Pagès, *Le Grand Électeur et Louis XIV, 1660–88* (1905) is a fine diplomatic study, understandably written more from the view of Paris than Berlin.

Relevant material in German on Frederick William is extensive, although not as much as might be expected. What follows is merely an introduction to it. Most important figures in German history have merited solid lives, written at the end of the nineteenth century and based on the published and unpublished central government records. In Frederick William's case there is M. Philippson, *Der Große Kurfürst von Brandenburg*, 3 vols (Berlin, 1897–1903). This study, together with H. Prutz, *Aus des Großen Kurfürsten letzen Jahren* (Berlin, 1897), has provided the starting point for all further work on Frederick William. Almost as useful is J.G. Droysen, *Geschichte der preußischen Politik* part 3, vols I–II (Leipzig, 1861–5) – the wealth of archival material employed in this history more than compensates for its natural pro-Prussian bias. Particularly because of the losses caused by the Second World War, an exhaustive collection of archival documents on Frederick William's reign, assembled by several editors, is indispensable: *Urkunden und Aktenstücke zur Geschichte des Kurfürsten Friedrich Wilhelm von Brandenburg*, ed. by Die Preußischen Kommission bei der Preußischen Akademie der Wissenschaften, 23 vols (Berlin-Leipzig, 1864–1930). The best, and most comprehensive, modern biography of the Elector is by E. Opgenoorth, *Friedrich Wilhelm, der Große Kurfürst von Brandenburg. Eine politische Biographie*, 2 vols (Göttingen, 1971–78). Shorter, but with merits of its own, is another scholarly biography, *Friedrich Wilhelm, der Große Kurfürst, Eine politische Biographie* by L. Hüttl (Munich, 1981). These lives provide excellent bibliographies of the German materials on Frederick William and his reign. Other extensive bibliographies can be found in R. Dietrich, ed. *Die politischen Testamente der Hohenzollern* (Cologne, 1986) and in the third volume of the valuable collection of previously published articles on Prussian history, edited by O. Büsch and W. Neugebauer *Moderne Preußische Geschichte, 1648–1947*, 3 vols (Berlin, 1981). Valuable research works in German published since these are P. Baumgart, ed., *Ständetum und Staatsbildung in Brandenburg-Preußen, Ergebnisse einer Internationalen Fachtagung* (Berlin, 1983); A. Nachama, *Ersatzbürger and Staatsbildung: zur Zerstörung des Bürgertums in Brandenburg-Preußen* (Frankfurt-am-Main, 1984) and C. Fürbringer, *Necessitas und Libertas. Staatsbildung und Landstände im 17. Jahrhundert in Brandenburg* (Frankfurt-am-Main, 1985). There is also a collection of modern scholarly articles on Frederick William edited by O. Hauser *Preußen, Europa und das Reich* (Cologne, 1987).

INDEX